MW01280286

Environmental Challenges for Higher Education

**Friends Committee on
Unity with Nature**

This book is a collection of papers presented at the symposium,
"Sustainable Development in Higher Education—
A Challenge for Educators by the Year 2000,"
June 25, 1994, William Penn College, Oskaloosa, Iowa,
sponsored by Friends Association for Higher Education
and Friends Committee on Unity with Nature.

To our students,
who have shared with us,
taught us, and inspired us.
To our families,
who have been patient and helpful,
and have critiqued manuscripts.
To members of our two publications committees,
who have provided guidance and valuable insights.
To the Shaw-North Foundation for its tangible support,
which made completion of this project possible.

—From the editors

Environmental Challenges for Higher Education
Integrating Sustainability into Academic Programs

Edited by

Robert L. Wixom
Lisa L. Gould
Susan Schmidt
Louis Cox

A project for educators by

Friends Association for Higher Education
    and
Friends Committee on Unity With Nature

1996

Supported by
The Shaw-North Foundation.

Published by
Friends Committee on Unity with Nature
179 N. Prospect St.
Burlington, VT 05401-1607 USA.

Additional copies may be ordered from the above address.

Library of Congress Catalog Card Number: 96-86853

ISBN 1-881083-03-9 pbk.

10 9 8 7 6 5 4 3 2 1

Printed in the United States of America on recycled paper.

Prepared with the advice of the following representatives from:

**Friends Association for Higher Education
Publications Committee:**
Michael Heller
Roanoke College, Salem, Va.
Joseph Mathews
Temple University, Philadelphia, Pa.
Michele Lise Tarter
Eastern Illinois University, Charleston, Ill.
Susanne Weil, clerk
Whittier College, Whittier, Calif.

For further information on FAHE, please write:
Friends Association on Higher Education,
P.O. Box 18741
Greensboro, NC 27419

**Friends Committee on Unity with Nature
Publications Committee:**
William Beale
Sunpower, Inc., Athens, Ohio
Louis Cox, clerk
Charlotte, Vt.
Lisa L. Gould
Rhode Island Natural History Survey, Kingston, R.I.
Jack Phillips
St. Cloud State University, St. Cloud, Minn.

For further information on FCUN, please write:
Friends Committee on Unity with Nature
179 N. Prospect St.
Burlington, VT 05401-1607

FAHE and FCUN are 501(c)(3) organizations.

Financial assistance for the preparation and publication of this book was provided by a generous grant from the Shaw-North Foundation, 1106 Foulkeways, Gwynedd, PA 19436.

Contributors

William M. Alexander, Professor Emeritus of
World Food Politics,
California Polytechnic State University
Stanley Becker, Associate Professor of Population Dynamics,
Johns Hopkins University
Ted Bernard, Professor of Geography,
Ohio University
Leonard Brown, Professor of Geography,
Wittenburg University
Stephen Collett, Director,
Quaker United Nations Office
Kathryn W. Hansen, Associate Director,
Iowa Division United Nations Association
Hazel Henderson, International Development
Policy Analyst and Fellow,
World Business Academy
William L. Howenstine, Professor of Geography and
Environmental Studies,
Northeastern Illinois University
M. Patrick McAdams, Assistant Professor of Natural Sciences,
William Penn College
Sally B. Merrill, Associate Professor of Philosophy,
Purdue University
Susan Schmidt, Assistant Professor of English and
Environmental Studies,
Brevard College
Robert L. Wixom, Professor Emeritus of Biochemistry,
University of Missouri
Jora Young, Director of Science and Stewardship,
The Nature Conservancy, Florida Regional Office

Contents

Acknowledgments

Many individuals have made tangible contributions to the development of this book. Several wonderful reference librarians at the University of Missouri's Ellis Library provided frequent invaluable advice on search strategies, on-line searches, interlibrary loans, and always cheerful comments/ideas. "Hats off" to **Brenda G. Blevins, Janice L. Dysart, Rachel S. Greeley, Axie A. Hindman, Diane E. Johnson, Nancy T. Myers** and **Paula L. Roper**. Several members of the University of Missouri Environmental Affairs Council (**Peter N. Davis**, law; **Susan L. Flader**, history; **Clark J. Gantzer**, soil science; and **Philip J. Shocklee**, campus facilities) shared over several years their insights, ideas, and comments. Many chapters were read and polished by qualified advanced students: **Julie Angelica, Laurence Buckley-Rohrer, Amy Lamprecht, Jennifer Parker, Raegan J. Rinchinso** and **Curt Wohleber**. Former MU students **David G. Wixom** and **Richard L. Wixom** were frequent sounding boards for ideas. Several faculty members reviewed carefully the chapter in their areas: **Dr. John K. Dickinson**, Professor Emeritus of Sociology, Boston University; **Dr. Suresh C. Tyagi**, Professor of Biochemistry/Medicine, University of Missouri; and **Dr. A. G. Unklesbay**, Professor Emeritus of Geology and former Vice President for Administration, University of Missouri. One author (R.L.W.) appreciates helpful discussions with **Job S. Ebenezer, Noel Pavlovic, Melvin E. West** and **Cal DeWitt** (see chapter 14 for their backgrounds); and **Ed Dreby, Michael Dunn**, and **Robert Schutz**, members of Friends Committee of the Unity with Nature. Outstanding secretarial skills were provided by **Rosemary Crane** and **Charlie Talmage**.

Faculty know that students come and go every four years; they receive and participate in their higher education and are now "out there" in the world at large. Our students may not be aware of how much they contribute to the education of faculty; for the comments in chapter 11, one author (R. L. W.) is profoundly in debt to the student leaders in the Earth Week Student Coalition and Environmental Affairs Council, both at the University of Missouri; each fruitful association covered a one- to two-year period with **Christine M. Doerr, Michelle D. Grigsby, Angela Hogan, Phil Howard, Julie Huddle, Tim Neal, Amy M. Petterborg, Michael E. Stansberry, Chris White**, and dozens of other MU students for shorter periods of campus environmental work.

Thanks also to **Dori Blacker** of Cranston, R.I. and **Ruah Swennerfelt** of Charlotte, Vt. for their work in indexing this volume.

We hope we have distilled the best for future readers and presented these essays and appendices in a clear, reasonable manner.

Permissions

Reprinted by permission of Pantheon Books, a Division of Random House, Inc.: Excerpts from *Sex, Economy, Freedom & Community* by Wendell Berry. Copyright © 1993 by Wendell Berry.

Reprinted by permission of North Point Press, a division of Farrar, Strauss, & Giroux, Inc.: Excerpts from *What Are People For?* by Wendell Berry. Copyright © 1990 by Wendell Berry.

Reprinted by permission of North Point Press, a division of Farrar, Strauss, & Giroux, Inc.: Excerpts from *The Wild Birds: Six Stories of the Port William Membership* by Berry, Wendell. Copyright © 1985, 1986 by Wendell Berry.

Reprinted by permission of W.W. Norton & Company: Excerpt from *State of the World* by Lester R. Brown. Copyright © 1990.

Excerpts used by permission of Oxford University Press: "Morning Has Broken." Words by Eleanor Farjeon. In *The Children's Bells.* Copyright © 1957.

Reprinted by permission of Elsevier Science, Oxford, England: "New Markets and New Commons." *Futures*, Vol 27, No 2, by Hazel Henderson.

Reprinted by permission of Oxford University Press: Excerpts from *A Sand County Almanac* by Aldo Leopold. Copyright © 1947.

From *Braided Lives* by Marge Piercy, published by Summit Books. Copyright © 1982 by Marge Piercy and Middlemarsh, Inc. Reprinted by permission of the Wallace Literary Agency, Inc.

Reprinted by permission of Feminist Press at the City University of New York. *Daughter of Earth,* by Agnes Smedley. Copyright © 1973.

Reprinted by permission of Union of Concerned Scientists: "World Scientists' Warning to Humanity." Copyright © 1994.

Reprinted by permission of the United Nations: "Principles on Population and Development" in *Population and Development,* Volume 1, Programme of Action adopted at the International Conference on Population and Development, Cairo, September 5-13 1994. Copyright © 1995.

Our Common Future, World Commission on Environment and Development (Gro Harlem Brundtland, chair). Copyright © 1987 by World Commission on Environment and Development. Used by permission of Oxford University Press.

Reprinted by permission of Simon & Schuster: Excerpt from *New Eyes for Invisibles* by Rufus Jones. Copyright © 1943.

A Far Off Place by Laurens Van der Post. Copyright © 1974 by Laurens Van der Post. By permission of William Morrow and Company, Inc.

Emerson was saying in his library one evening that Harvard College now teaches all of the branches of learnng. "Yes," said Thoreau, who had just graduated, "all the branches but none of the roots!" I am all for getting down to the **roots of life**. To miss those things that form and fortify the inner nature of the person is to miss the best thing there is here on earth. To enjoy simple beauty; to share in the creation of what ought to be; to enlarge the area of truth; to be the kind of person who will be essentially good in this world or in any other possible world, is to possess greater riches than the gold of Ophir. An education that trains a person to enjoy such durable wealth and riches partakes of the noblest art that has so far been discovered in this world. To be a teacher who knows how to enlarge the depth and scope of a person's life is the best gift there is.

—Rufus Jones, *New Eyes for Invisibles*

Preface

Lisa Lofland Gould[1]

> *I have learned that when knowledge and love become one,*
> *a force has been created that nothing can break.*
> —Agnes Smedley, *Daughter of Earth*

As you read this book you will come across many definitions of the word *sustainability*. The word sustain comes from the Latin *sub*, up from under, and *tenere*, to hold—in other words, to *support*. This word sustain has been used in many different ways. It can mean to suffer, as in "to sustain an injury or loss." It can mean to affirm the validity of an idea, as in the legal term, "objection sustained." To sustain can be to prop up, maintain, prolong, endure, prove, or confirm. But it has one more definition that to me comes closest to what we are groping for as we explore the issues of sustainability in this book: "to support the spirits or vitality of; to encourage, inspirit" (Morris 1969). Practices and systems that are not sustainable are hasty, discouraging, draining vitality from people and the earth. They do not "inspirit."

If I were to recommend just *one* book on the issues surrounding "sustainability" (from sexual behavior and community life to economics, conservation, social justice, peace issues, and Christian earth stewardship) it would probably be Wendell Berry's *Sex, Economy, Freedom, and Community* (1993); if called for a second recommendation, it would be Berry's *What Are People For?* (1990). Few current writers challenge us—educators, students, religious leaders, and citizens—as cogently as Wendell Berry. In all his writings, both prose and poetry, Berry brings us back home—to our

---

[1] **Lisa Lofland Gould** is a biologist (M.S. zoology, 1972) and Executive Director of the Rhode Island Natural History Survey. She serves on the Steering Committee of Friends Committee on Unity with Nature and is a member of Westerly (R.I.) Monthly Meeting of the Religious Society of Friends.

own locale, our own families and friends, our own place on the planet—
and summons us to create sustainable patterns *here and now*.

> In order to make ecological good sense for the planet, you must make eco-
> logical good sense locally. You *can't* act locally by thinking globally.
>
> No one can make ecological good sense for the planet. Everyone can make
> ecological good sense locally, *if* the affection, the scale, the knowledge, the
> tools, and the skills are right.
>
> The right scale in work gives power to affection. When one works beyond the
> reach of one's love for the place one is working in and for the things and
> creatures one is working with and among, then destruction inevitably results.
> An adequate local culture, among other things, keeps work within the reach
> of love. (Berry 1993)

Berry reminds us that our actions—even (or especially!) the seemingly
most ordinary—driving a car, enjoying sex, using a computer, purchasing
food, watching television, turning on a lamp—have consequences, consequence to ourselves and to the others in our community and beyond.
When our behaviors become abstractions—when we can no longer connect
our actions with their effect on others, when they have gone beyond "the
reach of love"—then communities begin to disintegrate.

> Abstraction is the enemy *wherever* it is found. The abstractions of sustainabil-
> ity can ruin the world just as surely as the abstractions of industrial econom-
> ics. Local life may be as much endangered by those who would 'save the
> planet' as by those who would 'conquer the world.' For 'saving the planet'
> calls for abstract purposes and central powers that cannot know—and thus
> will destroy—the integrity of local nature and
> local community. (Berry 1993)

But of course, our modern lives do reach beyond our local communities and affect lives all around the globe. How we avoid turning those
effects into mere abstractions, reducing human and non-human lives to
numbers in government reports, is one of the great challenges of our time.
Fortunately, we have been given a great gift to meet this challenge: the gift
of imagination. Imagination allows us to go deep into other lives, and to
begin to understand. Marge Piercy (1982) expresses it vividly:

> I live among people who think that analyzing something is action, who think
> that if they have dissected why they have done something that makes it per-
> missible to do it again, who think that a label gives possession, that when
> they have identified a sharp-shinned hawk they know something of
> hawkness—wooing high in the air and sinking with talons locked, swooping
> on live prey and tasting the fresh blood spurt hot, feeling with each extended

feather the warm and cold shift of the winds and the sculpture of the invisible masses of moving air. Dealing in words, I try to remember how far they go and where they leave off. Hungry for food for my brain, I try to remember all the other ways of knowing that coexist.

—Marge Piercy, *Braided Lives*

I hope that the pages of this book will lead us beyond abstractions and academic theorizing, opening us to new ways of understanding and new possibilities for action. On the global scale, geographer **Stephen Collett** (chapter 1) and environmental educator **Robert L. Wixom** (chapter 2) give us detailed information on the inner workings of the United Nations and related organizations, tools for us to understand how the world's peoples are attempting to bridge cultural and political divides, reaching toward the common goals of protecting our earthly home and developing more healthy relations among one another. Economist **Hazel Henderson** (chapter 3) explores emerging paradigms in global economics, paradigms which may lead us away from exploitative economies and toward "win-win" situations.

In chapter 4, geographer **William Howenstine** urges us to take a broad, interdisciplinary approach to the study of natural resources, understanding that "natural" systems and human culture function together. Demographer **Stanley Becker** (chapter 5) also informs us of the indivisibility of culture and environment; there will be no happy end to population growth and the subsequent effects on the earth's ecosystems and human cultures without an improvement in the status of women and involvement of men in family planning. Of equal importance, Becker reminds us of good Quaker practice: seeking always to act out of love, listening with the ears of the Spirit to all involved.

The theme of interrelationships continues in chapter 6 as geologist **M. Patrick McAdams** stresses the need for a long-term perspective of the human place in time and on the earth, and how this perspective can deepen students' understanding of energy resources, politics, economics, peace issues, and ecological studies.

With chapter 7, geographer **Ted Bernard** and environmental scientist **Jora Young** describe a California county and what can happen when people seek to reconnect with each other and the land, moving beyond social and political differences to forge new visions. Continents away in Kerala, India, world food scientist **William Alexander** (chapter 8) describes the exciting possibilities that can occur when people collectively search for ways to sustain their values and way of life. And geographer

Leonard Brown (chapter 9) tells us how new approaches to development—approaches that take into account the social structures and economies of the people being affected—have helped a Honduran community become healthy and self-sustaining.

In chapter 10, social activist **Kathryn Hansen** encourages the academic community to be more directly involved in educating the public, seeking new ways to disseminate the information needed by citizens to make informed decisions. **Robert Wixom**, in chapter 11, offers numerous resources to help students and faculty develop active, thoughtful campus environmental programs. And he reminds us of the "other ways of knowing": a love for the Earth can be made whole only through intimate experience with the beauty and integrity of natural places.

As we move into the humanities, ethics philosopher **Sally Merrill** (chapter 12) reflects on the spiritual basis for ideas of sustainability, and on the necessity to recognize and celebrate the interconnectedness of all life. In chapter 13, nature writer **Susan Schmidt** explores three works of modern literature that depict the disintegration of local communities as people become disconnected from one another and their roots with the land and sea.

Finally, in chapter 14, **Robert Wixom** introduces some of the connections being forged between environmental concerns and the religious communities, and provides many useful organizational and literary resources.

And so we are challenged to transform our knowledge and understanding of social and political systems, science, economics, literature, art, demographics, spiritual beliefs—all that we have discussed in these proceedings—into loving action. We are summoned to inspire—to inspirit!—our students and each other to be fully present in our communities and then to share the lessons we learn from one another beyond the bounds of our communities. And we must help our students—and one another—understand that the process will be slow, because transforming ourselves—and that is where we must begin—is never easy.

In a novel by Laurens Van der Post (1974), a boy remembers, after their deaths, words spoken by his father Ouwa, and a beloved Matabele elder, 'Bamuthi:

> It was only by education and re-education and patient exhortation and evocation and change of heart and imagination that men could be permanently changed. You could not punish men into being better; you could not punish societies into being better; you could not change the world by violence and by frightening people into virtue by killing off their inadequate establish-

ments. The moment was upon us when we had to accept without reserve that the longest way round in the human spirit was always the shortest way there. . . . There was no shortcut to a better life on earth. Impatience and shortcuts were evil and destructive. There were no shortcuts to the creative, there was no magic in creation except the magic of growth. Creation was growth and growth was profoundly subservient to time laws of its own, which could not be broken without destroying the process and bringing down disaster upon all. And here the sonorous voice of 'Bamuthi joined that of Ouwa, the deep bass echo coming from the cliffs of Amageba, where the evening shadows gather in the ancient mountains and where his spirit was believed to have gone, reiterating again and again, "Remember, Little Feather, patience is an egg that hatches great birds. Even the sun is such an egg. *Hamba Gashle!* Go slowly, because if you go slowly, good things will come to you and you will walk to the end of the road in peace and happiness."

Our challenges are great, and our sense of urgency keen. Let us sustain one another with patience, wisdom, and love.

Literature Cited

Berry, Wendell. 1990. *What Are People For?* San Francisco: North Point Press.
———. 1993. *Sex, Economy, Freedom and Community.* New York: Pantheon Books.
Morris, William, ed. 1969. *The American Heritage Dictionary of the English Language.* Boston: Houghton Mifflin Co.
Piercy, Marge. 1982. *Braided Lives.* New York: Summit Books.
Smedley, Agnes. 1973. *Daughter of Earth.* New York: Feminist Press at City University of New York.
Van der Post, Laurens. 1974. *A Far-Off Place.* New York: William Morrow & Co. [This book is the sequel to Van der Post's 1972 novel *A Story Like the Wind.* They form one complete story, so should be read in sequence.]

Foreword

Morning Has Broken

Morning has broken like the first morning;
Blackbird has spoken like the first bird.
Praise for the singing!
Praise for the morning!
Praise for them, springing fresh from the Word!
Mine is the sunlight!
Mine is the morning born of the one light
Eden saw play!
Praise with elation,
Praise every morning,
God's recreation of the new day! [1]

Morning has broken . . . God's re-creation of the new day! Much has happened to this Earth, its rain, its sunlight, this Garden. This Earth, our physical home, provides us with food, air, water, fiber and other required resources for life. The Earth, as God's re-creation, also sets the boundaries of our spiritual home.

For many years humankind has ruthlessly exploited and wasted the Earth's resources. We have also partially begun to recognize these human mistakes and to discern appropriate, feasible, corrective measures. These opposing directions seesaw up and down, back and forth. Early scientific evidence frequently is viewed with skepticism; mature scientific judgment may take years to accumulate and disseminate. At any place or moment in time, we do not know the balance. It may take years of study and hindsight to be reasonably certain of a teetering balance, or the gradual slide to destructive processes, or the slow climb to constructive measures.

What is certain is that humankind has a choice: we can make conscious, hopefully rational decisions that will affect the balance. That choice

---

[1] Words by Eleanor Farjeon, 1931.

will be affected by a search for true relationships and causes—by the role of the scientist—the imaginative seeking of new visions—the role of the artist and writer—and the creative distribution of these findings—the role of the educator.

This book and its preceding symposium were planned for educators and their students, who will become tomorrow's leaders. Despite what some "gloom and doom" environmentalists say, the latter may lead us in restoring harmony. Time is running out to reverse the damage caused by mankind's destructive processes, but it is not too late for faculty and their students to influence decision-makers at successively higher levels, in local institutions and at regional, national, and international levels.

Friends Association for Higher Education (FAHE) and Friends Committee on Unity with Nature (FCUN) were mindful of these considerations in planning an earlier symposium, "Sustainable Development in Higher Education—A Challenge for Educators by the Year 2000." This symposium was held June 25, 1994 at William Penn College, Oskaloosa, Iowa, as a part of the FAHE annual meeting. The goals of FAHE and FCUN are stated in appendix A. The objectives for the above symposium and now this resultant book are:

1. To understand the crucial interacting roles of the United Nations, the UN Conference on Environment and Development, the UN's Council for Sustainable Development, the UN International Conference on Population and Development, and non-governmental organizations (NGOs), leading to constructive roles for citizens and educators.
2. To decipher present environmental perceptions, and to connect specific academic disciplines with the general educational objectives as related to the relatively new concept (or vision) of "sustainable development" (or "sustainability").
3. To identify resources for these teaching tasks, bearing in mind their multidisciplinary nature. *How can the challenge and themes of the United Nations Conference on Environment and Development (UNCED), the UN* Earth Charter *and UN* Agenda 21 *be presented effectively to today's college students, i.e., our leaders for tomorrow?*

Before and after the symposium, several thinkers and theologians have designated the Earth as "our Garden"—an extension of the initial Garden of Eden. This Garden, our Earth, is ours to waste or to nurture, to damage or to cultivate, to ignore or to love. We use this metaphor as an introduction—*Morning has broken. . . . Praise for the sweetness of the wet garden. . . . Praise with elation, praise every morning. . . .* A new day has begun! From this foreword, we proceed from chapter to chapter, from one gifted author to another, from one academic discipline to another. We invite the reader to join us in the common search for understanding, for the vision to lead us in specific steps and for guidance from the Light within. *Mine is the sunlight! Mine is the morning, born of the one light Eden saw play!* The hymn reminds us of another opportunity to mend our adverse human practices. The task of educators is to inspire those who will restore and nurture the Garden.

—R.L.W.

I. Over-all Presentations

1. The Continuing UNCED Vision and Process

Stephen Collett[1]

Your task is really to convince the world that the sense of hope that was generated by the Rio process was not hope misplaced. We must show action, we must show results, results in the integration of the economy and ecology in decision making, results in the transition to sustainable patterns of consumption in the management of population growth, results in the alleviation of poverty and in human resource development, results in the quality and integrity of land, fresh water and marine and biotic resources, results in reducing threats to life support systems, results in the improvement of the conditions of health in human settlements, and in the increased flow of finance and technology for the shift to sustainable development.

—Nitin Desai, United Nations Under-Secretary-General for Policy Coordination and Sustainable Development,

Abstract

As a major step to consolidating nearly four decades of consciousness-raising about our interaction with the environment, the 1992 United Nations Conference on Environment and Development (UNCED or "Earth Summit") has set in motion a wide process to engage the world's citizens and their respective governments in turning the focus of human development toward sustainability. From the local to the national and international levels, new concepts of partnership and responsibility are building momentum, with economic, political and even spiritual ramifications. Many aspects of this multifaceted and integrative process are relevant to higher education today.

---

[1] **Stephen Collett,** a graduate of Haverford and Wilmington colleges, is a development geographer (MA, University of Colorado, 1973). He has taught, researched, written, and advocated on issues of global development and sustainable economics. Since 1986 he has been director of the Quaker United Nations Office at UN Headquarters in New York, where he specializes on questions of disarmament, regional security, and sustainable development.

Introduction for UNCED

As the twentieth century draws to a close, humankind finds itself in the imprudent position of having a decade or two—a short moment in time—in which to change the guiding perception of our role and our behavior as a species on planet Earth. The alternative, we are coming to understand, is to live in a world where human numbers will increasingly overwhelm the earth's capacity to absorb our impact and produce for our needs. Only in the past few decades have we begun to read the signs that the natural systems upon which we depend are being dangerously degraded and deranged, and that some may be slipping beyond our capacities of repair or adaptation. Toxic pileups, the loss of soils and soil fertility, shortage of fresh water and ruinous changes in the atmosphere and climate are the outcome of the global development trajectory of the past century. The new code by which we must learn to live—we as individuals and as a global society—is sustainability, or sustainable development.

Some have argued against attaching the word "development" to sustainability, as though the two formed an oxymoron. But without an emphasis on development, the concept is too narrow to convey our purpose. It is not that development will stop, but that it needs redirection. It is too elitist to say that now, we in our own close, comfortable circle have enough and can simply rest on our gains. Most of the world still does not have enough. The reorganization of our production and consumption patterns, and the development of a global society, must become our "development" focus.

The moment of opportunity is short because we are only just becoming aware of this wake-up call, and are more or less responsive to it—a point to which we will return in this volume of essays. The antecedents of the message are much closer in time and weight to Rachel Carson than to the Reverend Thomas Malthus, whose 1798 essay on population predicted that a geometric population growth could not be supported by an arithmetic increase in food production. Malthus's prediction has been proven wrong so far by dint of science, technology, and agriculture. That may change in the future. It was Rachel Carson who led us to consider our interwoven role in the mesh of life that embraces us as a species, and thereby the limits imposed by a fixed natural base.

The evidence pushing us, unwilling as we are, toward change has mounted quickly and steadily since the publication of Carson's *Silent Spring*. It is the result of innumerable individual studies on our environmental impact around the world, and of the broadening analysis and comparison of their conclusions. Much of the initiative for the direction of science and the globalization of environmental awareness has been the ongoing work of international scientific bodies (e.g., the International Council of Scientific Unions, the International Geographic Union, the International Union for the Conservation of Nature), working with and through the United Nations. Already in the 1950s, the United Nations Educational, Scientific, and Cultural Organization (UNESCO) initiated the Man and the Biosphere program, which led over the following years to the UN Conference on the Human Environment in 1972 in Stockholm, Sweden.

The Stockholm conference put environment on the intergovernmental policy agenda to stay, no small accomplishment in itself since the environment is not mentioned in the UN Charter. It also stimulated mechanisms such as the creation of national ministries of environment and the codification of environmental standards in countries that had participated, with Europe and North America in the lead.

Many developing countries, however, did not participate in the Stockholm conference and felt for some time afterward that the issues raised there were primarily relevant to industrialized societies. Furthermore, they suspected that environmental protection could be used as yet another banner—along with free trade, open markets and population control—under which continued neo-colonial exploitation would be marched through their regions.

Despite the Stockholm agreements and a number of sectorally-focused conferences on food, population, water, drylands, and the seas, by the mid-1980s the Earth's vital signs were signaling that we were losing the race against environmental deterioration. The UN's Economic and Social Council called for another serious look at the relationship between environment and development, and established a commission to that effect in 1984 with Norwegian Prime Minister Gro Harlem Brundtland serving as chair. The Brundtland Commission found and described a bleak dynamic of degradation in its 1987 report to the UN General Assembly. However, the commission was also able to describe a different path, one toward sustainability, sketching examples in areas of industry, farming, energy, and transportation. Also, the World Commission on Environment and Development recommended that a second international conference on the environment be convened. Hence, after the 1988 approval by the UN General Assembly, the Earth Summit was held in Rio de Janeiro in June 1992.

The four years of preparation for the Earth Summit was an intense period of collection and analysis of data and worldwide experiences. Four preparatory conferences, known as "prep cons" were held. From this work was produced a picture of the current situations, options for moving toward sustainability, and policy recommendations. The result was a document, called *Agenda 21* (as in the twenty-first century), which has a vast scope, encompassing nine major environmental issues and some twenty-three aspects of socio-economic dynamics and behavior that have an impact on the environment.

For three critical issues, *Agenda 21* details the agreed parameters and appropriate approaches and identifies responsibilities and action to be taken at local, national, regional, and global levels. Dealing as it does with such complex issues and variable time frames, *Agenda 21* is open-ended, in that its conclusions and directives are to be reviewed and reevaluated periodically.

Two critical elements emerged for governments as they first examined the relationship between environment and development and then fixed on the approaches and commitments they would undertake at the Earth Summit. Both elements involve new concepts of partnership. One is the need for a revised and revitalized relationship between the countries of the North and the South. The new North/South partnership needs to be infused with a sense of sharing one finite resource base. Also, the North needs to recognize that its rapid industrialization bears the chief responsibility for global environmental deterioration. In turn, if the South, with its increasing population, is not accorded a greater share of global development capital and new technologies, its growing impact on the environment could quickly exacerbate an already dire situation.

The second critical partnership, which distinguishes itself by the regularity and centrality of its appearance in *Agenda 21*, is the necessity of empowering communities to take responsibility for sustainable development in the local environment. The vast majority of decisions and actions affecting the environment are taken at the local level, from the removal and consumption of resources to the handling of toxins and wastes. If local communities do not practice sustainable development, it does not occur. Not only does sustainability need to inform government planning and economic policy-making, it reveals a new rationale for employing basic human rights as the foundation for development. Citizens and communities, if they are to be empowered, have rights to information, participatory decision-making, compensation, review, and referendum on policies that affect them.

Empowering individuals in communities and forging a new
North/South ethic are the centerpieces of *Agenda 21;* in Rio de Janeiro,
more than 150 governments signed the conventions on protection of
climate and biodiversity. To educators, these themes will find resonance in
many components of what we already consider our core curriculum, but
they should now push us, in the newer context of the profound environmental threats and challenges we face, to reevaluate and rededicate our
energies around these issues. This challenge is the purpose of the present
volume of essays.

The significance of the Earth Summit was briefly caught by the media
in 1992. Three years later, governments appear to be slowly implementing
the commitments they agreed to in Rio de Janeiro. Certainly the financing
which developing countries had hoped would follow on the Rio agreements has not been forthcoming. On the other hand, the Earth Summit
has spawned a range of vital activity which is building momentum among
both governments and citizens. Certainly the Rio conference established
the standards by which we will be judged by future generations. The canon
of sustainable development provides a kind of general theory we have not
had before and which will not tolerate inertia for long.

Follow-up to UNCED

Despite allegations of delay, the 1992 Earth Summit agreements did
not just disappear into the briefcases of the negotiators after being signed
by their heads of state and government in Rio de Janeiro. Much of the
action agenda relies on new forms of cooperation and review among
communities, businesses and various levels of government, which take
some time to evolve. Furthermore, several important mechanisms at the
international level will help guide and encourage their growth. They include: a new high-level intergovernmental body, the Commission on
Sustainable Development (CSD); new forms of interagency and interde-
partmental consultation to guide the UN system-wide approaches; and new
components of international law which will work to hold governments on
a set course of action to protect the global climate, biodiversity, and the
world's drylands.

The Commission on Sustainable Development (CSD)

The first General Assembly after the Earth Summit established the Commission on Sustainable Development (CSD) in the fall of 1993, as the
central review mechanism for *Agenda 21*. Meeting three weeks or so each
spring in New York, the CSD brings together heads of environment ministries (the Environmental Protection Agency in the United States) and those

of other sectors such as industry, agriculture, energy, trade and finance to review progress in implementing the Rio agreements and to plan continuing international cooperation. Each year the commission focuses on a changing set of issues from the forty chapters of *Agenda 21* (see appendix E), and is preparing for a full five-year progress review on the Rio agreements to be held as a special session of the General Assembly in 1997 (see chapter 2, table 5).

Important tools for the CSD are reports which countries are invited to submit each year concerning their national experience in applying *Agenda 21* priorities and programs. This function is spawning a new dialogue within each country between government agencies and the actors in the non-governmental sector. In over ninety countries, national forums for sustainable development have been created to promote implementation and review in a collegium of interests from the various levels in the national sphere of activity. While governments are writing the national reports, citizens and their NGOs who are increasingly attuned to the global agenda for sustainability are considering these reports.

Representatives of numerous non-governmental organizations and their networks—spanning local to international levels—attend the CSD each year, bringing expertise to issues on the annual agenda and interpreting current global perspectives in reports back to their regions. This role for public participation in the CSD mirrors what has developed around the work of the UN Commission on Human Rights over the decades. There, non-governmental representatives bring cases to the Human Rights Commission and its sub-bodies for review and submit information on subjects on the commission's agenda. To improve the effectiveness of both parties, this interactive process between citizens and governments needs to be deepened and strengthened in the field of sustainable development.

UN System-wide Focus on Sustainable Development

A major purpose of raising an international conference on environment and development to the level of a summit meeting is to bring the multitude of divisions in the governmental and intergovernmental spheres together in a common exercise. The divisions of national states into ministries and departments, and also the divisions of the international organizations, are renowned for their inherent diversity of interest.

The Earth Summit was unprecedented in its demands on the divisions of government, few of which would be unaffected by its outcome, to play a new game of consultation and interaction; first, to determine and then negotiate their national interests in the range of issues, and second, to coordinate the implementation and follow-up of the UNCED agreements. Although environment ministries still play the primary role in dealing with questions of sustainable development, each year a new set of issues is brought to the table at the CSD, calling for a multi-sectoral, interactive approach by the branches of government. Durable initiatives to move our societies toward sustainability will require that this interactive model become the rule rather than the exception within governments, and within the United Nations.

At the UN, the UNCED process established a continuing practice of system-wide interagency reporting and consultation to support the CSD, for example, in preparing the background documentation for issues on the year's agenda. With a history of competition and turf-battling among the semi-autonomous UN agencies, real collaboration remains a goal toward which to work. These agencies are, however, showing evidence of increasing cooperation in dealing with complex issues like the sustainable use of forests where portions of the problems and their solutions are managed by different agencies: forestry and soils in the Food and Agriculture Organization, biodiversity in the UN Environment Programme, and perspectives on social interactions with forests in the UN Education, Science and Cultural Organization. Sustainability is a lesson with many tutors: each body in the system must study it in concert with the others to understand the complex and decisive interactions between environment and development.

The Environmental Frontiers of International Law

Last, the UNCED process has advanced international environmental law on a scale matched only by the human rights field several decades ago (the work of governments at the UN to codify human rights has now produced a body of some thirty-five conventions, covering particularly heinous violations of human rights and vulnerable groups).

Two conventions were prepared and signed at the Earth Summit by 154 countries (not necessarily the same ones): the *Convention on Climate Change* and the *Convention on the Protection of Biodiversity*. A third convention, the *Convention on Combating Desertification*, was called for at UNCED, negotiated in the following three years, and adopted in Paris in June 1994. This triad covers what may be the most prominent features of the codification of environment/development law.

Convention on Climate Change. The Convention on Climate Change is an example of the codification of issues for the management of particular substances. As the climate problem demonstrates, particulates, even though otherwise fairly innocuous, can skew processes as large as climate if they are released in sufficient quantities. The commonality is that these problems can be largely controlled through legislation and standard-setting at regional, national and local levels. Environmental problems of this nature are already addressed by a number of national and regional codes for the control of toxins and toxic wastes in general, and may find new applicability in a convention to ban the production of fissile materials, presently being discussed.

Convention on the Protection of Biodiversity. The Convention on the Protection of Biodiversity calls attention to environmental considerations in decisions involving all manner of state and private interests, from the inclusion of indigenous people in forest regimes, to the protection of manatees from speedboat enthusiasts, and to both increase food production and sustain natural ecosystems.

Convention to Combat Desertification. The Convention to Combat Desertification has been called the first development convention. It recognizes that the state of dryland soils and soil fertility is a global issue, with ramifications ranging from climate change and biodiversity protection to the looming crisis in food security, which is pervasive in some countries and increasingly imminent in others. And it centers strategies for environmental protection in the empowerment of local communities in the fragile drylands. The model of the Convention to Combat Desertification is not that of limited interests controlling local resources, as in the challenge to national and state authorities in the American southwest, but that of a holistic approach based on integrating local needs with environmental carrying capacities. Factors as diverse, yet related, as local livelihoods and international trade are identified in this treaty as the stabilizing elements. In an inventive model, the convention proposes a system of national-level consultative bodies bringing together national ministries, multilateral and bilateral donors, and representatives of local communities and related NGOs. Their mission will be to formulate sustainable programs for donor and recipient partnership to give long-term support for community management of drylands' resources.

Conclusion

Substantial interdisciplinary information and a wealth of ethical and epistemological issues need to be addressed in our era for questions of the relationship between environment and development. In addition, there is the overlying motivation to educate the generation that will be trained in the next decade or two; it is they who will make (or not make) the historic difference.

Education in sustainability would do well to recognize that the relationship of our society to global environmental limits is not merely practical; there is a spiritual aspect to explore and celebrate. I will close with a quote on this subject by Gilbert F. White, from his acceptance address for the Cosmos Club Award in 1993, one of a long string of honors awarded to this Quaker dean of the role of human behavior in the earth sciences:

> The essential point, I believe, is that people around the world in the 1990s are perceiving the earth as more than a globe to be surveyed, or developed for the public good in the short term, or to be protected from threats to its well-being both human and natural. It is all of those in some degree, but has additional dimensions. People in many cultures accept its scientific description as a matter of belief. They recognize a commitment to care for it in perpetuity. They accept reluctantly an obligation to come to terms with problems posed by growth in numbers and appetites. This is not simply anxious analysis of economic and social consequences of political policies toward environmental matters. The roots are in a growing solemn sense of the individual as a part of one human family for whom Earth is its one spiritual home.

[Editor's note. The reader is referred to related information in chapter 2 and appendices B, C, and D.]

2. Environmental Principles for the Garden

Robert L. Wixom[1]

Whether in Asia or America or the South Sea Islands, the earth is the larger context of survival. All human professions, institutions and activities must be integral with the earth as the primary self-nourishing, self-governing, and self-filling community. To integrate our human activities within this context is our way into the future.

—Thomas Berry, *The Dream of the Earth*

Abstract

Environmental concerns may be expressed in the classroom, in the home, in the local community, or at the regional, national, and international levels of organization; they can focus on ideas, principles, problems, practices, interacting relationships, the scientific base for understanding, achievements and organizational resolution. Many scientific books attest to the diverse character of the subject. This chapter places primary emphasis on the principles and related structures in the United Nations and other organizations that may lead to significant environmental achievements.

Introduction

The following survey of events that followed the 1992 Earth Summit may alert the reader to some unfamiliar environmental events, some policy decisions, and current communi-

---

[1] **Robert L. Wixom** is a graduate of Earlham College and the University of Illinois (Ph.D., biochemistry, 1942). He has taught and conducted research on amino acid and protein metabolism/ nutrition and biomedical information retrieval in the departments of biochemistry, the University of Arkansas School of Medicine, and the University of Missouri School of Medicine and College of Agriculture; currently he is professor emeritus of biochemistry. He has had a lifelong interest in environmental concerns, hiking, and camping. For the past six years he has served as an advisor or co-advisor for several student environmental organizations, as co-initiator and first chair, the University of Missouri Environmental Affairs Council (1991-1994), and as current chair of its Campus Environmental Awareness Committee.

cation facets. On the other hand, this approach may be too brief for those unfamiliar with these subjects; in that case, the appended key cited literature may be useful.

With a flowing sense of history, we have moved from the Big Bang to the present Information Explosion (figure 1). After decades of telephone, radio and television, we have entered the era of daily fax, e-mail, the Internet, and electronic information transfer. In this hurtling race of the developed world, we have also been depleting our non-renewable resources and increasing pollution of our precious air, water and soil. From 1970 to the present, we have heard the persistent message to "reduce, reuse, and recycle," but the academic literature has gone far beyond this and other slogans in examining crucial environmental issues. The future is unpredictable, although several possible scenarios are depicted in figure 1: possible nuclear war, disease, continuation of present (probably unsustainable) life styles, and transformation to a sustainable society. Some environmental issues must be resolved on a local, regional, and/or national basis; others such as global warming, loss of tropical rainforest, and overpopulation require integrated, international recognition and resolution. To narrow our focus, this chapter concentrates on the policy developments related to the recognition and the developing principles in the international arena; the initial emphasis is on the work of the United Nations—its conferences, planning and detailed work in New York City and elsewhere. The United Nations Association (1995) has listed some fifty achievements of the United Nations, which have been grouped here into six clusters (table 1). Hereafter, this introduction examines the UN's role in promoting development and simultaneously protecting the environment

Figure 1. Where is Human Society Going?

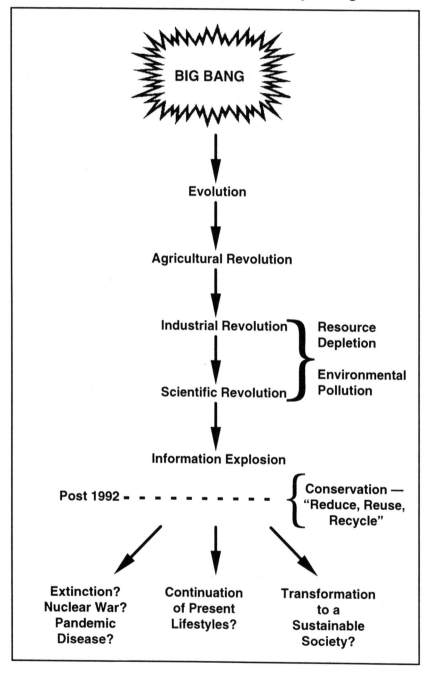

Table 1. The United Nations—50 Years of Achievement

Over-all Subject Clusters *	Subareas
Promote peace and security	5
Improve health of children, women, refugees, etc.	13
Enhance trade, investment, economic reform, workers' rights, etc.	6
Promote human rights, international law judicial settlements and women's rights	4
Facilitate free flow of information/ global communication	3
Promote development and Protect environment {	↑ UNDP ↑ UNEP ↑ African development ↑ Safe drinking water ↓ Natural disasters ↓ Ozone layer depletion ↓ Global warming ↓ Overfishing ↓ Deforestation ↓ Pollution ↑ World's oceans....11
Miscellaneous	8
Total	50

*Derived from a list of 50 areas (United Nations Association 1995)

The United Nations has sponsored many conferences, which have been diverse in size and breadth of subjects covered and frequently overlooked by the general media; table 2 lists four recent key conferences. A Habitat II Conference is being planned. The emphasis in each has been to achieve consensus despite disparate ideas and cultures among the nations. Though the final reports on the last two conferences were not available at the time of this writing, many preliminary reports indicate the subject matter of each reflects a partial overlapping, sequential, and integrative nature as world concerns have grown from 1987 to 1995.

Table 2. Some Key United Nations Conferences

June 3–14, 1992	United Nations Conference on Environment and Development (UNCED) or "The Earth Summit," or "Rio Conference" (preceded by four "Prep Cons" in 1989–92), Rio de Janeiro
Sept. 3–15, 1994	United Nations International Conference on Population and Development (ICPD) or "Population Conference," or "Cairo Conference" (preceded by world population conferences in 1927, 1974, 1984, and three "Prep Cons" in 1990–94), Cairo
Mar. 6–12, 1995	United Nations World Conference on Social Development, Copenhagen
Sept. 4–15, 1995	United Nations World Conference on Women, Beijing

[Note. The subject content of each reflects an overlapping, sequential, and integrative nature as time and world concerns have grown.]

The Growing Description of Sustainable Development

Words and concepts change in meaning over time, and such is certainly the case with "sustainable development." The dominant model for economic development in Third World countries from the 1950s through the 1970s was major dams, heavy industry, construction projects, and reliance on the Green Revolution (for example, see Korten 1990; Piel 1992; Tolba 1992). The 1972 UN Conference on Human Environment in Stockholm stated:

> Man is both creature and molder of his environment, which gives him physical substance and affords him the opportunity for intellectual, moral, social and spiritual growth. In the long tortuous evolution of the human race on

the planet, a stage has been reached when, through the rapid acceleration of science and technology, man has acquired the power to transform his environment in countless ways and on an unprecedented scale. Both aspects of man's environment, the natural and man-made, are essential to his well being and to the enjoyment of basic human rights—even the right to life itself. (Stockholm Conference, 1972)

Hence the Stockholm conference placed economic development and environmental degradation on the international agenda, but little was achieved during subsequent years.

Sustainability has its origin in the French verb *soutenir*, "to hold up or support." *The Oxford English Dictionary* defines sustainable as "capable of being upheld, maintainable, to support life, nature, etc., with needs." B. J. Brown et al. (1987) reviewed the diverse, transient and elusive nature of the term, and its use over many decades. Prior to the *Brundtland Report*, Brown et al. (1987) mention other more or less equivalent terms—"sustained use of the biosphere," "ecological sustainability," "maximum sustained yield," "sustainable agriculture," "sustainable energy," and "sustainable society." More recent, and maybe equally diverse, descriptions of sustainable development or sustainability follow.

By the 1980s, significant limitations and even disasters from earlier policies and practices were finally being recognized. Drawing on several earlier critiques, the United Nations in 1983 initiated the World Commission on Environment and Development, chaired by Gro Brundtland of Norway; they suggested a new model of "sustainable development," which they described as an approach "to meet the needs of the present without compromising the ability of future generations to meet their own needs" (Brundtland 1987).

Herman Daly in *Steady State Economics* (1991) described the terms "steady state economics," "throughput," "optimal allocation," and "optimal scale" that led him to distinguish between growth and development.

Growth refers to expansion in the scale of the physical dimensions of the economic system, while development refers to qualitative change (improvement or degradation) of a physically nongrowing economic system in a state of dynamic equilibrium maintained by the environment. The limits due to physical and biological resources make sustainable growth a future impossibility. By contrast, sustainable development implies a level, not a rate of growth, of resource use.

From Daly's emphasis on an operational approach, he concludes that "for renewable sources, harvesting rates should not exceed regenerative rates and that waste emissions should not exceed the renewable assimilatory capacity of the environment. . . . Nonrenewable sources should be exploited, but at a rate equal to the creation of renewable substitutes" (Daly 1991).

Lester Brown wrote in *Saving the Planet* (1991) that sustainable development was:

> development toward an economy that has a population in balance with its natural support systems, an energy system that does not raise the level of greenhouse gases, and a level of material demand that neither exceeds the sustainable yields of forests, greenlands, or fisheries, nor systematically destroys other species with which we share the planet.

In 1993, President Bill Clinton prepared Executive Order #12852 to establish the President's Council on Sustainable Development (PSCD) and suggested another, though similar, description: "economic growth that will benefit the present and future generations without detrimentally affecting the resources or biological systems of the planet" (PCSD 1995).

Another definition, from a New Mexico group, stated, "We interpret sustainability to mean a condition in which natural systems and social systems survive and thrive indefinitely" (Euston and Gibson 1995).

A recent modification of the above concept is "sustainable human development," which was defined by the United Nations Development Programme as "development that generates growth, but also equitably distributes the fruits of that growth. It empowers women, increases people's choices and opportunities, and protects and regenerates the environment. In short, sustainable human development is pro-poor, pro-jobs, pro-women, and pro-environment" (Speth 1995).

The definition of sustainable development in the *Brundtland Report* (1987) has its share of critics. Two recent critics, Wackernagel and Rees (1996), provide an alternative and perhaps a more precise planning tool, called "ecological footprint." This approach

> accounts for the flows of energy and matter to and from any defined economy and converts these into the corresponding land/water area required from nature to support these flows. This technique is both analytical and educational. It not only assesses the sustainability of current human activity, but is also effective in building public awareness and assisting decision-making.

These authors provide vivid examples of its use for analysis, prediction and decisions making. There is no question that the term "sustainable development" will continue to evolve.

United Nations Initiatives

United Nations Conference on Environment and Development (UNCED).

In 1989 the UN General Assembly adopted the report, *"Our Common Future"* (Brundtland 1987), and started the institutional machinery rolling for the 1992 Earth Summit (figure 2). Between 1989 and 1992, many reports from scientific, national government, and NGO sources (an NGO is a "non-governmental organization" that has an interest in one or more UN issues; there are about 900 NGOs) flowed into the United Nations. Lerner (1991) has recorded keen observations of some of the NGO leaders in the pre-UNCED period, "conversations with architects of an ecologically sustainable future." His book provides insight on how NGOs develop and function in a complex world. Lerner's book should be read in the context of the political and economic considerations of the pre-1992 era as expressed by Al Gore, then senator from Tennessee and now vice-president of the United States (Gore 1992). In a valuable, timeless statement, Gore wrote:

> When considering a problem as large as the degradation of the global environment, it is easy to feel overwhelmed, utterly hopeless to effect any change whatsoever. But we must resist that response, because this crisis will be resolved only if individuals take some responsibility for it. By educating ourselves and others, by doing our part to minimize our use and waste of resources, by becoming more politically active and demanding change, each one of us can make a difference. . . . We each need to assess our own relationship to the natural world and renew, at the deepest level of personal integrity, a connection to it. And that can only happen if we renew what is authentic and true to every aspect of our lives. (Gore 1992)

In preparation for the 1992 United Nations Conference on Environment and Development (also known as the "Earth Summit"), national reports, United Nations reports, and NGO reports had to be condensed, integrated, and made ready for inspection by the national delegations prior to the four preparatory conferences (shortened to "Prep Cons") that took place from 1989 to 1992. The UN Secretariat staff worked quietly and diligently to resolve different scientific, cultural and national viewpoints and to condense the massive paper flow to a manageable size with an organized structure. The United Nations Conference on Environment and Development was held June 3–14, 1992 in Rio de Janeiro, Brazil (United Nations 1992).

20

Figure 2. Paradigm Shift, UNCED, and Beyond

Two University of Missouri students and I spent five days at the United Nations in March 1992 to attend Prep Con 4. Some 100 to 200 NGOs were present daily throughout the six weeks of Prep Con 4. We met in the early morning for a briefing and tried to keep up with the daily paper flow, buttonholing delegates, attending workshops, and observing the daily prep con proceedings. When there was general agreement, the chair stated that it was approved. If one or more delegations disagreed, that section, paragraph, or even a word was "bracketed"; in other words, it was held over for later modification and compromise. Evidently the Prep Cons relied on the negotiation approach, and had rarely a vote or a difficult fifty/forty-nine split! Bracketing led to consensus, but for some areas it led to some innocuous statements. A long-time UN observer remarked that most national delegates are astute, "seasoned diplomats who know how to try to achieve common ground by persuasion and negotiation." This process of reaching decisions prevailed also at the Earth Summit and other subsequent conferences.

Following in the steps of the *Brundtland Report*, the goals of the Earth Summit were to find a balance between the forces of economic development and environmental protection, leading to an amplification of the term "sustainable development." The Prep Cons and the UN Secretariat organized the early agenda of the Earth Summit along the lines of the twenty-one Working Issues (Valentine 1991). (Table 3 relates these twenty-one issues to some twenty-four or more academic disciplines. The possibility for interdisciplinary study abounds!)

Question/Query: Do we teach about the "21 Working Issues" and related facets for the students in our classes and citizens at large?

Building on the many preliminaries, the Earth Summit adopted twenty-seven principles in a document labeled, "The Rio Declaration on Environment and Development," also known as the *"Earth Charter"* (United Nations 1993). Several principles focus on the concept of sustainable development:

Table 3. The "21 Working Issues" Considered at UNCED, Rio de Janeiro, June 3–14, 1992*

Working Issues	Related Academic Disciplines
Biodiversity	Biology, Wildlife, Natural Resources
Biotechnology	Biochemistry, Microbiology, Molecular Biology
Climate change	Atmospheric Sciences, Geography
Deforestation	Forestry, Natural Resources
Desertification	Geography
Economic Instruments	Economics, Public Policy
Education/ Information	Education, Journalism
Environment and Health	Medicine, Health-related Sciences
Financial Resources	Economic, Finance
Freshwater Resources	Biology, Wildlife, Natural Resources
Institutions	Sociology, Public Policy, Political Science
Legal Aspects	Law, Political Science
Living Marine Resources	Biology, Natural Resources
Marine Pollution Engineering	Sciences, Biology
New/ Renewable Energy Resources	Economics, Engineering, Natural Resources
Ozone Layer	Atmospheric Sciences
Poverty and Environmental Degradation	Economics, Sociology, Rural Sociology
Technology Transfer	Engineering, Sciences
Toxic Waste Disposal	Engineering, Sciences
Transboundary Air Pollution	Atmospheric Sciences
Urban Environment	Sociology, Geography

*Derived from Mark Valentine, *Introductory Guide to the Earth Summit* (1991)

Principle 1:   Human beings are at the center of concerns for sustainable development. They are entitled to a healthy and productive life in harmony with nature.

Principle 20: Women have a vital role in environmental management and development. Their full participation is therefore essential to achieve sustainable development.

Principle 21: The creativity, ideals and courage of the youth of the world should be mobilized to forge a global partnership in order to achieve sustainable development and ensure a better future for all.

Principle 25: Peace, development and environmental protection are interdependent and indivisible.

All twenty-seven principles in the *Earth Charter* are listed in appendix B.

The 5,000 government delegates at the Earth Summit produced a 294-page book, *Agenda 21,* in which the earlier twenty-one Working Issues evolved into forty chapters (United Nations 1993) (see appendix C for the outline of *Agenda 21*). Due to its intrinsic content and historic precedence, *Agenda 21* should be placed in all academic libraries and included as source material in many university/college courses.

The 1992 agreements set the focus for subsequent international discussion, negotiation, and treaty-making. Not yet treaties, these international agreements are a major early step in preserving our shared heritage, the global commons; however, "international diplomacy is a slow business. Most treaties take years and years to negotiate, ratify and implement" (French 1992).

Simultaneous with the above negotiations, many individuals and their respective organizations (NGOs) felt that their government delegations were not addressing basic environmental problems. They believed that environmental solutions began within local citizens groups and communities that have been (or will be) affected by environmental degradation and misdirected development (Rome et al. 1993). Some 18,000 individuals from around the world attended a parallel meeting in Rio de Janeiro, the NGO Global Forum (Rome et al. 1993). They simultaneously negotiated forty-six NGO alternative treaties, which are available upon request (Rome et al. 1993). Topics range from biodiversity to deforestation to urban environment (see table 4). These NGO treaties are an expression of many people from both North and South and from many diverse cultures. "They come from the grassroots and are for the grassroots." An excellent practice is to read them side by side with the forty chapters of the official *Agenda 21* (United Nations 1992). Another suggested educational approach is to read the alternative *Peoples Treaties* (Rome et al 1993) and *Agenda 21* simultaneously with the detailed behind-the-scenes accounts of the Earth Summit provided by Rogers (1993) in *The Earth Summit: A Planetary Reckoning,* and in *The Road From Rio* (McCoy and McCully 1993). A relevant *Bibliography on the Earth Summit and Related Environmental Subjects,* containing 205 post-1990 references, is available (Wixom 1993).

Table 4. NGO Alternative Treaties
(from the NGO Forum, Rio de Janeiro, June 3–14, 1992)

Declarations & General Principles
• The People's Earth Declaration   • Rio de Janeiro Declarations   • The Earth Charter   • Ethical Commitment
NGO Cooperation & Institution Building
• Rio Framework Treaty on NGO Global Decision Making   • Treaty for NGO Cooperation and Sharing of Resources   • Communication, Information, Media and Networking Treaty   • Treaty on Technology Bank   • Treaty of the People of the Americas   • Code of Conduct for NGOs
Alternative Economic Issues
• Treaty on Alternative Economic Models   • NGOs "Treaty" on Transnational Corporation   • Alternative Treaty on Trade and Sustainable Development   • NGO Debt Treaty   • Capital Flight and Corruption   • Treaty on Consumption and Lifestyle   • NGO Poverty Treaty
Ocean & Marine Issues
• Pollution of the Marine Environment   • Minimizing Physical Alteration of Marine Ecosystems   • Protecting the Sea from Global Atmospheric Changes   • Marine Biodiversity Treaty   • Marine Protected Areas Resolution Concerning Guanabara Bay

Global Environmental Issues
• Alternative NGO Agreement on Climate Change • Forest Treaty • Treaty Regarding Arid and Semi-Arid Zones • Treaty on "Cerrados" (Scrubland) • Citizens Commitments on Biodiversity • Draft Protocol on Scientific Research Components for the   Conservation of Biodiversity • Citizens' Commitment on Biotechnology • Treaty on Energy • Treaty on Waste • Treaty on the Nuclear Problem
Food Production
• NGO Sustainable Agriculture Treaty • NGO Food Security Treaty • NGO Fresh Water Treaty • Fisheries Treaty
Cross-Sectional Issues

• A Global Women's Treaty for NGOs Seeking a Just and
    Healthy Planet
• NGO Treaty on Population, Environment and Development
• Youth Treaty
• Treaty in Defense/ Protection of Children/ Adolescents
• Treaty on Environmental Education for Sustainable Societies/
    Global Responsibility
• Treaty Against Racism
• NGO Treaty on Militarism, the Environment, and Development
• Treaty on Urbanization
• International Treaty between NGOs and Indigenous Peoples

Note. The full alternative treaties and commentaries are available in a looseleaf notebook, "The People's Treaties from the Earth Summit" for $20.00 from CNSD, c/o *Commonweal,* Box 316, Bolinas, CA 94924, or $1.00 per single treaty.

United Nations Commission on Sustainable Development (UNCSD). The fifty years of UN history may be divided into three periods:

1. 1940s—Initial hope for global peace
2. 1950s-80s—The decades trapped in Cold War politics
3. 1990s—Pressing environmental issues as a relatively new concern at the United Nations.

With this background, the programs of the UN Environmental Programme (UNEP) and UN Developmental Programme (UNDP) helped build the pre-1992 foundation for UNCED. After UNCED, the UN General Assembly initiated the UN Commission on Sustainable Development (UN Yearbook 1993). UNCSD, the heir to UNCED, reorganized the earlier forty UNCED chapters into five cross-sectoral (or overlapping) issues, and four sectoral issues and prepared a timetable for their evaluation (table 5). Thus by 1997, the UNCSD will have reviewed all forty chapters of *Agenda 21* with the goal of producing a 1997 report to the UN General Assembly. Reports submitted annually to UNCSD by national governments "are the main basis for monitoring progress and identifying problems faced by countries. By 1995, some seventy-five governments reported having established national sustainable development commissions or other coordinating bodies. . . . To help countries formulate policies for sustainability and regulate their impact, *Agenda 21* recognized the need for a set of internationally accepted indicators" (United Nations, *In Focus,* 1995). UNCSD plans to have a "menu of indicators" for use in the 1997 reports to UNCSD.

Quakers (Friends) are fortunate to have the Quaker United Nations Office (QUNO), which is physically located across the street from the United Nations (at 777 UN Plaza, New York, NY 10017). The QUNO *Briefing Paper* series and *In and Around the UN* series provide excellent current and concise reports of on-going diplomacy at the United Nations. Examples are the reports (Hunter 1993; Collett and Roberts 1994; Mason 1995; Collett 1995) that appeared months before the official *United Nations Yearbook* and weeks before the UN's

Table 5. Review of Agenda 21 by UNCSD

Five Cross-Sectoral Clusters

Chapters	Subject Areas
2-5	Critical Elements of Sustainability (Poverty, Consumption, Population, and Health)
33	Financial Resources and Mechanisms
34-47	Education, Science, and Technology (Technology Transfer, Biotechnology, Education Science Awareness and Training, Capacity-Building)
8, 38-40	Decision-Making Structures in Sustainable Development (Legal Instruments, Institutions, Information, Integration of Environment and Development
23-32	Roles of Major Groups in Sustainable Development (Children, Youth, Women, Native People, Workers, Farmers, Businesspersons, Scientists, etc.)

Four Sectoral Issues

Year for Review	Chapters Covered	Subject Areas
1994	6, 7, 18, 21	Healthy Human Settlements and Freshwater
1994	19, 20, 22	Toxic Chemicals and Hazardous Waste
1995	10-15	Land, Desertification, Forests, and Biodiversity
1996	9-17	Atmosphere, Oceans, and All Kinds of Seas

Department of Public Information articles in *In Focus.* Another way to keep current is a subscription to the bimonthly newsletter, *CSD Update,* with many specific, valuable and current details; it is available from the CSD Secretariat, United Nations. The Institute for Sustainable Development (Winnipeg, Canada) has a valuable, thorough newsletter, *Earth Negotiations Bulletin.* Thus, the "spirit of Rio lives on" in the specifics of workshops and intersessional committee meetings (United Nations, *In Focus,* 1995). Negotiation, persuasion, and the search for mutual agreement continues quietly on a weekly basis at the United Nations, but the media has tended to ignore these incremental, though necessary, environmental steps.

UN International Conference on Population and Development (ICPD). The features of the Earth Summit, namely the emphasis on consensus, the principles developed, the Programme of Action, and the participation of NGOs, set the pattern for the next UN conference, the 1994 UN International Conference on Population and Development in Cairo. Several older population organizations that had a continuing concern with overpopulation and overconsumption were joined now by many new groups. One hundred and seventy-nine nations were represented in Cairo; 11,000 participants were present! Though some may remember from the media several disagreements in Cairo, ninety percent of the ICPD documents were agreed upon prior to Cairo. Friends and many others will applaud two of the accepted fifteen principles of the ICPD (United Nations 1995):

Principle 1. All human beings are born free and equal in dignity and rights.
Principle 4. The full and equal participation of women in civil, cultural, economic, political and social life at the national, regional and international levels and the eradication of all forms of sex discrimination are priority objectives of the international community.

The full fifteen principles of ICPD may be found in appendix D.

The final consensus document of this UN Conference on Population and Development—Programme of Action of ICPD (United Nations, ICPD 1995) has sixteen accepted chapters, which should be read particularly by those educators with an interest in population and those who are reaching out to the young men and women—our students—who will be faced with the problem of the population explosion. A variety of classroom approaches might be used to supplement this original report.

Rapid population growth cannot and should not be considered as a single focus. Lester R. Brown, president of the Worldwatch Institute, notes that with increasing population come falling water tables, shrinking cropland area, lack of further net benefit from fertilizer and declining yields in fisheries; the world's stocks of rice, corn, wheat, and other cereals have fallen to the lowest level in two decades (L. Brown 1995). In addition to the information and trends described in their earlier books (*Population, Resources and Environment*, Ehrlich and Ehrlich, 2d ed. 1972; *The Population Explosion*, Ehrlich and Ehrlich, 2d ed. 1990), Ehrlich, Ehrlich, and Daly (1995) confirm these factors and expand on several other related adverse factors, such as diminishing genetic diversity of crops and their wild relatives, and increased ultraviolet radiation. Family planning is essential, but not sufficient; women's equity in income, education, and health is crucial to lower fertility rates and prevent the environmental degradation that accompanies over-population. Ehrlich, Ehrlich, and Daly (1995) propose a "global ethical revolution"; values, vision, and education are part of that revolution.

Question/Query: Do we educators teach our students—our future leaders—about the above issues and the relevance of UNCED, UNCSD, ICPD, Earth Council, PCSD, UNDP, UNEP, etc., as readily as we do about the presidency, Congress, EPA, NIH, NSF, DOE, etc.? We live more and more in an interdependent, globalized world.

Other Responsive Chords for the UNCED Message

United Nations Environment Programme (UNEP). The UN Environment Program, begun in 1972, has grown slowly, mostly unheeded by western media. Mostafa K. Tolba, executive director of UNEP (1976-1992), and other UNEP leaders recognize the complexity of their task, as simplified in figure 3. Their UNEP report, *Saving Our Planet—Challenges and Hopes* (Tolba 1992), describes and documents common environmental problems: atmospheric pollution; fresh water resources, and water quality; land degradation and desertification; deforestation and forest degradation; loss of biological diversity; and environmental disasters, toxic chemicals, and hazardous wastes. Their *Development Activities and the Environment* includes agriculture and food production, industry, energy production and use, transport, and tourism.

UNEP recognizes that such human conditions as population growth and development, settlements, health and peace, security, and the environment are interrelated; they are complex and interact in diverse patterns in different countries. "The dismal economic predicament of developing countries both causes and aggravates environmental despoliation. This in turn makes economic and structural reform difficult to achieve" (Tolba 1992). "Almost all wars have one basic strategy: destruction of the enemy's life-support systems so that their armies and peoples can be defeated. . . . Studies of the arms race and development have stressed the fact that each competes for the world's finite resources. . . . " (Tolba 1992). General awareness of the above signifies that the world's citizenry has changed. "Evolution in public perception of environmental issues, increased public awareness and the activities of different national and international NGOs gave impetus to many actions in the past two decades to protect the environment. . . . The 1990s are witnessing not only a more vigorous interest, but also an important transformation in thinking." More people now accept the need for strategies to live off "nature's interest," rather than "nature's capital" and recognize the principle of intergenerational responsibility and equity (Tolba 1992). The necessity of leadership and higher education is implicit, though unstated, throughout this book. On the constructive side, Tolba's *Priorities for Action* propose regulatory measures by 1995; assessment by 1995, 2000, and 2010; steps for environmental management by 1995, 2000, and 2010 and integration of environmental economics (Tolba 1992).

United Nations Development Program (UNDP). With the background of UNCED's *Agenda 21*, the UN Development Programme, which had formed in 1965, underwent major review in 1994, leading to significant changes in its goals and programs. UN Secretary General Boutros Boutros-Ghali (1991 to date) encouraged their crucial role, saying,

> As the UN celebrates its 50th anniversary (Oct. 24, 1995), it is faced with challenges of unprecedented urgency and complexity. Following the end of the Cold War, economic and political transition has given rise to new conflicts. The long-standing challenges of the eradication of poverty and protection of the planet's resources for future generations are taking on new dimensions and a new sense of urgency. Peace and development deserve equal priority on the United Nations agenda. Without peace, there can be no development, when so many of the world's people continue to live without adequate food, safe water or shelter and lack access to education, health care and a means of sustainable livelihood. As the UN's leading organization for coordinating and providing grant funding for development cooperation, the UNDP plans a crucial role in shaping an effective and unified UN response to today's development challenges. . . . (Speth 1995)

Figure 3. Connections of People and the Environment*

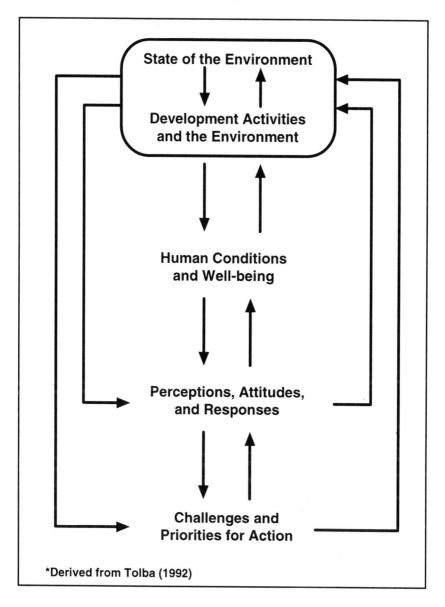

State of the Environment

Development Activities
and the Environment

Human Conditions
and Well-being

Perceptions, Attitudes,
and Responses

Challenges and
Priorities for Action

*Derived from Tolba (1992)

In 1994, the UNDP's executive board endorsed a proposal, "Initiatives for Change," to make sustainable human development the organization's guiding principle. These initiatives seek "to eradicate poverty, to create jobs and livelihoods, to empower women and to regenerate the environment. . ." (Speth 1995). The magnitude of the initiatives is enormous; UNDP cooperates with more than 170 countries. Some 45,258 people are involved in carrying out UNDP goals at the international, national, and local levels, helping developing countries take charge of their own development. The challenges in *Agenda 21* and the *Earth Charter* are being seriously approached by UNEP and UNDP; evaluation of these programs must wait until a later date.

World Summit for Social Development (WSSD). The UN World Summit for Social Development took place in Copenhagen, March 6-12, 1995, and was attended by 185 national delegations, including eighteen heads of state (*Popline* 1995). They "made a clarion call for concerted international action in solving three of the world's more compelling problems—worsening poverty, joblessness and underemployment, and the disintegration of societies. A key ingredient in the solution formulated at this summit was people-centered development" (Speth 1995; Reardon 1995).

UN sources report that fewer than ten percent of the world's people participate fully in the political, economic, social and cultural institutions that shape their lives, particularly the marginalized and rural dwellers (Reardon 1995). Dr. Nafis Sadik, secretary general of the UN International Conference on Population and Development and executive director of the UN Population Fund, concluded that the approval of 180 out of 185 national delegations provided a seal of "legitimization of the Cairo Program of Action (ICPD). . . . Investing in people is the key to balanced, sustainable growth and sustainable development and includes broadening opportunities for people and enables them to realize their potential as human beings." Rapid population growth is one of the main reasons the international community has been unable to stem the tide of world poverty (*Popline* 1995) (UNDP 1995). The official UN report is not available at this date.

United Nations World Conference on Women (UNWCW). The UN World Conference on Women was held in Beijing September 4-15, 1995. The media gave more coverage to this conference than to most of the others—perhaps due to controversies with the Chinese authorities and the presence of First Lady Hillary Rodham Clinton—but none of these conferences have received adequate media coverage. An overall UN report is yet to be published; for an excellent pre-Beijing report, the reader is referred to the QUNO *Briefing Paper* (Mason 1995; United Nations 1995), the short post-conference summary in QUNO's *In and Around the UN* (Collett 1995), and other similar NGO communications.

These conferences, by planning and by hindsight, were cumulative; each building on the preceding one, each integrating the concepts and practices of the earlier ones into a new tapestry. To summarize, many in the world community have recognized the interrelated environmental issues in these and other conferences and have begun the long process of healing the Garden.

United States Initiative

President's Council on Sustainable Development (PCSD).

To develop the United States' response to UNCED and "fulfill U.S. commitments related to *Agenda 21*" (PCSD 1995), President Bill Clinton appointed in June 1993 a President's Commission on Sustainable Development (PCSD), which has met subsequently four times per year.

The twenty-five members of PCSD include representatives from environmental organizations, government departments, and the private corporate sector. They divided into eight task forces (table 6), with an additional 450 task force members and met frequently at the quarterly public meetings of the PCSD. They accept the earlier description of sustainable development. The PSCD feels that the nation should make "a national commitment to economic prosperity, ecological integrity and social equity." Their Vision Statement declares:

> Our vision is of a life-sustaining Earth. We are committed to the achievement of a dignified, peaceful, and equitable existence.
>
> A sustainable United States will have a growing economy that equitably provides opportunities for satisfying livelihoods and a safe, healthy, high quality of life for present and future generations.

Our Nation will protect its environment, its natural resource base, and the functions and viability of natural systems on which all life depends. (PCSD 1996)

Table 6. Eight Task Forces: Working Groups of PCSD*

	Number of Members
Principles, Goals, and Definitions	(10 +1)
Eco-Efficiency	(11 + 35)
Energy and Transportation	(9 + 60)
Natural Resources	(10 + 42)
Population and Consumption	(9 + 18)
Sustainable Communities	(10 + 120)
Sustainable Agriculture	(9 + 12)
Public Linkage, Dialogue and Education	(6 + 59)

*Derived from PCSD Status Update (1995)

The April 1995 *PCSD Status Update*, with fifteen principles, was revised to give sixteen principles in the "We Believe Statement" within their Final Report (February 1996), two of which state:

Item 2. Change is inevitable and necessary for the sake of future generations and for ourselves. We can choose a course for change that will lead to the mutually reinforcing goals of economic growth, environmental protection, and social equity.

Item 16. Citizens must have access to high-quality and lifelong formal and nonformal education that enables them to understand the interdependence of economic prosperity, environmental quality, and social equity—and prepares them to take actions that support all three.

(See appendix E for the full sixteen principles.)

A closer inspection of the two sets of Principles shows a shift to a more conservative viewpoint in the intervening year, perhaps reflecting the November 1994 national elections. The Final Report, published in February 1996, also has a commendable set of ten Goals. A copy may be obtained by writing the U.S. Superintendent of Documents.

Grassroots Initiatives

Earth Council. In 1993, concerned international environmental leaders proposed facilitating the work of the world's approximately 10,000 NGOs, some weak and slim on resources. Thus the Earth Council was initiated and headquartered in San Jose, Costa Rica, with Maurice F.

Strong, the former secretary general of UNCED, as the vigorous chair. The council has twenty-one members from political, business, scientific, and other NGO sectors of the worldwide civil society. They identified three needs that the Earth Council should address:

1. To provide information and empower civil society organizations
2. To monitor, review and assess the implementation of the Earth Summit results
3. To promote public awareness and support for the needed transition to more sustainable patterns of worldwide development (Earth Council brochure)

Several specific programs in each category are described in table 7. The Earth Council is in touch with sustainable development groups in 117 countries and two regions, leading to an invaluable directory of these groups (Silveria 1995). The council reports that more than forty national governments have formed broad-based national entities to develop strategies and approaches for sustainable development (Silveria 1995). For further information, write to: Alicia Barcena, executive director, Earth Council, Apdo 2323-1002, San Jose, Costa Rica.

Citizens Network for Sustainable Development (CNSD). From 1990 to 1992, the U.S. Citizens Network for UNCED worked to learn about, contribute to, and influence the developing UNCED. Their successor NGO, the Citizens Network for Sustainable Development, publishes a quarterly *CNSD Newsletter*. Their objectives include:

1. Define and articulate the meaning of sustainability.
2. Develop an agenda to create sustainability.
3. Provide a forum on issues of sustainability.
4. Serve the diverse constituencies working on sustainability.

The CNSD has held annual meetings of its comprehensive and quite diverse member organizations, with participants from citizens groups, academia, state governments and federal governments. Many of the prepared lectures, discussion summaries, participants present and organizations involved have been recorded in their *Conference Proceedings* (Porter et al. 1992; Taylor et al. 1993; and Hansen et al. 1994). The second conference at Louisville, Ky. (Taylor et al. 1993) was mainly sponsored by the governor of Kentucky and included the presence of many CNSD leaders and members. These proceedings are great raw material for students to decipher the process of networking and group decision-making. The heart of the CNSD's strength lies in its nineteen ongoing Network Working

Table 7. The Earth Council's Three Programmes*

Mission	"The mission of the Earth Council is to support or empower people in building a more secure, equitable, and sustainable future."

Programmes	**1. Earth Monitoring and Reporting**
	   a. Earth Reports
	   b. Sectoral Assessments
	   c. People's Earth Monitoring Systems
	
	2. Facilitating People's Initiatives
	   a. Networks of National Councils on Sustainable Development
	   b. Empower Civil Society Institutions and Major Groups
	   c. Ombudsman-type Function and Networking
	   d. People's Funding for Sustainable Development
	
	3. Public Education and Awareness
	   a. Earth Charter
	   b. Development and Dissemination of Information
	   c. Public Forums and Hearings
	   d. Contributions to Major Events and Ongoing Negotiations Related to Sustainable Development

*Derived from Earth Council leaflet (1995)

Groups, which range from biodiversity to principles/ethics (see table 8); these working groups follow and communicate the developments at PCSD, UNCSD, and ICPD. Perhaps the reader would like to join one of these working groups, participate and benefit from the exchange. For further information, contact this writer or write directly to CNSD (Sharyle Patton, CNSD, c/o Commonweal, P.O. Box 316, Bolinas, CA 94924).

Pertinent to many NGOs is the excellent detailed book by David C. Korten, *Getting to the 21st Century–Voluntary Action and the Global Agenda* (1990). From a wealth of thirty years' experience in academia, governments, foundations and overseas, Korten describes three interrelated global crises of the 1980s, the "decade of denial": poverty, environmental failure and social violence. Now the 1990s show the potential for development in the arenas of justice, sustainability and inclusiveness. From these bases, Korten traces the historic changes in NGOs from relief and welfare and community development to sustainable systems development and people's movements. "There are at least four critical roles for voluntary action within the broader framework of a people's development movement: catalyzing the transformation of institutions, policies and values; monitoring and protesting abuses of power; [and] facilitating reconciliation and providing essential community services." In contrast to a social organization based on hierarchy (control, stability and bureaucratization), networking is "the organizational mode of lateral communication, self-direction, rapid adaptation and social movements. It frees the flow of creative and voluntary energies. . . [and becomes] the primary cohesive force of the just, sustainable, and inclusive society. It is the foundation of people power and the driving force of transformation" (Korten 1990). Korten has many other valuable perceptions on the role of NGOs as catalysts for transformation, as witnessed later at UNCED, IPCD, and subsequent UN conferences (table 2). For a careful analysis of the strengths and weaknesses of NGOs, McCoy and McCully (1994) describe how NGOs met the earlier challenges of UNCED and continue to negotiate in UNCSD. McCoy and McCully (1994) state, "The challenge now to NGOs is to demonstrate that they have the flexibility, skill, creativity and energy to engage international institutions and their governments as genuine professional and political peers." McCoy, as one of four co-chairs of CNSD, writes from direct experience and should be heeded.

Question/Query: *Do we, as educators, teach our students about the views of citizens groups and minority expressions, the approach of networking, and other tools of communication, as contrasted with the main emphasis on official government, national or international positions and statements?*

Conclusions

Over the past two decades, there has been a "paradigm shift" in our concerns for the environment (as depicted in figure 1). While Native Americans and other indigenous people have a strong, long-standing sense of connectedness to the Earth, now many more people express loving care for our planet Earth, our Gaia. Individuals, citizens groups, and governments are urging change. We—society and its members—have made progress,

Table 8. Outline of Citizens Network for Sustainable Development

Executive Committee Co-Chairs

Dianne Dillon-Ridgley (President's Council on Sustainable Development)

Don Edwards (Washington, D.C.)

Michael McCoy (New York City/ UN Liaison)

Sharyle Patton (Administration/Memberships
Commonweal   Phone 415/868-9720
P.O. Box 316   Fax: 415/ 868-2230
Bolinas, CA 94924   E-mail: mlerner@igc.apc.org

Citizens Networks—Regional and State

Great Lakes	California
New York City/	Idaho
UN Liaison	Iowa
Northeast	New Mexico
Northwest	Oregon
Southeast	Washington, D.C.

Citizens Network Working Groups

Arctic	Indigenous Issues
Biodiversity	Japan/US Agenda 21 Project
Commission on Sustainable Development	Population and Consumption
Consumption/Production/Jobs	Presidents Council on Sustainable Development
Economics	Principles/ Ethics
Education	Sustainable Agriculture
Forest Issues	Sustainable Communities
Human Settlements	Women/Youth

but we have a long way to go, for two factors are still missing in the developed world: large numbers of citizens pressing for change, and political will.

Some may know and have carried out the following; others are invited to do so:

1. Identify and learn the fundamental relationships of environmental issues and ecology.
2. Express these concepts in your home, your place of residence, your academic institution (or workplace) and your daily life.
3. Join an environmental organization. Some good ones prevail in academia, cities, states and nationwide. Each of us can "recycle, reuse and reduce," but some of the environmental challenges seem to be too large for individual effort. Work with others!
4. Nurture your spiritual resources, and your vision of a sustainable world. Share that vision with others!
5. Your ideas, your energy, your leadership, and your contributions are needed in a continuing struggle for:

   - A sustainable environment
   - Sustainable institutions
   - A sustainable world community.

Literature Cited

Brown, Becky J., et al. 1987. Global Sustainability: Toward Definition. Environment Management. *Int. J. For Decision Makers and Scientists,* 11:6, 713-720.

Brown, Lester R., et al. 1991. *Saving the Planet: How to Shape an Environmentally Global Economy.* Washington, D.C.: Worldwatch Institute.

Brown, Lester R. 1995. Facing Food Scarcity. *World Watch,* 8:6, 10-20.

Brundtland, Gro. 1987. *Our Common Future.* New York: Oxford Univ. Press.

Collett, Stephen, and Alice Roberts. 1994. Follow-up to the Earth Summit. *QUNO Briefing Paper,* Vol. 2, June.

Collings, Mark, ed. 1990. *The Last Rain Forest–A World Conservation Atlas.* Oxford: Oxford University Press.

Daly, Herman E. 1991. *Steady State Economics,* 2d ed. Washington, D.C.: Island Press.

Ehrlich, Paul R., and Anne H. Ehrlich. 1972. *Population, Resources, Environment–Issues in Human Ecology,* 2d ed. San Francisco: W. H. Freeman & Co.

———. 1990. *The Population Explosion,* 2d ed. New York: Simon and Schuster.

Ehrlich, Paul R., Ann H. Ehrlich, and Gretchen Daly. 1995. *The Stork and the Plow–The Equity Answer to the Herman Dilemma.* New York: G.P. Putnam's Sons.

Euston, Stanley, and William Gibson. 1995. *Gathering Hope–Sustainable Project for the Gazilian Road.* Santa Fe, N.M.:

French, Hilary F. 1992. *After the Earth Summit–The Future of the World Governance.* Washington, D.C.: Worldwatch Institute, Pamphlet 102.

Goldsmith, Edward, Nicholas Hildyard, Patrick McCully, and Peter Bunyan. 1990. *Imperiled Planet–Restoring Our Endangered Ecosystem.* Cambridge: MIT Press.

Gore, Al. 1992. *Earth in the Balance: Ecology and the Human Spirit.* Boston: Houghton Mifflin Co.

Hammond, Allen L., ed. 1992-93. *World Resources–A Guide to the Global Environment.* A report of the World Resources Institute, the United Nations Environment Programme, and the United Nations Development Programme. Oxford: Oxford University Press.

Hansen, Kathryn W., and Mary Steinmaus, eds. 1994. *Two Years after UNCED–Exploring Partnerships for Sustainable Development.* Proceedings of a CNSD Conference, July 20-24, 1994, Davenport, Iowa.

Hunter, Amy. 1993. Establishment of the UNCSD. *QUNO Briefing Paper.* Vol. 1, March.

Kirder, Uner, ed. 1992. *Change: Threat or Opportunity.* 5 vols. New York: United Nations Development Programme.

Korten, David C. 1990. *Getting to the 21st Century–Voluntary Action and the Global Agenda.* West Hartford, Conn.: Kumarian Press.

Lean, Geoffrey, et al. 1990. *World Wildlife Fund Atlas of the Environment.* New York: Prentice Hall.

Lerner, Steve. 1991. *Earth Summit. Commonweal and Friends of the Earth.* Bolinas, Calif.: Common Knowledge Press.

MacNeill, Jim, et al. 1991. *Beyond Interdependence: The Meshing of the World's Economy and the Earth's Ecology.* A report to the Trilateral Commission. Oxford: Oxford University Press.

McCoy, Michael, and Patrick McCully. 1993. *Road from Rio–An NGO Action Guide to Environment and Development.* Utrecht, Netherlands: International Books and World Information Service on Energy.

McNeely, Jeffrey E., et al. 1990. *Conserving the World's Biological Diversity.* Gland, Switzerland: World Resources Institute; International Union for Conservation of Nature and Natural Resources; Conservation International; and the World Wildlife Fund, co-publishers.

Mason, Ruth. 1995. An Agenda for Women's Empowerment. *QUNO Briefing Paper* Vol. 1, June.

Munro, David A. 1991. *Caring for the Earth–a Strategy for Sustainable Living.* Gland, Switzerland: 2nd World Conservation Strategy Project.

Myers, Norman. 1991. *The Gaia Atlas of Future Worlds–Challenges and Opportunities in an Age of Change.* New York: Anchor Books/Doubleday.

Myers, Norman, ed. 1993. *Gaia–An Atlas of Planet Management,* rev. ed. New York: Anchor Books.

Piel, Gerard. 1992. *Only One World–Our Own to Make and to Keep.* New York: W.H. Freeman and Co.

Population Institute. 1995. *Popline,* 17:2, March.

Porter, Catherine, Tom W. Carroll, and Tracy A. Dobson, eds. 1992. *The Citizens Respond–The Earth's Summit and Beyond: Convergence of Knowledge and Action for Change.* Proceedings of a U.S. Citizens Network on UNCED Conference, September 25-27, 1992. East Lansing: Michigan State University.

QUNO Prepares for the 4th World Conference on Women. *In and around the UN.*, July 1995. New York: Quaker United Nations Office.

President's Council for Sustainable Development. 1995. *PCSD Status Update.* Washington, D.C.: President's Council for Sustainable Development.

———. 1996. *Sustainable America.* Washington, D.C.: President's Council for Sustainable Development.

Reardon, C. 1995. Promises–To Keep. *Choices–The Human Development Magazine.* United Nations Development Programme, 4:1, 4-7.

Rogers, Adam. 1993. *The Earth Summit–A Planetary Reckoning.* Los Angeles: Global View Press.

Rome, Alexandra, Sharyle Patton, et al. 1993. *The People's Treaties from the Earth Summit.* Bolinas, Calif.: Common Knowledge Press.

Sigma Xi (Forum on Global Change and the Human Prospect). 1992. *Global Change and the Human Prospect: Issues on Population, Science, Technology and Equity.* Research Triangle Park, N.C.: Sigma Xi–The Scientific Research Society.

Silveria, Diomar. 1995. *Directory of National Council for Sustainable Development.* San Jose, Costa Rica: Earth Council.

Speth, James G. 1995. Building a New UNDP–1994-95. *UNDP Annual Report.* New York: United Nations Development Programme, Division of Public Affairs.

Taylor, Diana, et al., eds. 1993. *From Rio to the Capitols. Proceedings of a CNSD Conference, May 25-28, 1993.* Louisville, Ky.

Tolba, Mostafa K. 1992. *Saving Our Planet–Challenges and Hopes.* United Nations Environment Programme, Nairobi, Kenya. New York: Chapman and Hall.

Train, Russel E. 1993. *Choosing a Sustainable Future.* Washington, D.C.: Island Press.

Union of Concerned Scientists. 1993. *World Scientists' Warning Briefing Book.* Cambridge: Union of Concerned Scientists.

United Nations. 1992. *Agenda 21–The Programme of Action for Sustainable Development.* New York: United Nations.

———. 1993. *The Global Partnership for Environment and Development.* New York: United Nations.

———. 1993. *Yearbook of the United Nations.* New York: Martin Nijhoff Publishers.

———.1995. *Report of the International Conference on Population and Development–Programme of Action, Cairo, Egypt, September 5-12, 1994,* Vol. 1. New York: United Nations.

———.1995. Sustaining the Future. *In Focus,* Vol. 1. New York: United Nations (DPI/SD/1686–April 1995-2M).

———.1995. Briefing Papers on Women; Rural Poverty (IFAD); International Migration (INSTRAW); Education Empowers (UNESCO); Refugees

(UNHCR); Population (UNFPA); and Social Progress (UNIDO). New York: United Nations.

United Nations Association. 1995. *The U.N.–50 Years of Achievement*. New York: United Nations Association.

Valentine, Mark. 1991. *An Introductory Guide to the Earth Summit*. San Francisco: U.S. Citizens Network for UNCED.

Wixom, Robert L. 1993. *Bibliography of the Earth Summit and Related Environmental Subjects*, 205 mainly post-1990 references cited. Columbia: University of Missouri.

3. New Markets and New Commons
Opportunities in the Global Casino

Hazel Henderson[1]

The goal is a harmony between the human economy and nature that will preserve both nature and humanity, and this is a traditional goal. The world is now divided between those who adhere to this ancient purpose and those who by intention do not— a division that is of far more portent for the future of the world than any of the presently recognized national or political or economic divisions.

The remarkable thing about this division is its relative newness. The idea that we should obey nature's law and live harmoniously with her as good husbanders and stewards of her gifts is old. And I believe that until fairly recently our destructions of nature were more or less unwitting—by-products, so to speak, of our ignorance or weakness or depravity. It is our present principled and elaborately rationalized rape and plunder of the natural world that is a new thing under the sun.

—Wendell Berry, *What Are People For?*

---

[1] **Hazel Henderson** is an international development policy analyst and forecaster and a Fellow of the World Business Academy. She served on the original Advisory Council of the U.S. Office of Technology and Assessment. She held the Horace Albright Chair, University of California, Berkeley, 1982. She is on the board of Appropriate Technology International, the Worldwatch Institute, and advisor of the Calvert Social Investment Fund. She is a member of the Social Venture Network and limited partner of the Global Environment Fund. Her latest book is *Paradigms in Progress* (Indianapolis: Knowledge Systems, 1991). This article first appeared in: *Futures,* 27 (2): 113-124, 195, Elsevier Science Ltd., Great Britain. Printed with permission of Elsevier Science Ltd.

Abstract

The United Nations is well positioned for the global changes of the Information Age now engulfing nation states. The UN role and tasks—as global norm-setter, broker, networker, convener, and peace-keeper—are ideally suited to today's world of linked "infostructures" and distributed power, influence and knowledge typified by the emerging global civil society. The UN can serve all these emerging "electronic commons," including today's global financial casino. Technological, social, and economic contexts for this new global agenda are described together with some new market opportunities in new public/private partnerships to serve the global commons.

Introduction

Currency speculation and the inability of the global securities and financial industry to address the mounting risks to all players, national and international, is a classic example of how events and technology render economic textbooks obsolete. Economic theory is highly articulated concerning markets and various market failures. But economics has consistently overlooked the commons and their allocations theories—except when commons can be owned as property. Today, most of the governance and allocation issues perplexing human societies involve the global commons. Interestingly, today's now-integrated, twenty-four-hour global casino is transforming itself from a classic free market place of win-lose competition to a new form of electronic commons, where each "rational actor's" self-interested behavior can endanger the entire system—unless rapid cooperative, collective action is taken. Recent examples illustrate the vulnerability of tightly interlinked global financial systems operating without overall rules, such as Germany's Herstatt Bank failure and the U.S. savings and loan crisis. Both these episodes were addressed by cooperative agreements and government intervention. The more recent losses by banks and corporations in derivatives and hedging strategies raise concerns that risk reduction for individual players increases risks in the whole financial system which will require new global rules. Even otherwise free market economists, including Fred Bergsten, Jeffrey Sachs, and Lawrence Summers, are urging the formation of a "GATT for investment and finance" (for example, "Beyond Bretton Woods," The *Economist* October 1, 1994 and The *Economist* October 8, 1994). Clearly, the UN has a key role in fostering such innovations.

Today, information technology innovations have created a global financial casino where as much as $4 trillion of "virtual securities" (*derivatives* of underlying real stocks, bonds, commodities, and currencies) are traded each day—bringing new uncertainties such as raids on the dollar, sterling, and other major currencies and scenarios of financial collapse. Worried central bankers and national politicians, trying to stave off such scenarios, are left with failing textbook economic remedies to support their domestic economies and currencies (such as raising interest rates or buying efforts). These national players, handicapped by eroding national sovereignty, maneuver painfully toward the *social innovation* needed to match the advance of the global casino's computer and satellite-based *technological innovation* (Henderson 1993). The UN in its preeminent role as global norm-setter, broker, networker, and convener is well suited to fostering such social innovations in the new electronic commons.

In today's financial markets, bankers, brokers, bond and currency traders themselves—along with growing numbers of finance ministers, parliamentarians and regulators—see the need for new rules to create more orderly capital and currency markets. Such new market regimes can inspire confidence, such as the "circuit breakers" introduced on Wall Street after the 1987 stock market crash, which now damp the effects of program trading. Finance ministers acknowledge the loss of domestic controls as well as diminished tax revenues which came with the financial deregulation of the 1980s. Bond markets more concerned with inflation than unemployment limit "pump priming" projects and jobs while reducing options for social safety nets. Some central banks have even tried to join the derivative trading game—on occasions with heavy losses. Only global agreements on capital investment, currency exchange stabilization and restructuring the International Monetary Fund (IMF), World Bank, and the World Trade Organization (WTO) can address today's paradoxes so well described by Jeffery Sachs in The *Economist* (for example, "Beyond Bretton Woods," The *Economist* October 1, 1994 and The *Economist* October 8, 1994). However, his prescriptions for closing "the big holes (that) remain in the legal fabric (which) may yet threaten global economic systems," fall far short of addressing the dilemma of national governments squeezed between currency speculators and bond traders on the one hand and the perils of domestic protests of IMF structural adjustments, on the other. Sachs assumes "in 1994 the world is closer than ever before to the global *cooperative* [emphasis added] free market arrangements championed fifty years ago by the visionaries who met at Bretton Woods." However, cooperative agreements do not emerge automatically from free markets and must be designed by human rather than invisible hands.

The Social Innovation Lag

The 300-year evolution of Western industrial societies involved a continuous lag between technological innovations and the social innovations needed to accommodate their societal assimilation. From the spinning jenny and the steam engine, to the automobile and computer, such technologies have always outpaced and eventually called forth responding social innovation: double-entry bookkeeping and accounting protocols, national currencies and central banks, standardization of rail gauges, highway signs and electrical fixtures. The computer industry, now automating services sectors worldwide, underpins today's global casino. The UN—itself a major social innovation—is well suited to development of the legal infrastructure of this electronic commons. Computer industries are still in their competitive, market expansion phase—facing many paradoxes of technological evolution often experienced at this stage of the innovation cycle: incompatibility and mismatches between software, operating systems, etc. This diversity of design—originally a competitive advantage to individual firms—begins to hinder further market expansion into more system-wide applications. The other major paradox is joblessness, poverty, and thus loss of consumer purchasing power. Market competition (or in game-theory terms, win-lose strategies) begins to disorder social structure and also *limits* market penetration. Incompatibility often leads to chaotic conditions, for example, in the early railroads and multiplicity of bank-issued currencies, or the separate development in the 1970s of a dozen or so different machine-readable product code systems. Paradoxically, textbook market theory inhibits the social innovation response which could distribute the fruits of technological productivity more widely via new tax policies *and* widen market penetration. Such social innovations are seen as "interference in free markets." In France, Minitel terminals were distributed freely by government—achieving much more rapid acceptance of computers than in the U.S. France has also a widening debate about shortening work weeks to reduce rising unemployment (The *New York Times* 1993). Systems approaches view the win-lose market framework as simply entering a transition phase where cooperation (i.e. win-win strategies) could expand opportunities for all, as well as by standardizing a regulatory regime, now at the global level, as I have detailed elsewhere (Henderson 1988).

Today, it is not surprising that social efforts are still lagging in the control of the rate and direction of technological innovation. Western societies are still unsuccessful in channeling these now powerful institutionalized technological drives toward systemic, social, and ecological goals. Social inventions arise in response, such as the U.S. Office of Technology Assessment, founded in 1974, on whose original Advisory Council I served until 1980. Nowhere is this widening lag in social innovation more visible than in the growing gap between the explosion of computerized global financial trading (over ninety percent of which is speculation) and the so-far feeble efforts of finance ministers, bankers, and international bodies, such as the Bank for International Settlements (BIS) and the IMF, to create the needed regulatory regime. This new regulatory framework is now essential and must be global and as "real-time" as the markets themselves. Minimally it should resemble the functioning of the Securities and Exchange Commission (SEC), which regulates Wall Street in the U.S. Other similar capital market regulations in other countries will need to be harmonized into a single "Global SEC." Many ad hoc efforts are on-going behind closed doors in studies underway at the IMF, the BIS, at meetings of the G-7, and in academia, such as the "Rethinking Bretton Woods Symposium" at American University, June 1994 (Griesgraber 1994). Even Bankers Trust chairman Charles Sanford envisioned the restructuring consequences of global information networks which can now bypass banks—allowing entrepreneurs seeking capital to simply upload their business plans onto the Internet (The *Economist* March 26, 1994). Similarly, I have predicted that financial TV channels will offer "The Venture Capital Show," "The Initial Public Offering Show," etc., complete with "800" numbers to complement existing electronic trading systems, such as Instinet, AutEx, and Reuters. National legislators can only respond to global speculation, hedging, and derivatives with ineffective domestic legislation. Market responses are equally sub-optimal, such as increasing the contracting out of hedging and risk-management activities to banks (including Bankers Trust and Tokai Bank Europe) or private consulting firms such as Emcor Risk Management Consulting, USA, the largest player (Boulding 1968). This out-sourcing is driven by the complexity and costs of the computer programs and "rocket science" experts in such hedging strategies—now beyond the capabilities of most company treasurers. Such out-sourcing creates even greater risk to the system as a whole since the few providers of such services may lead to a de facto "cartelization" of them.

Thus, today's looming global financial crises have deep systemic roots based in the paradigms which underlie industrialism and still drive the so-called "post-industrial" Information Age. No wonder traditional banking and financial leaders are unable to transcend their competitive models to visualize needed social innovations. Only new paradigms—beyond reductionism, the Puritan ethic and nationalistic competition—can allow social innovation to catch up with rampant technological innovation, whether in computerized hedge programs and global financial markets or the globalization of today's arms markets and industries. Such new paradigms need to extend beyond individualistic economic textbook models of maximizing self-interest as "rational" behavior and global competitiveness of such actors in a "level global playing field" of few rules and "free trade." Regulation is opposed by equating free enterprise technological evolution as "natural as ecosystems," while invoking chaos theory and system dynamics to "prove" that regulatory intervention to deal with rising poverty and joblessness is too unpredictable. It remains to be seen whether today's chaotic global financial casino and other new technological domains in cyberspace will be even more unpredictable without some regulatory intervention. It is never a matter of *either* rules and regulations *or* freedom and markets. In human societies rules for interaction are fundamental—it is only a matter of who, what, when, why, where, and how we choose to regulate ourselves. The invisible hand is our own.

Today's abstracted world trade/global competitiveness model has alienated financial markets from the real economy of "Main Street" (where actual people in real factories produce real shoes or build real houses and grow real food). Thus, the global casino now spinning off into cyberspace—divorced from any understanding of the whole picture: human societies with people working, cooperating and competing, while interacting within webs of other species and ecosystems in a fragile, ever-changing biosphere. Thus, the needed paradigm shifts are toward systems and chaos theory and other interdisciplinary, dynamic change models, informed by psychological reintegration to overcome the pervasive fear/scarcity-based strategies of economics. There are now conditions for the shift of our present financial systems from pervasive GNP-based "trickle-down" economic growth typified still in the Bretton Woods institutions to diversified, decentralized "trickle-up," sustainable development; the latter restores incentives to mutual aid, cooperative informal sectors, and the development of agreements and rules on managing global commons.

These paradigm shifts begin with rethinking scarcity, abundance, needs and satisfaction, and lead inevitably to wholesale re-definitions of money, wealth, work, productivity, efficiency, and progress. A prerequisite of this new world view is the understanding that money is not scarce and that its apparent scarcity is itself a major social regulatory mechanism: a social innovation, which when functioning well provides a beneficial circulatory system for wider human exchange and purchasing power beyond face-to-face barter. As Boulding (1968) noted, there are three basic kinds of human interactions:

1. *Threat*, based on fear
2. *Exchange*, barter and reciprocity
3. *Love*, based on gifts, altruism, and more comprehensive, long-term value systems.

Many of the operating principles derived from industrial paradigms remain unexamined: technological innovation is widely encouraged and subsidized; social innovation is suspect (as "planning") and occurs only after crises, such as the Great Depression. The UN itself emerged only after the experience of two ghastly world wars. National societies are assumed to be divided up into a private sector (market competition) and a public sector (government and non-profits) with a "Berlin Wall" inhibiting interaction (buttressed by anti-trust laws). Government is enjoined from "competing" with private sector business. Much creativity and inventiveness is dammed up behind such rigid definitions and restrictive institutions which keep operational the competitive nation state-based industrial paradigm that is now moving toward its logical conclusion: global economic warfare. In pre-industrial and traditional societies, most land and natural resources were held communally, for example, "the commons" or village green (as the common grazing land of feudal England was known). Garrett Hardin, in "The Tragedy of the Commons," pointed out the problem that occurred when individuals could maximize their self-interest by putting more of their sheep to feed on the commons—leading to overgrazing that destroyed the commons for all (Hardin 1968). Hardin failed to dispel the confusion among economists between the commons as "property" and the commons as "closed systems" which are accessed collectively (for example, Aguilera-Klink 1994) (See figure 1).

Figure 1. Differing Views of Markets and Commons

Economists	Futurists/systems
Markets	**Open Systems**
Private sector	
• Individual decisions • Competition • Invisible hand • Anti-trust	• Divisible resources • Win-lose rules • (Adam Smith's rules)
Commons	**Closed Systems**
Public sector	
• Property of all • Monopoly under regulation • Consortia	• Indivisible resources • Win-win rules • Cooperation • Agreements

Note. One must remember that all such schematizations are, at best, approximations and often culturally arbitrary.

Either communities could agree on rules to fairly access the commons—or it could be enclosed as private or group property and plots could be traded in a market. In either case, issues of equity and freedom always have to be adjudicated, while the poor and powerless tend to be denied fair access. The world's oceans, the air we breathe, the planet's biodiversity are also commons—not property. They can only be managed with agreed-upon rules to prevent exploitation. This is now true for the emerging electronic commons. The concept of private property, as I have detailed elsewhere (Henderson 1988), is derived from the Latin word *privare:* all those goods, lands, and resources that individuals wished to *withhold* from the community and *deprive* to common usage.

Today, commons are still widely evident in traditional agricultural societies and many developing countries. Indeed, the march of industrialism has involved the enclosure of commons begun by force in seventeenth-century Britain, when peasants were driven off common lands by the Enclosure Acts, as described by Karl Polanyi in *The Great Transformation* (Polanyi 1944). Today, market forces seek to enclose such declining commons as ocean fish stocks (by arbitrarily allocating property rights to fisheries) and biodiversity (by continually encroaching on natural habitats and by patenting life forms and species)–thus short-changing future generations via current market discount rates. Such preempting of commons and simply declaring them as "common property" or "markets" by fiat denies due process to indigenous people who have fostered such resources and biodiversity for generations. Markets are the focus of economic textbooks, since economics arose as an epistemological justification for early capitalism and industrialization. The concept of commons is still barely examined, even in much more recent "green" economic texts, except as common *property* (Henderson 1991). The global electronic commons of finance, computer and other communications networks are still widely viewed as "markets."

From a systems viewpoint, "markets" are merely open systems with abundant resources that can be used individually and competitively, while commons are closed systems, where resources are used indivisibly, such as national parks, air, oceans, satellite orbits, and the Earth's electromagnetic spectrum (see figure 1). From the economic textbooks' standpoint, these commons conceived of as "common property" can only be rationally managed if *owned* by somebody. Thus, economists rely on private ownership and property rights schemes as "market-based regulations" (e.g., taxes and subsidies) leading them, for example, to lobby governments to set up "markets" as those in the Clean Air Act of 1991, allowing polluting companies to sell and trade their "licenses to pollute" the common air to other companies. The rhetoric used borders on schizophrenia, i.e., markets versus "command and control" (a straw man in the post-communist world) and a false dichotomy, since such pollution "markets" are *set up* by new regulations and require costly monitoring and enforcement of total emission levels. Needless to say, many local citizens groups point out that these polluting companies did not "buy" the air and have no right to sell a common resource such as air, which is a condition of *survival* and protected as a human *right* along with liberty and the pursuit of happiness (for example, in the U.S. and others' constitutions). Today's issues of markets-versus-commons (and regulations) still concern equity, accountability, democratic access to public assets and essential services. Debates on the information superhighway typify the now bankrupt "public-versus-private/market-versus-regulation" polarization. Even Wall Street analysts schizophrenically characterize the cut-throat and still privatizing telecommunications sectors as "balkanized and fragmented" and "needing national standardization" in order to develop further. This state of affairs typifies the myriad players in the global casino: banking, brokerage, and insurance services which now are merging, ad hoc groups such as the Paris Club, as well as the International Organization of Securities Commissions (IOSC), the BIS and its 1988 Basle Accords, the Committee on Inter-Bank Netting Schemes, etc. (Cooper et al. 1993). These public and private sector actors in today's global casino can be convened with the help of the UN to create broader agreements on currency regimes at a new "Bretton Woods" conference, as many groups, including the Volcker Commission, are now proposing.

More systemic theoretical frameworks can help reconceptualize today's great globalizations and the restructuring processes they engender: the globalization of industrialism and technology, of finance and information, of work and migration, of human effects on the biosphere, of the arms race, and the emergence of global consumption and culture (Henderson 1991). Concepts that provide the context for the rise of information societies and the eclipse of industrialism and its now dysfunctional economic paradigm include:

1. The shift from human progress as equated with quantitative GNP growth (to more complex qualitative goals of quality of life and sustainable development), requiring new scorecards such as the Human Development Index (HDI) of the United Nations Development Programme, and my Country Futures Indicators (CFI) and its first version for the U.S.: the Calvert-Henderson Quality-of-Life Indicators. The reclassification of the "economy" beyond textbook public-versus-private sectors and market-versus-regulations is necessary, as well as expanding the mapping of productive sectors to include the unpaid, informal economy and the undergirding of productivity by nature, as well as the rise of the global civil society.
2. A systems view of markets as open systems and commons as closed systems (see figure 1), to clarify policy options and new strategies. Economic textbooks need to reflect systems theory and teach how to recognize when markets saturate (i.e., all niches are filled), and they turn into commons. A sure sign of the need to reorganize a market from a *win-lose* competition to broader *win-win* rules for all players is the pervasive appearance of cut-throat competitiveness, i.e., *lose-lose*, such as today's competitive global economic warfare or conflicts over the Earth's cluttered electromagnetic spectrum, or increasing global arms sales which make no one more secure (Henderson 1986). Most institutions geared to meeting today's

needs and those of future sustainable development will require re-structuring and cooperative linking in networks and consortia of *both* public and private actors and institutions. There will be as many new types of enterprise charters, providing new incomes and jobs, as human imagination can devise: from joint stock companies and employee stock ownership plans, worker-owned enterprises, non-profit institutions, private/government corporations (such as the World Bank and Intelsat) and new UN agencies, such as the proposed Development Security Council, to community development banks, cooperatives, and networks of cooperating small businesses, such as those in Italy and Denmark (figure 2).

Figure 2. Exploring the Evolving Global Playing Field

New Markets	New Commons
• Telecom services	• Space, Earth systems science
• Desert greening	• Electromagnetic spectrum
• Pollution control	• Oceans, water resources
• Renewable energy	• Atmosphere, ozone layer
• Recycling, eco-resources management	• Security, peace keeping
• "Caring" sector (day care, counseling, rehabilitation, nursing)	• Forests
• Infrastructure (extending transport, telecommunications, etc.)	• Health
• Eco-restoration, bio-remediation	• Global economy
• Peacekeeping, risk-assessment services	• Global electronic commons

Breakup of the Global Money Cartel

Today we see the rise of non-money, information economies (local, regional, and global networks for barter, counter trade, reciprocity, and mutual aid) wherever macro-economic management is failing in societies (Henderson 1991). In G-7 countries, Russia and Eastern Europe, all challenged by the global casino, people are creating their own local information societies of mutual aid on the Internet and other networks where users are increasing twenty-five percent per month. Businesses in high unemployment and poverty areas are issuing discount coupons and other scrip, just as cities all over the U.S. did during the Great Depression of the 1930s. In the 1990s' Information Age, democracy is now sweeping the planet as people everywhere can see on satellite TV how politics, economics, money, and cultural traditions interact to control human affairs from the global to the local level. A global civil society made up of millions of citizens groups now linking electronically is challenging both governments and corporations, as a third "independent sector." New demands include reducing work weeks to thirty hours so as to share the fruits of automation, or for guaranteed incomes for all citizens so as to maintain purchasing power (Henderson 1994a). Many in governments and at the local level are realizing the implications of the global Information Age: money and information are now equivalent—if you have the one, you can get the other. In fact, information is often more valuable. Today, money often *follows* information (and sometimes *misinformation*) and markets are no longer so "efficient." Indeed, psychology and game theory now often explain markets better than economics, as the latest Nobel awards in economics attest.

Thus, the global money monopoly is breaking up, even as its casino becomes more unstable with bouncing currencies, derivatives, and increasing volatility. Socially innovative governments can now go around the money monopoly and conduct sophisticated barter and counter-trade deals directly (as do corporations) using computer-based trading, systems similar to those that Chicago's commodity traders use. Indeed, one-quarter of all world trade is already done this way according to industry estimates. Thus, the "need to earn foreign exchange," which hung over governments like a sword of Damocles, can now be lifted and the IMF must face up to this new game it can never control. Complicated four-, five-, and six-way trading deals between multiple partners can be executed with almost the ease of money. Computers keep the audit trails of who promised to "pay" for which commodity in exchange for what other commodity on what dates—which is what money is and does anyway.

Today, calls for democratizing and restructuring the World Bank, the IMF, and the WTO, and opening up the still-private BIS, have grown out of new evidence of the irrelevance of structural adjustments (The *Economist,* October 1, 1994) and the failure of the economic approaches in the United Nations Third Development Decade. These demands culminated in the 1994 clashes in Madrid between developing and industrial countries over fairness and Special Drawing Rights (SDRs) to the global, grassroots campaign, "Fifty Years is Enough," to actually shut down the World Bank. Protests will become more strident as more people see that money is not in short supply and that credits and liquidity often follow politics and could be made available more widely and equitably—not just to governments to shore up alliances and to pander to bond traders and other special interests. Democratic reformers seek wider access to credit for private groups, local enterprises, villages, and many other NGOs and communities for "trickle-up" development. Such campaigns will persist until the political assumptions of the Bretton Woods institutions are teased out of their economic models and their relationships with governments, banks, securities traders, stock exchanges, and bond holders are made clearer.

Local Information Commons as Safety Nets

As the crises swamping macro-economic management become more evident worldwide, people at local grass roots are rediscovering the oldest, most reliable safety net: the non-money, information economy. Over half of all the world's production, consumption, exchange, investments, and savings are conducted outside the money economy—even in industrial countries (for example, some eighty-nine million American men and women volunteer an average five hours each week, saving taxpayers millions in social programs). No wonder World Bank and other development projects failed since they overlooked these non-money sectors. Meanwhile, many OECD countries face eleven percent average unemployment rates, while economic "shock treatment" still roils Eastern Europe and Russia, and debt problems worsen in "developing" countries.

Independent, urban money systems have always flourished whenever central governments mismanaged national affairs. Such alternative currencies, which fostered local employment, are catalogued in *Depression Scrip of the United States* (1984) documenting the hundreds of American cities and others in Canada and Mexico which recovered from the 1930s unemployment by issuing their own money. Most economic textbooks excoriate such informal local economies as backward or inefficient and ignore the rich history of such information-based alternatives to central banks and national currencies. Earlier examples were based on the theories of economist Silvio Gesell and included the city of Worgl in Austria and the Channel Islands of Jersey and Guernsey off the southern coast of Britain. All three became enclaves of prosperity and survived botched national policies of the period. Today, Jersey and Guernsey still survive as examples of how independent, local credit and money systems can maintain full employment, public services and low inflation. Economists and bankers, after fighting such local initiatives, today may need to rely on them to stabilize sputtering national economies.

Today, ordinary people are not sitting idle, hoping that macro-economic managers can help them. Local communities see the confusion at the top and are not waiting. In Russia, as the ruble declined, barter and flea markets became pragmatic substitutes. Oil flows from Kiev, Ukraine to Hungary to purchase trucks, while Russian engineers design power plants in exchange for Chinese coal. The big lesson for the Information Age is being learned: information can substitute for scarce money. Information networks operate barter systems in the U.S. worth $7.6 billion per year. The number of U.S. companies engaged in barter services has increased from 100 in 1974 to 600 in 1993 (*At Work* 1993). These barter companies, according to *At Work* newsletter, range from the Barter Corporation, a trade exchange network in the Chicago area, to Ron Charter of Costa Mesa, California, which exchanges recycled appliances and sports equipment for Green Card credits good toward payment for goods and services at more than 200 participating businesses in Orange County. Some of these exchanges are for education and health care of employees. Goods bartered range from trucks, office furniture, and carpeting to clothing, travel hotel rooms, dental and optical services. At the local level, barter clubs now keep track of credit, investment, and exchange transactions. These information networks function like commodity exchanges, just as payments unions and trade agreements do for governments. These non-money and scrip-based economies are leading indicators signaling the decline of macro-economic management.

Such decentralized, local ingenuity still alarms bankers and central monetary authorities. Some local "currencies" and ad hoc alternative economies in the past have been stamped out by governments as illegal or tax dodges. Yet whenever local producers and consumers are faced with hyper-inflating national currencies or jobless economic growth policies, they resort to such pragmatic ways of clearing local markets, creating employment, and fostering community well-being. These new local information societies are not only attempts to create safety nets and home-grown economies, but are a resurgence of kinship systems. Thus they are understood better from anthropological and cultural perspectives than as "economic" or merely financial/currency systems (an excessively reductionist view). These local information societies are rooted in the informal economy and derive from traditional societies and their systems of reciprocity, mutual aid, and self-reliance and based on attempts to re-knit community bonds, work, and relationships (for example, Hyde 1979; Shiva 1989; Salins 1972; and Polanyi 1944). Now that information has become the world's primary currency, both on international computer trading screens and in local PC-networks and exchange clubs, people were at last beginning to understand money itself (Henderson 1994b). The implications of the new global information currency were shattering all our former assumptions about central banks, money, credit, liquidity, and trade. This fast-moving information had end-run fiscal and monetary tools, and called into question how deficits should be calculated and other macro-economic management models, statistical apparatus, and conventional measures of progress such as money-denominated Gross National Product (GNP) and Gross Domestic Product (GDP) (Henderson 1991).

New Markets to Serve Both Global and Local Commons

The United Nations itself is best positioned to serve this new global Information Age. The UN is now the world's de facto "super power"—being called upon daily to assume even larger burdens of peacekeeping from Bosnia and Somalia to Cambodia, Cypress, and El Salvador. Yet member countries making these demands include the richest G-7 countries and are collectively in arrears by almost a billion dollars in paying their dues to the UN. Secretary General Boutros-Boutros Ghali has noted in *Agenda for Peace* (1993) and *Agenda for Development* (1994) that a strengthened UN, which can meet the new burdens, requires more secure and predictable financing. The UN Charter mandates these dues. Logically, it should impose penalties on arrears and be able to collect taxes, for example, on arms trading and currency speculation, which could yield sufficient revenue to fund all the UN programs from peacekeeping to health, education, children's and humanitarian aid (*UN Development Programme* 1994). Issues of restructuring the UN for greater accountability are crucial to its new role. The UN, acting as a convener and broker, can continue its vital service to the international community by assisting in organizing global commons, thus fostering the formation of new markets to *serve*, not *control* them. Markets, as the Chinese and others know, are good servants but bad masters, and social markets are emerging in most OECD countries.

Industrialism, now worldwide, is about labor-*saving*—resulting in jobless economic growth, corporate downsizing and automation worldwide. At the same time, deficit-strapped governments are unable to continue serving as employers of last resort (via military spending, public works, jobs, and welfare). Only rebalancing tax codes toward neutrality between labor and capital can stem wasteful and often irrational capital investments and reduce the heavy burden of payroll taxes. Globally, capital markets can be made more efficient by shifting taxes to resource depletion, inefficiency, waste, and pollution, while reducing income and payroll taxes (calibrated to meet each country's tax code differentials between labor and capital). Such a tax formula could correct prices (by internalizing social and environmental costs) and run economies with a leaner mixture of resources, energy and capital, and a richer mixture of employment. Globally, taxation of currency speculation (collected automatically by all governments as proposed in the 1970s by James Tobin) is winning much support. This tax should be less than the 0.5 percent originally proposed, since the volume of speculation is now so huge. Some currency traders are comfortable with a tax of .003 percent or less, even though their trades often involve spreads of only a few basis points.

There are few good arguments against the UN being able to issue its own bonds. The $700 billion of socially responsible investment demonstrates that many globally-concerned investors and bond traders could make a viable market in such UN bonds. This would recognize that the UN has become a mature global institution which provides its 186-member countries with indispensable services. Unfortunately, a high-level Advisory Group on UN financing convened by the Ford Foundation in 1993, representing many players in the now-dying global financial order (including former central bankers Paul Volcker of the U.S. and Karl Otto Pohl of Germany's Bundesbank), rejected many such pragmatic new UN funding mechanisms. Nevertheless, the debate about democratizing the global financial system in the Information Age has been joined. Social innovations to enhance UN functions and provide secure financing will be debated at the UN World Summit for Social Development in Copenhagen, March 1995.

Many new markets and new commons will provide opportunities in the emerging global playing field (see figure 2). For example, a new public/private agency, the United Nations Security Insurance Agency (UNSIA), could provide a substantial source of revenue for peacekeeping and peace making while providing to member states more security for less money (Kay and Henderson 1995). Initial calculations suggest that this new UNSIA (a newly-organized global commons) could eventually cut countries' defense budgets by as much as fifty percent; provide enormous new markets for sub-contracting insurance companies; and allow former defense budgets to be redirected toward investments in health and education—now recognized, at last, by economists to be keys to development. New agreements can raise the floor under this global playing field by building on the girders already in place, such as the *Agenda 21* treaties and other UN agreements, so that we can build a win-win world where the *most ethical* companies and countries can prosper—together with the growing global civil society.

Literature Cited

Aguilera-Klink, F. 1994. Some Notes on the Misuse of Classical Writings in Economics on the Subject of Common Property. *Ecological Economics*, April 1994: 221-228.

Beyond Bretton Woods. The *Economist*. October 8, 1994.

Boulding, K. E. 1968. *Beyond Economics*. Ann Arbor: University of Michigan Press.

Cooper, R. N., S. Griffith-Jones, P. B. Kenen, J. Williamson, et al. 1993. *The Pursuit of Reform*, edited by J. J. Tenuissen. The Hague, Netherlands: Forum on Debt and Development (FONDAD).

Griesgraber, J. M., ed. 1994. *Rethinking Bretton Woods*. Washington, D.C.: Center of Concern.

Hardin, G. 1968. The Tragedy of the Commons. *Science*. December 12, 1968.

Henderson, H. 1986. Riding the Tiger of Change. *Future Research Quarterly*.

———. 1988. *Post-Keynesians—Not Much Better, in Politics of the Solar Age*. Indianapolis: Knowledge Systems.

———. 1991. From Economism to Earth Ethics and Systems Theory (chap. 3); Beyond GNP (chap. 5); and The Indicators Crisis (chap. 6) in *Paradigms in Progress*. Indianapolis: Knowledge Systems.

———. 1993. Social Innovation and Citizen Movements. *Futures*, 25(3): 322 [April 1993].

———. 1994a. Changing Faces of Work, the 4th Lowell Hallewick/Personnel Decisions, Inc. Lecture, University of Minnesota. April 13, 1994.

———. 1994b. Information: The World's New Currency Isn't Scarce. *World Business Academy Perspectives*, Berrett-Koehler (Fall 1994)

———.1995. New Markets and New Commons: Opportunities in the Global Casino. In *The United Nations: Policy and Financing Alternatives*. Special issue of *Futures*, 27(2): 113-124, March. Kiddington, England: Elsevier Science Ltd. U.S. edition 1996, $12.95 (P & P included), from the Global Commission to Fund the United Nations, 1511 K St. NW Suite 1120, Washington, DC 20005.

Hyde, L. 1979. *The Gift*. New York: Vintage Press.

Kay, A. F., and H. Henderson. 1995. United Nations Security Insurance Agency (UNSIA). Available upon request from: P.O. Box 5190, St. Augustine, FL 32085-5190. USA

Polanyi, K. 1944. *The Great Transformation.* Boston: Beacon Press.

Salins, M. 1972. *Stone Age Economics.* Chicago: Aldine Publishing Co.

Shiva, V. 1989. *Staying Alive.* London and Atlantic Highlands, N.J.: Zed Books

The *Economist.* March 26, 1994.

———. (October 1, 1994)

The *New York Times.* November 22, 1993, A-1.

United Nations Development Programme. 1994. *Human Development Report.* New York: United Nations.

II. From the Life Sciences/ Physical Sciences

4. A Resources Approach to Sustainability

William L. Howenstine[1]

The way we are, we are members of each other. All of us. Everything. The difference ain't in who is a member and who is not, but in who knows it and who don't.
                                                              —Wendell Berry, *The Wild Birds*

Abstract

The concept of "environment" must be seen to include both the natural environment (both abiotic and biotic factors) and the socio-cultural environment (both population and cultural factors). Sustainable development is dependent upon a holistic understanding of the resources/resistance functions of our total environment. We in higher education are challenged to practice this understanding in our teaching.

Introduction

That elusive concept "sustainability" appears in several forms and represents a variety of challenges. For example, maintaining a "sustainable ecosystem" can suggest holding the status quo if one is talking about a large natural area such as a tallgrass prairie or a tropical rainforest. To sustain such ecosystems is to leave unhindered the long-standing processes such as prairie fires or forest nutrient cycling. To restore them is to restore the processes that created them, but no more. On the other hand, "sustainable development" shifts

---

[1]**William Howenstine** received an M.A. in education from Western Reserve University in 1951 and a Ph.D. in conservation from the School of Natural Resources at the University of Michigan-Ann Arbor in 1959. He has been working with environmental concerns and environmental education throughout his professional life, in camping and outdoor education programs and in higher education. A member of the Religious Society of Friends since 1951, he worked with community development projects for the American Friends Service Committee in Mexico (1964) and Peru (1965-66). In June 1996 he retired after 35 years of teaching geography and environmental studies at Northeastern Illinois University in Chicago.

the emphasis from sustaining an ecosystem to sustaining the processes of change which we label "development."

Elusiveness creeps into both of these cases, in that natural ecosystems (even those called "climax") have changed over time because of climatic and geologic alterations, and sustainable development, to the extent that it incorporates use of nonrenewable natural resources, would seem to have some eventual upper limit.

Sustainability must be dependent upon the presence of certain factors which may be labeled "resources"; for example, an oak savanna ecosystem in the midwestern United States will be sustainable only if its essential resources of precipitation, temperate climate, and fire are maintained. A human ecosystem, such as a mining community in the Rocky Mountains, may not be sustainable once its mineral resource has been depleted. Commonly the word "resource" is used as a synonym for "natural resource" (just as the word "environment" is frequently used as a synonym for "natural environment"). I believe, however, that we educators would be well advised to use these words more carefully, in recognition of the complexity of resource factors.

The Resource/Resistance Duality

An environmental factor functions positively as a benefit to the organisms of a community or negatively as a resistance, hindrance, or cost. Thus, in the sustainable development of the American Midwest, the rich prairie soil has functioned as an important natural resource, and the steel moldboard plow which broke the prairie became an important cultural resource. The first European settlers, however, might have viewed the prairie as a resistance, almost impossible to plow, dangerous in the fire season, and frightening in its windswept expanse. John Deere's new plow, as a marvelous new cultural resource, helped to convert the prairie into an international breadbasket of grain production. However, to the native prairie ecosystem and to today's practitioner of ecological restoration, the plow can be seen as a negative factor threatening the very survival of the prairie ecosystem.

In short, the same factor in the environment might function positively for some members of a community and negatively for others. Or it may function positively at one time and negatively at other times. Notice the interesting change of value our society is placing on the wolf. Once feared, hated, and exterminated from much of the land, it is now being protected, admired, and even restored to some ecosystems. It was once a resistance to almost everyone, but now is becoming viewed increasingly as a resource.

To make matters more complex, the same factor of the environment might function simultaneously as a benefit (or resource) for a community and as a cost (or resistance). A road into a rainforest might bring the economic advantage of lumbering or tourism, but in the process destroy the resource base for future economic endeavors. A road into the rural fringes of a metropolitan city might function as a resource for people wanting to live in the country and commute to work in the central city, but by bringing more and more people, it can destroy the very rural amenities which those city migrants sought.

This duality of function assumes tremendous proportions when we look at the grand schemes for "sustainable development," such as major dams, airports, housing projects, and irrigated agriculture. Even social institutions or values such as free trade, public education, or family planning can be viewed as resources or resistances, depending on one's perspective.

A Typology of Environmental Factors

Accordingly, practically anything in our environment can be viewed as a resource or as a resistance. But what does our environment really include? To equate "environment" with "natural environment" would be a gross oversimplification. If we are to work meaningfully toward "sustainability," we must be cognizant of our total environment (See figure 1).

Some factors of the environment seem to most of us to be clearly "natural." Wildlife, precipitation, and old-growth forests fall into this category. Other factors seem more clearly to be "human." Technological inventions, such as the internal combustion engine, and population factors such as a high birth rate, illustrate this human side. (I have heard arguments that since humans evolved along with all existing life, we and all we have developed are essentially "natural." To me, however, the development of culture by the human species marks such a separation in the stream of evolution that it warrants separating human characteristics from the "natural.")

Natural Environment. To many of us, the natural environment is simply "nature" with its living and non-living components. This distinction between life and its non-living, physical environment is an important one, as seen in the increasing global concern over loss of biodiversity. A stream that is polluted can be cleaned up. Metals that have been dispersed through mining can be reconcentrated and used again through recycling. A species of life, however, once exterminated, is gone forever. Consider the passenger pigeon, probably the most common bird in eastern North America 150 years ago, and an important economic resource. This pigeon is now nothing more than a textbook illustration to most wildlife resource students.

Therefore, because life is a special creation that is so irrevocably delicate in its manifestation, its diverse forms should be labeled as the *biotic* natural environment. The rest of the natural environment, including such things as minerals, climate, and topography, can therefore be labeled the *abiotic* natural environment.

The Socio-Cultural Environment. When looking at those factors of our environment that are directly human, there is an important distinction between cultural factors per se and certain aspects of population that are less directly "cultural." For example, when striving for sustainable development of a developing nation, the culture, as manifested in technological developments, social institutions, and values, is critically important, but so are population density, the natural rate of increase, and the dependency ratio (proportion of children and aged persons). Thus, it is useful to distinguish between cultural factors and population factors within the total framework of the socio-cultural environment.

Putting these factors together leads to a classification as follows:

Figure 1. Factors of the Human Environment

Natural factors (the natural environment)		Sociocultural factors (the human environment)	
Abiotic factors air, water, climate, minerals, topography	**Biotic factors** plants, wildlife, primitive forms of life	**Population factors** density, rate of increase or decrease, age structure, sex and race composition	**Cultural factors** language, religion, institutions, mores, values, technology

The Integrity of the Environment

The reader may now be aware that there are no sharp boundaries between these several environmental factors. Where does one place soil, or the oceans? Their components of minerals, temperature, gravitational movements and currents can be labeled abiotic, but soil and ocean are full of life.

Two countries with very similar cultures may have very different population densities or population growth rates, that impact differentially upon sustainable development programs. But are not those population differences due to subtle differences in culture or to some critical factors of the natural environment? The reality is that the environment is one integrated whole. We can separate out various factors for analytical purposes, but in reality all the factors are connected. Any one factor is meaningless apart from the state and condition of other factors. Thus, to know that a small population of an endangered plant exists in a natural ecosystem says nothing about its sustainability, without knowing such factors as the presence or absence of pollinators, the existence of exotic invasive species, the degree of pollution in the ecosystem, or the size of the refuge. In a much more complex way, the "sustainable development" of a nation is related to a multitude of interacting natural and socio-cultural factors. Nonetheless, a full awareness of the various factors that make up our environment is crucial for sustainability, as we shall see.

Implications for Sustainability

For those who would seek sustainability, either of an ecosystem or of a development process, a knowledge of the many factors that might impinge on that system or process is essential, as is the realization that these factors interact holistically. Also important is the understanding that these factors function both positively and negatively, as resources and resistances, in highly complex ways.

Thus an economist who looks at human populations solely as a labor force for industrial development, the engineer who plans a dam without consideration of its impact on species diversity, the biologist who tries to protect an endangered species with disregard for the cultural values of the neighboring people, the chemist who introduces a pesticide without thinking of its ramifications in the food chain—all represent the narrow view that has too often thwarted sustainability.

Aside from having this holistic view of the environment, those working with sustainability should have a clear understanding of the special role of culture. Human culture has demonstrated the ability to speed up enormously the processes of nature that existed even before we appeared on Earth. Thus soil erosion, topographical modifications, climate change, species and ecosystem extinctions, and biogeochemical cycling have all experienced exponential increases of occurrence due to human culture. These are culturally-caused resistances. But, at the same time, as noted in the case of the John Deere plow, our culture can produce a resource function that did not exist before. Ecotourism, which provides income from viewing trees and wildlife instead of killing them, is a cultural development. The greater perfection of solar energy technology promises to make the sun an even more important resource to countries poor in fossil energy. The development of new political institutions to replace the centrality of the present nation state is, perhaps, one of the most hopeful ways by which culture can enhance the resource base.

Implications for Higher Education

The implications for those of us in higher education seem to me to be clear, simple, and threatening. If we teach about and work for sustainability, whether for a local natural area or for a foreign nation, it seems clear that we must strive to look at the whole environment and understand as well as possible its complex oneness. This concept seems simple when one realizes the arbitrary and artificial nature of all classification. Why should the integrity—the wholeness—of the environment and its resource and resistance functions be any surprise?

But such integration is threatening, because our academic upbringing has led many of us to become so "disciplinocentric." As "educated people" we can easily see the dangers of racial, religious, and national prejudices. However, as most prejudiced people do not admit to their prejudgments, neither do we. Too often we confine ourselves narrowly within our academic disciplines. Seldom do we team-teach a seminar; seldom do we invite a colleague from a different discipline to our classes to present the perspective of that discipline on an issue. Too often we compete with them for fiscal resources. From a resource perspective, "sustainability," however defined, will never be achieved without the valuable contributions of all disciplines. The multidisciplinary nature of this book instructs that we should help reinforce this approach in our own institutions. The natural sciences, the social sciences, and the humanities all have roles to play in developing a culture that optimizes the resource potential of our total environment.

A model for integration I use in my teaching is three-dimensional tic-tac-toe. We all know that one wins an ordinary one-dimensional game of tic-tac-toe by establishing a straight-line relationship with three "Xs" or three "Os". We can compare this to a scholar who establishes a relationship among three environmental factors. Similarly, three-dimensional tic-tac-toe uses four transparent plane surfaces. The winner of this game establishes a straight-line relationship of four markers, but the line of markers may be on any one of the plane surfaces, or cut down in a straight line through all four planes. I liken the four planes of tic-tac-toe to the four factors of our environment. The bottom plane is made of the abiotic factors; the second plane, the biotic factors; the third plane, the population factors; and the fourth plane, the cultural factors. Focusing play primarily on one plane would be like a biologist who tries to achieve a straight line with his/her markers solely on the second layer, or the sociologist who works only on the fourth layer. Maybe other educators would like to try this approach.

Problems of sustainability, I believe, will be solved only by *finding relationships that cut across all four planes of the environment.* As educators we might have more fun playing the game in multidisciplinary teams that look at the challenge cooperatively, utilizing the varied perspectives that each of us can bring from our respective disciplines. Hopefully our students, having experienced such an integrated approach to issues of sustainability, will be in a better position to meet the challenges of sustainable development as we move into the twenty-first century.

[Note. Several of the themes in this chapter are complemented by sections in chapters 2 and 11.]

5. Population Concerns for Higher Education
A Friend's Perspective

Stanley Becker[1]

World population is growing at the unprecedented rate of almost 100 million people every year, and human activities are producing major changes in the global environment. If current predictions of population growth prove accurate and patterns of human activity o the planet remain unchanged, science and technology may not be able to prevent either irreversible degradation of the environment or continued poverty for much of the world.
—Preface to a joint statement of the Royal Society of London and the United States National Academy of Sciences, February 1992

Abstract

About ninety million persons are added to the planet each year, or 220,000 per day, three per second. Rapid population growth is the most important problem facing us at the end of the twentieth century. About 200 million couples in the world want to limit their family size but do not have access to modern contraception. Improving the status of women is crucial to lowering fertility. Men need to be more involved in family planning. We all need to seek solutions and provide training about the problem of rapid population growth.

Introduction

The population of the world reached one billion in 1830. The second billion was reached in 1925, the third in 1960, the fourth in 1974 and the fifth in 1987. We are currently adding about *ninety million persons per year* (United Nations 1993). But population

[1] **Stanley Becker** is Associate Professor in the Population Dynamics Department of the Johns Hopkins University School of Public Health in Baltimore, Maryland. He teaches demographic methods and does research mainly on fertility and child mortality in developing nations. Recently he has begun research on male involvement in family planning and particularly condom use. He has traveled among the Religious Society of Friends under the concern about rapid population growth and the future of the planet. He serves on the Steering Committee of Friends Committee on Unity with Nature and clerks the FCUN Population Subcommittee.

growth is far from uniform around the globe. We live in a demographically divided world—over ninety percent of the growth is in developing nations. The good news is that the growth rate is dropping as fertility declines in many nations. Thirty years ago the average number of children per woman for the whole world was 5.0; today it is 3.3. In developing nations the average thirty years ago was 6.0, and it is now about 4.0 children per woman (Demeny 1986). To stabilize population the rate must be about 2.0. Most professionals would agree, however, it is easier to reduce the average from 6 to 4 than from 4 to 2. For more developed nations, fertility is close to or below replacement level: in Italy and Spain the mean fertility is about 1.5 children, and in the U. S. it is just about at the replacement level of 2.1 (Population Reference Bureau 1993). But the U.S. population is still growing by two million per year because of the baby boom echo and immigration (National Center for Health Statistics 1994).

Another problem is demographic momentum: even if fertility fell to 2.0 children per woman tomorrow, the world population would still grow by several billion persons because there are disproportionate numbers of young people waiting to begin childbearing. Hence the logic of the one-child family in China. The population level in the twenty-first century depends on the speed of decline in fertility. Hypothetically, if the child per family average declines to 2.5 then, all else being equal, the world population in 2100 would be nineteen billion. If it declines to 2.2, the population in 2100 would be eighteen billion; if it declines to replacement level of 2.06, the world population would be eleven billion (United Nations 1992). However, the actual level is 3.3 now. As the population grows from 5.7 billion today to 6.5 billion within a decade and possibly to ten or fifteen billion by 2050, it is likely that violent competition among humans for diminished resources will increase and destruction of the biosphere will continue. Our co-species on the planet will continue to be extinguished at an alarming rate, and the human death rate will likely rise. To avoid these negative outcomes we must stabilize human population very soon.

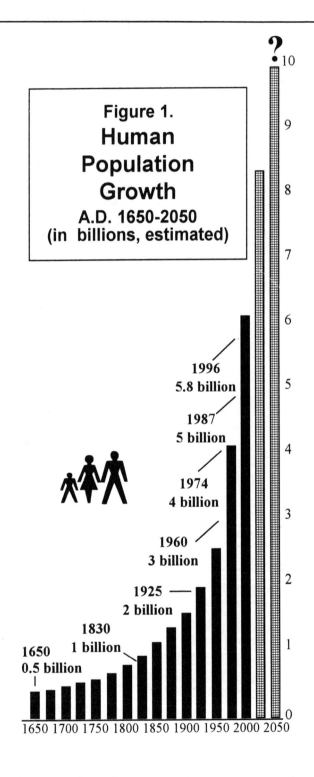

Figure 1.
Human Population Growth
A.D. 1650-2050
(in billions, estimated)

1996 5.8 billion
1987 5 billion
1974 4 billion
1960 3 billion
1925 2 billion
1830 1 billion
1650 0.5 billion

1650 1700 1750 1800 1850 1900 1950 2000 2050

The most important determinant of fertility levels is the percentage of couples using contraception. In the developed countries, seventy to eighty percent of couples use contraception, but in some nations of Africa less than ten percent use contraception. It is estimated that 100 to 300 million couples in the world want to space or limit their births, but lack access to modern contraception (Westoff and Ochoa 1991). If the global budget for family planning were doubled from $6 billion to about $10 billion annually, all the need for contraception could be met (United Nations 1994). This spending is a bargain! The bad news is that even if all this unmet need for contraception were met, this factor alone, by one calculation, would only reduce fertility about twenty-five percent of the way to replacement levels (Pritchett 1994). Thus, besides considering the supply of contraception, we must also consider increasing the demand for contraception. Changing couples' desired family size is more complicated. When women's status improves, then desired family size declines. In fact, the level of education of women has the most consistent and largest negative correlation with levels of fertility. We in developed nations have an obligation to provide these contraceptive technologies to the couples in the developing world who want to limit their family size but do not currently have access.

Unique Quaker Witness

Since Friends are typically poor at theology but are good at visioning and at practical religion, let's be visionary and practical. We want to leave a world to our children with less violence, less oppression, a more equitable distribution of resources and a preserved biosphere: in short, a better world. Quakers have a unique perspective on our relation to each other and to our natural surroundings, and on our relation to the divine power in the universe. I would like to consider two aspects of rapid population growth as related to our Quaker testimonies.

It is known that improving women's status is crucial for reducing both fertility and child mortality. As noted above, the most important variable in explaining fertility decline across all nations is the number of years of schooling that women have. More schooling yields fewer children, many fewer children. For example, in Ghana women with no education have an average of seven children, but women educated beyond middle school have only four children. Generally, fertility is low where the status of women is high. Women in the labor force outside the home have fewer children than those who stay home. Women who can discuss the size of their desired family and family planning with their spouses have fewer births than do those who do not discuss these matters. When women are given education and access to contraception, they choose to have fewer births.

What does population policy have to do with the Religious Society of Friends? We have a history of equality for women; we have the equality testimony. Women must have equal opportunity, equity in the workplace, and freedom from sexual domination. What about men? First and foremost, men need to be more responsible *vis a vis* their relationships to women and family planning. Men need to educate men that "sex on demand" is inappropriate in caring relationships. Men need to be made responsible for the children they father.

More men need to accept responsibility for using contraception. Too many men around the world refuse to use the condom because they say it reduces sexual pleasure. The AIDS epidemic provides even more reason to see the triviality of this excuse. In family planning, a male's vasectomy is considerably easier and safer to perform than a female's tubectomy; yet men are much less likely to choose sterilization than women in most nations of the world (Ross, Mauldin, and Miller 1993). We need to convince our Latin, Arab, and African brothers that vasectomy is an excellent choice for many of us. If more men in the world assumed reproductive responsibility, fertility would decline rapidly.

A second aspect of the population question relates to our destruction of the biosphere. The impact of humans on the biosphere can be summarized by this equation:

$$I = P \times A \times T$$

Environmental Impact = Population x Affluence x Technology,
   where:
   I is environmental impact,
   P is population size,
   A is the affluence of each individual or per-capita consumption
      of goods and services, and
   T is the technology or the quantity of resources consumed and
      pollution generated during production and consumption per
      unit of goods and services.

Note that higher population size and greater affluence per capita both lead to greater impact on the environment for a given level of technology (Ehrlich, Ehrlich, and Holdren 1977).

While population is rapidly expanding in developing nations, consumption of resources in developed nations is thirty to fifty times that in developing nations. Affluent North Americans have a problem of overconsumption. For example, to be blunt, while people are malnourished in other parts of the world, we too often take more food than we can eat and waste the excess. We drive our personal automobiles alone too often. We waste energy at the office and home. What does this waste have to do with population rates? Citizens of developing nations are now trying to emulate the lifestyle of western or northern nations. The worldwide reach of radio and television has led to what sociologists call a "revolution of rising expectations." This trend can clearly make the *per-capita* impact on the planet even worse. The world population alive today could not exist at the North American standard of living because many resources would be quickly exhausted.

Friends have two testimonies that speak to this disparity of resources allocation. First and again, the *equality testimony.* Friends World Committee for Consultation has a project called "Right Sharing of World Resources." If the world's per-capita income were divided equally, there would be about $4,000 per person per year. We in the U.S. would be quite poor indeed with only $4,000 per person. So what do we mean by "right sharing of world resources"? Do we have a "right" to a larger share of the resources than anyone else on the planet? I doubt if any of us, after prayerful consideration, could answer yes to that question.

Another Quaker testimony speaks to our condition in this regard— the *simple living* testimony. We know the benefits of simple living on the spiritual level—a centered life is less hectic. Simple living means not trying to do too many things. On the material level, simple living also has benefits. For example, a vegetarian diet is more healthy, costs less, and leads to less destruction of the rainforests, since a significant portion of the rainforest is cleared in order to raise cattle for beef exports. Right sharing and simple living are voluntary actions to equalize world resources.

Quakers, Population, and Higher Education

The American public is abysmally ignorant about population matters. In 1988 the National Geographic Society conducted parallel surveys in nine countries to assess basic geographic literacy. Only forty-three percent of Americans knew that the U.S. population was between 150 and 300 million. This ignorance is very sad. Higher proportions of adults in Sweden, Japan, Canada, Mexico, and France reported correct answers on the U.S. population size.

Why are Americans so poorly informed? One reason is the decline in geography classes in primary and secondary schools. Another is that population statistics are not necessarily covered in any required course for students at most colleges and universities. Indeed, demography is often considered a minor subfield of sociology, and ecology courses rarely deal with the complexities of human population growth. Only a dozen American universities have population centers.

Knowledge on population matters—and the teaching of that knowledge—is important; sometimes relationships may not be immediately apparent, or may even appear counter-intuitive. For example, students need to understand that even though the rate of population increase has been declining slightly, the actual number of persons added to the planet has been increasing each year for the past decade. The reason is that the population base has been expanding faster than the rate has been declining. A second example: it takes two abortions to prevent one birth! Reason: an abortion cuts short the pregnancy and the postpartum sterile period associated with breastfeeding, so women who have abortions will become pregnant again more rapidly, all else being equal.

Our school and college curricula should cover these subjects: the demographic transition; population distribution by age, sex, geographic area; demographic methods; stationary population and total fertility rate; population momentum; population programs; reproductive health, including sexually transmitted diseases and maternal morbidity and mortality; contraceptive technologies and abortion; ethics (e.g. incentives and disincentives); gender relations and the status of women. Given the gravity of the problem, population education must become more evident in our colleges and universities. Population concerns cut across disciplines, and nearly all disciplines can have contributions to solutions.

Here are some examples:

- Biologists can discover and develop new and better means of contraception.
- Statisticians can design surveys to measure fertility levels in developing nations and can document efficacy and continuation rates of contraception.
- Geographers and ecologists can document our impact on the biosphere.
- Sociologists can examine what is most effective for improving the status of women.
- Economists can consider the meaning of "right sharing of world resources."
- Lawyers and lawmakers can pass laws to provide universal coverage of safe contraceptive and abortion care.
- Psychologists can help us understand the barriers to contraceptive use among teens and other population groups.
- Artists can find creative ways to make us aware of the population problem.
- Business persons can help us find ways to make contraceptives available and affordable to everyone on the planet.
- Physicians, nurses and other health care providers can improve availability of high-quality services.

What Can We Do As Friends?

Friends can take several actions personally and publicly:

- Give prayerful consideration to population concerns.
- Educate ourselves, our families, our Meeting community, our students. Friends Committee on Unity with Nature has materials for leading sessions in Monthly and Yearly Meetings.
- Encourage Quaker organizations to give energy and guidance to this concern, e.g. American Friends Service Committee, Friends Committee on National Legislation, Quaker United Nations Office, and Friends World Committee on Consultation.
- Be agents for change in the wider society.

I would like to share two messages from worship in Monthly Meetings that I have visited. In the first Meeting someone offered the simple message: "Be sure to act out of love and not out of fear." In many circles, the impetus for stabilizing human population growth comes from a realization of the terrible consequences that will occur if we do not control our own growth. Ecological arguments about global warming, ozone depletion, and the disappearance of rainforests engender fear. But we must act out of love.

Second, someone in another Monthly Meeting shared about the difficulty of "loving my enemies" as Jesus preached (here we could view rapid population growth as the "enemy"). This Friend found three concrete things that help:

- *Do not get personal.* At several meetings I have visited under the weight of the concern about rapid population growth, I have been told of persons who stayed away from the session because they had large families and felt guilty or prejudged by me. This preconception should not happen.
- *Focus on the good for all concerned.* In many cases it is in the interest of all concerned (including the health of offspring and mother) to have only one or two children. And it is the good of future generations that we must also hold in the Light.
- *Have an image of a reconciled state.* What is the optimum population of the world? Perhaps the number which could live in 'eco-sustainability' with the planet, defined as living such that the state of the biosphere is not diminished for future generations.

Summary

We have a vision of a better world. Such a world must have a stabilized or even reduced population size. We must act now to slow the population rate to zero growth. Our motive must be love. We have two testimonies that give us a unique witness on this concern—equality and simple living. The first can lead us to work for improvement of women's status and to involve men to a greater extent in family planning. Simple living and right sharing can lighten our impact on the biosphere. Persons above age forty are old enough to have seen the world population double or even triple in their own lifetimes (the population in 1950 was only 2.5 billion and now we are 5.7 billion). While the problem seems complex and remote, we are blessed with the resources to help solve it. As persons of conscience, we must devote energy and guidance toward solutions for the sake of future generations. As educators we have a special role to play in education for social change.

Literature Cited

Demeny, P. 1986. The World Demographic Situation, in *World Population and U.S. Policy*, edited by J. Menken. New York: Norton and Co., 27-66.

Ehrlich, P. R., A. H. Ehrlich, and J. P. Holdren. 1977. *Ecoscience: Population, Resources and Environment*. San Francisco: Freeman.

National Academy of Science and Royal Society. 1992. Statement reprinted in *Population and Development Review*, 18(2):375-378.

National Center for Health Statistics, 1994. *Vital Statistics of the United States*. Vol. I *Natality* and Vol. II *Mortality*.

National Geographic Society. 1988. *Geography: An International Gallup Survey*. Princeton, N.J.: The National Geographic Society.

Population Reference Bureau. 1993. World *Population Data Sheet*. Population Reference Bureau.

Pritchett, L. H. 1994. Desired Fertility and the Impact of Population Policies. *Population and Development Review*, 20(1):1-56.

Ross, J. A., W. P. Mauldin, and V. C. Miller. 1993. *Family Planning and Population: A Compendium of International Statistics*. New York: The Population Council.

United Nations, 1992. *Long Range World Population Projections*. New York: United Nations. ST/ESA/SER.A/125.

———. 1995. *World Population Prospects: 1994 Revision*. New York: United Nations

———. 1994. *Programme of Action of the International Conference on Population and Development*. New York: United Nations.

Westoff, C., and L. Ochoa. 1991. Unmet Need and the Demand for Family Planning. *Comparative Studies No. 5*. Columbia, Md.: Institute for Resource Development.

6. Geologic Time and Sustainability

M. Patrick McAdams[1]

Hey mighty Brontosaurus do you have a lesson for us.
—Sting, The Police, "Walking in your footsteps," 1983.

Abstract

The study of geologic time and of the history of life as revealed by the fossil record are the two most significant contributions of the science of geology to modern thought. Even a glimpse of the immensity of "deep time" provides a different perspective from which to view the permanence of the deeds of humanity. The panorama of life as viewed through the fossil record provides a different perspective on the very permanence of humanity—a call to reorder our lives. My hope is to set this call against the backdrop of geologic time and the evolution of life.

Introduction

The "twenty-one working issues" of the United Nations Conference on Environment and Development (UNCED) lists academic disciplines with an educational corollary. Geology is absent from the list. Indeed, were it is not for dinosaurs and diamonds, geology would be nearly absent from the public consciousness. Of the twenty-three private colleges and universities in Iowa, only one offers a major in geology. Some do not offer a single geology course. Even at larger research institutions, undergraduate enrollment in geology courses is typically low. Consequently, even college-educated citizens are only minimally aware of geology and its potential contribution to discussions concerning the environment and development. My intent for this paper is to tempt the reader to explore the perspective on environment and development offered by geology and to inform the reader of my efforts to inject

---

[1] **M. Patrick McAdams** is an assistant professor of geology at William Penn College. He received his M.S. in geology from the University of Iowa. He is currently on leave from teaching to pursue interests in native plants, seed collection, and prairie restoration.

this perspective into the academic discourse of students at William Penn College.

Energy Resources

Contrary to popular opinion, most geologists do not look for rocks and fossils. They use fossils to find oil in the rocks. Perhaps the most concrete example of the role of geology in defining sustainability is provided by a geologist's analysis of oil reserves. In the late 1950s gasoline was less than thirty cents per gallon, cars had tail fins, and Saudi Arabia was a mysterious place of genies and sand seas. The first warning that modern technological society, based on fossil fuels, was not sustainable was published in the late 1950s. A geologist, M. King Hubbert (1969), argued that U.S. oil production would peak and begin a sharp decline in the early 1970s. Further analysis of the same type, applied to all fossil fuels, revealed that their production would peak and begin a sharp decline in the middle of the twenty-first century (Hubbert 1969). U.S. oil production did peak in 1971 and has declined since then. World oil production will probably peak and begin a sharp decline between 2000 and 2020. Fossil fuels that accumulated over a period of one billion years will have been consumed in about 1,200 years (Dott and Prothero 1994).

Majors in environmental studies at William Penn College are required to take twelve hours of earth science courses. Hence the origin, distribution, and past and future utilization of fossil fuel resources are explored in depth in the required courses "Physical Geology," "Historical Geology," and "Alternative Energy and Power in the Industrial Technology." These three classes give the environmental studies majors a clear understanding of the nature and limits of fossil fuels and some experience with alternatives. Students taking "Alternative Energy and Power" have constructed working solar cell rays, solar distilleries, and other similar devices.

Currently the Industrial Technology Department is investigating the technological and financial feasibility of constructing a wind-powered generator sized to provide the college's electrical needs as a practical study of alternative energy. They are collecting wind data on campus and are exploring funding options. A preliminary cost-benefit analysis by the local utility company suggests a five- to six-year payback on the investment.

The 1993 Persian Gulf War occurred when I was teaching a semester of physical geology. The war was a sobering example of the interrelationships between nonrenewable energy resources, economics, politics, and peace. Terrestrial and marine oil spills, oil fires and associated smoke plumes, the destruction of public water supplies, and deliberate or accidental releases of chemical nuclear or biological agents crystallized the image of war as environmental disaster. I attempted to integrate the Gulf War into the course through class discussions of the history of oil exploration and utilization, the geology of petroleum resources, and the environmental impacts of the war.

Each year I offer an "Introduction to Earth Science" course which includes sections on geology, astronomy, and atmosphere sections. Most of the students are non-majors using the credits for an elective or general education. The very broad scope of the course provides ample opportunities to discuss most environmental issues. Discussions have included ozone depletion, carbon dioxide and other "greenhouse" gases, and the short- and long-term effects of the Gulf War oil fires.

A majority of the "Introduction to Earth Science" students have a broad-brush awareness of most environmental issues; however, they lack specific information. Few know that ozone is triatomic oxygen. Although they know that chlorofluorocarbons affect the ozone layer, they do not know how, where, or why. Many confuse ozone depletion with greenhouse warming. Much of the class is devoted to providing depth to the students' understanding of these issues. Field trips often provide an excellent venue for improving students' knowledge base. We regularly tour the local recycling center, water treatment facility, waste water treatment facility, a coal-fired power plant, a landfill, and a wet corn-milling plant in Oskaloosa. Each provides ample factual information and sets environmental issues in a familiar and immediate local context. Class discussions broaden the scope of the experience. For example, the coal-fired generating plant naturally leads into a discussion of strip mining in Wyoming (interstate) and acid rain (international).

Geological Time

The contributions of geology to our understanding of energy and resources helped shape, in a very direct fashion, our concept of sustainability. The supply of fossil fuels is limited; therefore, a society powered by fossil fuels is not sustainable. However, few geologists consider these ideas a central contribution of the science. Most argue that the fossil record of the history of life and the associated geologic time scale ("deep time") are the most important contributions of geology to modern thought (Gould 1993). My purpose in the remainder of this paper is to explore the concept of sustainability from the perspective of "deep time." The fossils and the rocks that contain them are the record of the history of life on Earth.

Through the nineteenth century European and North American scholars assembled this data within the framework of time. In doing so they transformed scattered observation into a sequence of events, the panorama of life. At the same moment they created "deep time," which Hutton once said offers, "No vestige of a beginning, no prospect of an end" (Hutton 1795).

In 1654, Archbishop Usher pronounced that, based on biblical genealogy, the Earth was created in 4004 B.C. on October 23d. The Earth was then about 6,000 years old, a figure commonly cited by modern fundamentalist Christians. During the nineteenth century it became clear that the Earth's age was more likely tens or even hundreds of millions of years. By 1904, radiometric dates put the age of the Earth at 2.3 billion years plus. Additional scientific studies lead to the modern data for the Earth's age at about 4.5 billion years. Stretch your arm. From shoulder to fingertip is the 4.5-billion-year history of the Earth. Filing your nails removes all of recorded history. Clipping your nails removes *Homo sapiens*. The simple immensity of "deep time" juxtaposed against human concerns of sustainability gives pause for contemplation.

Evolution

Concurrent with the development of the fossil record came Charles Darwin's publication of *On the Origin of Species by Means of Natural Selection, or the Preservation of Favored Races in the Struggle to Survive* (1859). Darwin envisioned a continuum of life progressing from the origins in a warm little pond to *Homo sapiens*. This continuum was generated by natural selection operating on variations in the population. Individuals with a characteristic(s) that aided survival would tend to produce more offspring, and therefore that characteristic would come to dominate in the population (species). This vision suggested that the fossil record would provide evidence of phylogenetic gradualism. However, there were "missing links." Darwin lamented these "gaps" in the fossil record in this era and assumed that the record was imperfect; either the data were missing, irretrievably lost to the vagaries of nature, or not yet documented (Dott and Prothero 1994).

The current view of the fossil record is much different. Mayr (1942) argued persuasively that large, freely interbreeding populations have little chance to differentiate genetically. New species are not likely to arise from populations such as these. However, genetically isolated small populations tend to diverge rapidly from the ancestral population, giving rise to new species. Eldredge and Gould (1972) applied Mayr's allopatric speciation model to the fossil record with surprising results. Based on the allopatric model, they predicted that species would appear suddenly in the fossil record and persist relatively unchanged for long periods of time. This new model was christened "punctuated equilibrium."

The fossil record has examples of phylogenetic gradualism as envisioned by Darwin. However, most species do appear suddenly and remain unchanged for millions of years. Seemingly, once a successful species arises, it has an internal stabilizing mechanism. Species persist through significant environmental changes, suggesting that the process of natural selection is unable to affect large, freely interbreeding populations (Dott and Prothero 1994).

Darwinian views of the processes of organic evolution are deeply embedded in western capitalist culture. Competition eliminates a less "fit" business just as it eliminates a less "fit" genetic trait. Virtually every television "nature" show has the obligatory comments about "survival of the fittest." Hsu (1986) argued that Darwin's ideas of "natural selection," the "struggle for survival," and the "preservation of favored races" are merely reflections of his cultural biases. Darwin colored the natural world with a palette of views formed by the capitalist middle class of industrial England. In much the same fashion, Gould (1993) argues that our view of the processes of evolution as a progression from "lower" to "higher" life forms is a reflection of our egocentric nature and Judeo-Christian heritage.

Sustainability cannot be an end; it must be an evolutionary process. Just as different places and different cultures will require different sustainable practices, so will different times. This evolution of a sustainable society must proceed in concert with the evolution of the physical world. Therefore, it is important to examine our views of organic evolution. It is difficult for us to conceive and impossible for us to articulate a non-egocentric world view (Gould 1993). But by listening carefully to others, we can hear echoes of our own biases.

I use about one-third of my "Historical Geology" course to discuss the processes of evolution, either directly or indirectly. Ninety-nine percent of my students are from a Judeo-Christian culture; many from conservative fundamentalist backgrounds view evolution and religion as being mutually exclusive. Many view evolution as ungodly or even worse. Their factual knowledge of evolution is minimal and often incorrect (e.g., humans have evolved from monkeys). Textbooks, journal articles, videos and class discussions help bolster their knowledge base. The greatest challenge is to help students put religious beliefs and scientific views in proper context. Class discussions where students' views are aired openly help to foster a less dogmatic approach. I refrain from expressing any spiritual beliefs to promote a more open discussion and avoid an authoritative "solution." The lack of an answer from an authority changes learning from a goal-oriented to a process-oriented experience. Students learn the process of evolution by participating in the evolution of their own views of the topic.

In 1980 the geological and paleontological worlds were stunned by a publication which attributed the dinosaur extinction event to a large meteorite impact (Alvarez, Alvarez, Asaro, and Michel 1980). This hypothesis ignited a wave of public and academic interest and activity which continues unabated today. Aside from novels, theme parks and movies, this publication has and will have a lasting impact on scientific paradigms and society.

Death and extinction are integral parts of evolution. Without extinction there can be no room for evolution. Mammals and dinosaurs coexisted for 100 million years. For all of this time our ancestors were small, furry, mostly nocturnal rodents. The mass extinction event at the end of the Cretaceous terminated the dinosaurs and about one-half of all extant species. This catastrophic environmental and ecological disruption opened the way for the rapid speciation and radiation of the modern mammalian fauna. Major events in the history of life do not arrive on the slow and steady shoulders of phylogenetic gradualism. They arrive with a blast from space which punctuates the evolutionary process. Mass extinctions do not select the most favored races; only the lucky survive.

The Darwinian paradigm of natural selection and survival of most favored races suggests that extinction is a sign of failure (e.g., the dinosaurs were dumb slow beasts that deserved to be replaced by the intelligent, fast, and agile mammals). The post-Alvarez view is different. Even if we work hard, even if we do all the right things, even if we devise the most sophisticated sustainable society imaginable, our efforts may all come to naught. The fossil record is littered with the carcasses of long extinct life forms. Sooner or later *Homo sapiens* will join them. But that is not a sign of failure; it is only the next punctuation mark in the history of life. My hope is that by examining and incorporating this "deep time" perspective we can more clearly define and address the immediate issues of sustainability.

Literature Cited

Alvarez, L., W. Alvarez, F. Asaro, and H. V. Michel. 1980. Extraterrestrial Cause for the Cretaceous-Tertiary Extinction. *Science.* 208:1095-1108.

Darwin, C. 1859. *On the Origin of Species by the Means of Natural Selection, or the Preservation of Favoured Races in the Struggle to Survive.* London: John Murray.

Dott, R. H. Jr., and D. R. Prothero. 1994. *Evolution of the Earth* (5th ed.). New York: McGraw-Hill.

Eldredge, N., and S. J. Gould. 1972. Punctuated Equilibria: An Alternative to Phyletic Gradualism. In *Models in Paleobiology*, edited by T. J. M. Schopf. San Francisco: Freeman Cooper, 82-115.

Gould, S. J. 1993. Reconstructing (and Deconstructing) the Past, In *The Book of Life, An Illustrated History of the Evolution of Life on Earth*, edited by S. J. Gould. New York: W. W. Norton and Company, 6-21.

Hsu, K. J. 1986. Darwin's Three Mistakes, *Geology*, 14: 532-34.

Hubbert, M. K. 1969. Energy Resources. In *Resources and Man*. San Francisco: National Academy of Sciences, Freeman.

Hutton, J. 1795. *Theory of the Earth With Proof and Illustrations.* London: Cadell and Davies.

Mayr, E. 1942. *Systematics and the Origin of Species.* New York: Columbia.

III. From the Social Sciences

7. Seeking Sustainability
Community-Based Resource
Management in North America

Ted Bernard[1] and Jora M. Young[2]

A thing is right when it tends to preserve the, stability, and beauty of the biotic community. It is wrong when it tends otherwise.
—Aldo Leopold, *A Sand County Almanac* [1949] 1987

Abstract

Resource management is based on the conceit that humans are capable of managing the planet. Ecologist and land philosopher Aldo Leopold wrote that this role would prove self-defeating. To survive humans must become "plain citizens" in the community of life on Earth. Though Leopold never used the word sustainability, his writings provide the foundation for sustainable resource management.

Using a case study in Plumas County, California, we explore a newly-emerging resource management cropping up all over North America. Community-based and collaborative, it takes a small but important step in the direction Leopold suggested. In its design and practice, ecological integrity and stability are central. We examine elements of the new resource management, its evolution, and its relevance to university education.

[1] **Ted Bernard** is professor of geography and environmental studies at Ohio University. His research on village-level resource management and the consequences of rapid population growth in East Africa informs this paper and the larger project of which it is a part. He is a member of the steering committee of the Rural Action Network, a community-based sustainable development project in Appalachian Ohio, and serves on the Steering Committee of Friends Committee on Unity with Nature.
[2] **Jora Young** is director of science and stewardship at the Florida regional office of the Nature Conservancy. Her life's work as a designer and manager of natural area preserves began with degrees in botany and environmental studies at Antioch College and Ohio University. She has served on national planning commissions of the Nature Conservancy and has been a consultant in its projects in Mexico and Central America.

Introduction

Almost everything we need to know Aldo Leopold taught us. He may not have used the terms resource management or sustainability, but he clearly understood the pathway to righting the relationship between humans and the land. Integrity, stability, and beauty are the elements of Leopold's test for rightness. Integrity denotes wholeness and diversity in the land and its living systems. Stability implies nature's pace of change, where "the capacity of the land for self-renewal" guides decisions (Leopold [1949] 1987). Beauty inspires human awe and admiration, love and reverence. "It is inconceivable to me," Leopold wrote, "that an ethical relation to land can exist without love, respect and admiration for land and a high regard for its value" (Leopold [1949] 1987).

Though Leopold's land ethic, in Wallace Stegner's (1987) words, goes to the "heart of the matter" and has been known for almost fifty years, it has barely touched the actual practice of resource management. To Leopold, this would not be surprising:

> [Do] we not already sing our love for and obligation to the land of the free and the home of the brave? Yes, but just what and whom do we love? Certainly not the soil, which we are sending helter-skelter down river. Certainly not the waters, which we assume have no function except to turn turbines, float barges, and carry off sewage. Certainly not the plants, of which we exterminate whole communities without batting an eye. Certainly not the animals, of which we have extirpated many of the largest and most beautiful species. (Leopold [1949] 1987)

Resource management, the professional outgrowth of the American conservation movement, has philosophical roots in utilitarianism as articulated by British political philosophers Jeremy Bentham and John Locke. In the nineteenth century this came to be understood as a form of government which conducted itself "for the greatest good of society for the longest period of time." At the turn of the century Gifford Pinchot, President Theodore Roosevelt's first director of forestry, embraced utilitarianism as a way of fairly managing natural resources. Conservation, a term coined by Pinchot and others, was, in his view, "the most significant achievement of the T. R. administration" (Pinchot 1947). To Roosevelt and Pinchot, conservation meant development of natural resources, preservation of waste, and benefits for "the many" and not merely profit for "the few." Utilitarianism led to an institutional approach to natural resources. Fernie and Pitkethly, authors of a popular British text, write that the "success or failure of resource management is intrinsically tied up with institutional structures," and that resource management is primarily about "power and politics" (Fernie and Pitkethly 1985). The science most often employed is political science. American geographer David Greenland (1983) observes that resource management is woven tightly into a "spider's web" of socioeconomic and legal structures, and the energy and creativity of managers are often trapped in the web.

Efforts to develop and preserve natural resources have led resource managers to focus on impact and risk assessment, and cost-benefit analysis, defining "middle ground" between economic growth and preservation through both litigation and mitigation (Mitchell 1989). As a consequence, conventional resource management—utilitarian and hooked on growth and the elusive notion of progress—almost never deals with root causes. It does not ask why there is a web in the first place.

Conventional resource management is not working for anyone. Pro-environmental groups argue that resource management has been satisfied "to work within the system in ways that reinforce it instead of seeking the thoroughgoing social and political changes that are necessary to halt massive assaults on the natural world" (Sale 1986). Environmentalists allege that simple reform of resource management is a sell-out. In the world of Washington politics, the environment is just another "special interest." Conventional resource managers, argue critics, "are not successful even on their own terms. . . in stopping the onrush of industrial devastation. They are so caught up in compromise that they're actually going backward" (Sale 1986).

Pro-development groups have the opposite opinion. Reacting to the environmental movement, mining, logging, and ranching interests have formed grassroots groups dedicated to the "wise use" of resources. The so-called wise use/property rights movement, which includes unemployed loggers, off-road vehicle users, local government officials, and powerful industrialists, is reputedly out "to destroy environmentalism once and for all" (Helvaarg 1994).

> At its core Wise Use/Property Rights is a counterrevolutionary movement, defining itself in response to the environmental revolution of the past thirty years. It aims to create and mold disaffection over environmental regulations, big government, and the media into a cohesive social force that can win respectability for centrist arguments. . . . Simultaneously the movement pushes a more radical core agenda of "free-market environmentalism," "privatization," and the deregulation of industry. (Helvaarg 1994)

Between these poles of opinion are many shades of difference. It seems obvious that resource management has failed to stake out common ground. As one National Forest supervisor put it, "When we finished the forest plan and everyone was mad at us, we knew we had a good plan" (Thornton 1994).

Given the deteriorating state of natural resources, polarization is not only dysfunctional, it is dangerous. We do not have time for pitched battle. Polarized thinking must give way to a search for common ground. Leopold argued that we must take risks for the survival of the community—human and biotic. "All ethics so far evolved rest upon a single premise: that the individual is a member of a community of interdependent parts. . . . The land ethic simply enlarges the boundaries of the community to include soils, waters, plants, and animals, or collectively: the land" (Leopold [1949] 1987). If resource management continues to be bound by webs of conventional practice, if it can find no way to bring "warring parties" to the table, if it manifests no ecological courage, there is cause for despair.

Straws In The Wind?

Fortunately, despair is not the only theme. A few resource managers seem to comprehend the vast contradictions of their practice. Some are challenging decisions in their own agencies and firms. John Mumma, a regional forester for the U.S. Forest Service, spoke out against violations of environmental laws in the Forest Service's rush to "get out the cut." Though he was forced to resign, he is one of thousands of Forest Service employees who are placing ethics ahead of clear cutting in federal forests (Schneider 1992). Others are getting back to Leopold. Edward Pister, a lifelong fish and game manager in the California Department of Fish and Game, courageously refused to conduct his work simply for the pleasure of anglers and hunters. He felt responsible for the entire ecosystem: snakes, cacti, reptiles, and insects. At his retirement he wrote:

> More than a decade of field experience gave Aldo Leopold's words new meaning. Within the principles which he so eloquently set forth I found a rational basis for approaching and solving the problems that perplexed and seemed to completely overwhelm me. I felt I had within my grasp the basic components for making management programs address the entire biota, not simply the superficial popular demands which had so fully and frivolously consumed my time. (Pister 1987)

New language is emerging. Government agencies have been talking about ecosystem management. Business touts "cradle-to-cradle product stewardship" and "green technology." The United Nations has coined the paradoxical term "sustainable development" and, after the Earth Summit, President Clinton formed the President's Commission on Sustainable Development. Vice-President Al Gore's best-selling book argues convincingly that the environmental crisis is a crisis of spirit (Gore 1992). Religious leaders of all faiths have been engaged in international meetings on "peace, justice, and the integrity of creation" (Dowd 1991; T. Berry 1991; Massey 1989).

Even more intriguing than these shifts in the big institutions are changes in communities. Recycling has become part of mainstream American life (Hays 1987). Land trusts and private acquisition of ecologically threatened land are a national trend. Armed with shovels, brush cutters, seedlings, ecological awareness, and a good deal of hope, small brigades of volunteers have launched an environmental restoration movement (Stevens 1995). And, as people have begun to realize that American rivers are profoundly ill, watershed groups and stream teams have popped up everywhere (Bolling 1994; Doppelt et al. 1993).

Change is in the air, and we, the authors, wanted to discern whether it has substance. We wanted to know if the new language is merely talk. Are seeds of a radically different way of thinking about humanity's relationship with the Earth now being planted? Though we feared the worst—new language largely disembodied from practice—we embarked on a journey to find some places where a more sustainable approach to resource management might be taking root.

We have good news. Though rare, communities moving toward sustainable resource management can actually be found. A handful of projects, mostly in rural areas, piqued our curiosity. We read, inquired, and networked more. We cruised the information superhighway. Our list of communities grew from a handful to several dozen. From these, we narrowed our choices. We then set out to see them with our own eyes, to place them under a microscope, to learn some lessons. And always we questioned: would Aldo Leopold have found hope in the changes we were witnessing?

Our travels took us to New Mexico, Arizona, Oregon, and California; Ohio, Illinois, Iowa, and Wisconsin; Maine, Virginia, and Tennessee. Our case studies are: Monhegan Island, Maine; the Eastern Shore of Virginia; Chattanooga, Tennessee; Florida; Rural Action, Ohio; North Branch Prairie Project and Volunteer Stewardship Network, Illinois; the Menominee Reservation, Wisconsin; the Zuni Pueblo, New Mexico; the Malpai

Borderlands, Arizona and New Mexico; Plumas County, California; Mattole Valley, California.

In each place, we initially made contact with a few key people, did a quick reconnaissance to learn the geography and landscapes, visited projects and field experiments, and collected boxes of local documents, maps, and statistics. We then spent several days conducting semi-structured audiotaped interviews with employees, volunteers, politicians, government agency people, and friends and foes of projects in each community. When we returned home, we summarized what we found, looked critically both at details and general patterns and processes, and made comparisons among sites.

At this writing, we are still working toward a model that ties together these eleven communities in instructive ways (Bernard and Young 1996). What we report below is preliminary. Rather than encyclopedically cover each community, we present here a single case study which we believe to be illustrative of the thresholds many communities in North America could soon cross. In Plumas County, California, we think we have found what it might take to achieve sustainable resource management at the close of the twentieth century.

Plumas County: An Embryo of Sustainability

Setting

Tucked into the northern Sierra Mountains, Plumas County is paradoxically both one of the most scenic and ecologically impacted counties in California. Plumas County is rugged country with steep mountain passes and canyons, snow on the peaks until June in some years, fast flowing rivers, and upland mountain meadows. Here lie the headwaters of the Feather River, a river of inestimable value to California's urban and agricultural fortunes. An average of sixty inches of precipitation on westward slopes and good soils give rise to magnificent forests of Douglas fir, western red cedar, and ponderosa and sugar pine. Facing the vast expanses of the Great Basin, the dry eastern slopes, where precipitation is twenty inches or less, support Jeffrey and yellow pine and white fir.

Resource History

Plumas County people have always been tied to the land and its resources. The story begins with the Maidu and other Sierra Indians for whom this bioregion provided bountiful terrestrial and aquatic resources until the mid-nineteenth century. When John Muir walked through these upland meadows, he encountered Basque shepherds summering in the mountains with vast herds of sheep.

The gold rush of the mid-nineteenth century diverted the livestock keepers and drew prospectors from all over the world. When the gold had been tapped-out, when every stream had been panned, timber became the resource of choice. A settled ranching economy coexisted in the upland basins. Both activities profoundly changed both the watersheds and the living systems dependent upon them. Whole mountainsides were stripped by hydraulic mining; old-growth Douglas fir was clear-cut; and overgrazing and mining caused streams to incise their upper channels and become choked with sediment. Plumas County suffered a century of resource abuse.

By the mid-twentieth century, work in the woods and mills became the mainstay of the economy. Seventy-five percent of Plumas County is national forest. The Plumas National Forest has always been a working forest. In the prime years of the 1970s, over 300 million board feet of timber were cut per year from "the Plumas," making it one of the three most productive forests in the entire National Forest system. Here, as elsewhere in the west, logging moved aggressively into the last stands of old growth timber. Multinational timber operations, export pressures, and American consumption of forest products all pushed Congress and the Forest Service "to get out the cut." As late as 1991, 243 million board feet from big trees in the Plumas were coming to mills in northern California (Plumas National Forest 1994). As in all national forests in the past sixty years, forest fires were actively suppressed. Smokey the Bear profoundly disrupted his own habitat (Williams 1995).

With California's population growing tenfold in the first half of the twentieth century, Plumas County's water resources came into play. Southern California turned its thirsty attention toward the Feather and other northern rivers to irrigate crops, supply domestic needs, and generate hydroelectricity. Today, about thirty percent of the water used by farmers in the Central Valley and urban dwellers in southern California is Feather River water (Sheehan 1993). Plumas County has thus been inexorably drawn into California's unsustainable economy based on wasteful irrigation, runaway growth, urban sprawl, and high levels of water consumption.

Meanwhile, throughout the seventies and eighties, new people drifted into the mountains. Back-to-the-landers and urban refugees from San Francisco and Los Angeles migrated to Plumas County. A modest tourist industry blossomed. The newly-established Feather River Community College attracted teachers and students. Outsiders with different viewpoints brought the loud voices of the Wilderness Society and the Sierra Club. By the late 1980s these voices, with calls of "no more logging of old growth," "no more clear-cutting," and "beef is bad," confronted the logging and ranching cultures. Long isolated by topography and economy, Plumas County became another western place where fractious and inflammatory resource conflicts dominated the local political scene.

Coordinated Resource Management

In the capital in Sacramento, the state began to respond to statewide resource conflicts and deterioration. Mimicking a federal interagency agreement of 1980, California, in 1983, established a statewide Coordinated Resource Management (CRM) program. The working heart of CRM was a set of incentives for interagency cooperation, pooling funds, and staff and resource sharing (Sheehan 1994). Counties impacted from a century of mining and logging could apply for grants for watershed management and restoration to stem the loss of soil and silting of streams and reservoirs. CRM opened the door for county-level projects based on the idea of watershed restoration. "CRM has worked so well because individual members have been able to take the blinders off and see other people's viewpoints. We look at the environment and the watershed as a whole rather than the aspect we are narrowly concerned with" (Stine 1994).

The Plumas Corporation (known locally as "Plumas Corp"), a nonprofit economic and tourist development agency based in Quincy, saw opportunities for resource renewal and job creation in CRM. In 1985 Plumas Corp began coordinating stream restoration and erosion control projects. Two years later, they spearheaded a Memorandum of Agreement among seventeen partners, including the regional utility, Pacific Gas & Electric, and since have combined CRM funding with revenues from local, state, and federal sources to restore the upper reaches of the Feather River watershed (Sheehan 1993). It was a tentative, hands-on activism based on the principle that enhanced environmental quality and job creation were goals around which ranchers, loggers, back-to-the-landers, and tourism promoters all could rally.

CRM has continued to pour money into Plumas County projects. From 1985 to 1995, Plumas County received $2.7 million from PG & E and a variety of other sources, leading to tangible success on several fronts (Hamilton 1993; Sheehan 1995). Technically, the projects have begun to stem stream incision and bank erosion. Economically, they have pulled dollars into the county and created small businesses, jobs, and income for local contractors and recent high school and community college graduates.

Socially, they have drawn together an improbable cross-section of folk to work on locally designed and locally controlled resource management. People have learned to work together. They have begun to see each other in a new light. Hippies of the 1960s and fourth-generation ranchers, school children and resource agency professionals, back-hoe operators and environmental activists are laying the foundations for a culture of collaboration.

In less than a decade, Plumas Corp could boast of increased waterfowl populations in the upland meadows, improved spawning habitat for trout, enhanced forage production on ranches, and reduced erosion and stream incision. People could see and understand these changes. And not only local folk: so impressive were the results that Plumas County began to get national publicity and a steady stream of outside inquiries (Hamilton 1993; Little 1995). It was not that the projects in Plumas County were so technically sophisticated or innovative—stream restoration is happening in many places—but that they aroused community and ecological awareness in quite a new way: new language linked to new work. People seemed not only to be "talking the talk," but also "walking the walk." Perhaps as important, the door opened a crack, in increasingly dark economic times, to light a new path.

Hard Times

Even as CRM projects healed a few stream miles of the watershed, the economic lifeblood of Plumas County began to hemorrhage. In 1993, the U. S. Forest Service issued an interim plan to prevent the California spotted owl from becoming endangered like its northern cousin (Little 1995). In protecting this small and seemingly unobtrusive owl, the Forest Service effectively shut down logging operations in the Plumas. Output dropped from over 200 million board feet in the 1980s to less than thirty million in 1995 (Little 1995). Timber companies, following a much slower but no less significant trajectory, pulled operations from the region and replaced jobs with machines.

At the same time, the political steamroller of federal government downsizing rolled over the Forest Service. Just when the local economy was in greatest crisis, the preeminent resource manager in the region was forced to retrench. Between 1991 and 1994, Plumas National Forest headquarters and the ranger stations in the county lost 200 permanent and temporary jobs (Thornton 1994).

The economy and the community were in free-fall. Fear and despair led to finger-pointing and denial. Outraged locals railed against anyone not of their persuasion. Those dependent on timber denied that their industry, not the spotted owl, had been progressively undermining three generations of steady work. Angry yellow signs in towns declared, "I swear with my right hand on this stump, that my generation will be proud to be loggers" (Hamilton 1993). Friends of Plumas Wilderness argued that the spotted owl was a last gasp indicator of the sorry despoliation of Sierra forest ecosystems. California Women in Timber alleged that men in far-off office towers—timber magnates and environmentalist elites alike—were undercutting families whose livelihoods depended upon work in the woods and mills. Battle lines were clearly drawn. Someone's 44 magnum twice pierced the office windows of Michael Jackson, one of the most prominent critics of current forest practice, an environmental lawyer in Quincy.

The Quincy Library Group

Then emerged Bill Coates, a thoughtful leader, a conservative county commissioner and small business owner, and long a friend of the logging community. He quietly asked two key community leaders to meet with him: the de facto leader of the environmentalist community and an official from Sierra Pacific Industries, the largest logging operation in Plumas County (Little 1995). Their initial meeting was furtive. Coates understood that the future of the community depended upon resolving differences and envisioning ways to sustain the economy and its resource base.

Soon these three leaders began to meet openly at the Quincy Library. They invited anyone who desired to participate in drafting a consensus plan for the management of public forests and ultimately for the restoration of community pride and prosperity. The Quincy Library Group (QLG), as they came to be called, drew almost every sector of the community: environmental activists, timber company executives, National Forest Service professionals, representatives from California natural resource agencies, the Feather River Alliance for Resources and Environment (a "wise use" advocacy group), and California Women in Timber. Those who, for a decade, had worked on CRM projects, seemed especially anxious to be part of this collaboration. Representatives of the Collins Pine Company in nearby Chester came to tell the story of fifty years of successful sustainable stewardship of their 92,000-acre tract of forest. The Quincy Library Group met semi-monthly for more than a year, trying to envision a future in which both forestry and ecosystem integrity could coexist.

In November 1993, they arrived at a consensus document called a "Community Stability Proposal." The proposal sees production of timber as a function of restoration. It seeks to reduce fire hazards and sedimentation, increase populations of spotted owl, trout, and waterfowl, and protect roadless areas–goals that speak to ecosystem health rather than forest products. Instead of "talking timber quota, we are talking acres treated," said Michael Jackson, one of three QLG facilitators (M. Jackson 1994). The plan speaks of diversity in age-classes and species of trees rather than single species domination; of individual and group selection forestry rather than clear cutting; of stream restoration and protection rather than grazing and logging to the banks; of planning and management by watersheds rather than ranger districts; of a fire-resistant forest approximating pre-settlement conditions; and of roadless wilderness and scenic and riparian corridors (Quincy Library Group 1993).

The QLG plan is written in language of collaboration and partnership rather than winners and losers:

> We realize that our opinion is simply an educated opinion and may not be appropriate in the eyes of others. All other opinions have a reasonable possibility of being right. We also believe that we represent a very diverse group of local interests, each with a shared stake in the outcomes of these actions. (Quincy Library Group 1993)

By avoiding a set of watered-down agreements hammered out in an adversarial process, this radical document commits its authors to work toward short-term common goals while a longer-term plan is fashioned. It incorporates suggestions from Friends of Plumas Wilderness proposals of the 1980s, sustained yield forestry, and lessons from CRM projects. By focusing on ecosystem integrity and stability, it attends to community integrity and stability, and thereby pays homage to the essential beauty of these mountain landscapes and the people who use them. Aldo Leopold, who disdained plantation forestry as "growing trees like cabbages," would, we think, heartily approve (Leopold [1949] 1987).

What is especially striking is the sense of hope in this plan. Whereas the conventional Forest Service planning process ends up with local stakeholders at each other's throats and ready to lynch Forest Service planners, the QLG continues to work together. Given this collaboration, long-term sustainable resource management on the Plumas seems to have a fighting chance.

The story does not end here. In responding to the QLG plan, the Forest Service proved to be a substantial part of the problem. Its bureaucratic "spider web" and internal politics have thrown up barricades to change. Yet the Forest Service's own formal assessment of the QLG proposal proved the Quincy Library Group's assumptions to be correct. Based on that assessment, the Forest Service received funding from the U.S. Environmental Protection Agency for forest fire fuel reduction (thinning, removal of downfalls and control of fire-prone litter). Two years later, the Forest Service thus appears to be slowly coming into the QLG fold (Sheehan 1995).

CRM projects continue to attract funds for stream restoration. Plumas Corp has advanced the idea that the California Water Project and Los Angeles Basin residents are principal beneficiaries of a healthy Feather River watershed and therefore should be willing to invest in further restoration. If this principle is understood and acknowledged, a new era of water resource politics and economics will have unfolded in California. And CRM will have a reliable flow of funds to sustain restoration projects indefinitely.

The California spotted owl management guidelines, published in 1995, are being interpreted by most observers as devastating, even to the owl. Two Quincy Library Group women (one a Sierra Club president, the other an organizer for California Women in Timber) have evaluated the guidelines and recommended a new approach to protect the owl without sacrificing the forestry provisions of the QLG Proposal (Sheehan 1995). In sum, the community is now armed with a potent vision of a new kind of resource management. They have successful experience with collaboration and partnership. They possess a renewed sense of place. They are more confident about the future. Their optimism is infectious.

Sustainable Resource Management

In Plumas County, and in every other case we have studied, optimism is based not on fantasy but on experience. Much of this experience is embryonic and therefore fragile. But folks in our sample of communities seem to understand that radically different approaches are required to survive the resource problems they have inherited. From the people's descriptions of their own winning formulas, from the writings of Leopold and other visionaries, and from our own observations and life experiences, we present here a set of ideal characteristics that might typify communities who envision a sustainable future in that most sacred of places—their home.

Good Working Knowledge of the Ecosystem. Finely tuned ecological awareness and knowledge; an understanding of natural form and function; knowledge about natural elements, cycles, relationships, and processes—this is what Leopold meant when he advised resource managers to "think like a mountain" (Leopold [1949] 1987). Good knowledge of the ecosystem begins with a search for answers to management questions in the workings of nature. Variable and unpredictable, complex and mysterious, nature will be our teacher. If we can save some bits of wild nature relatively intact, we have a better chance of discovering how to live compatibly with this complexity and mystery. It therefore makes sense to take seriously Thoreau's dictum, "in wildness is the preservation of the world." Roadless areas and free-flowing streams in Plumas County hold clues for unlocking the mysteries of the Sierra ecosystem. Thoughtful study of these "wild" bits of nature will yield management plans with a chance of success. That's why the QLG proposal is so revolutionary. It explicitly intends "to create a forest that will more closely mimic the historic natural landscapes of the Sierra. . . " (Quincy Library Group 1993).

A Vision of Ecosystem Health. Closely allied to knowledge is ecosystem health. The key question is: What constitutes a healthy, functioning ecosystem? The answer must be based on solid data collected at carefully controlled local sites. The answer must also emerge from local history and geography, and, to a certain extent, from ecological intuition. The community must have a working concept of what "health" for their own ecosystem looks like.

Though the Quincy Library Group laid out a short term plan, it aimed in the long term to have an ecologically healthy forest. They understood the need to reduce the heavy cover of highly flammable understory trees, to stem the rate of stream sedimentation, to reduce forest fragmentation by closing some National Forest roads, to discourage large clear cuts, to encourage fish and wildlife protection and diversity, and to bring a diversity of native tree species back to the forest. Their proposal therefore not only assures an adequate timber supply but also promotes forest health and ecological integrity (Quincy Library Group 1993).

Commitment to Learning. Members of the community are students of nature. David Orr (1994a) writes that "students of nature" must know how the Earth works, basic ecology and thermodynamics, essentials of human ecology, the natural history of their community, and "the kinds of knowledge that will enable them to restore natural systems and build ecologically resilient communities and economies." Awareness and knowledge of these things teaches humility, for decisions will always be based not only on appreciation of the sanctity of nature but also on insufficient knowledge. Managers might plan their strategies as testable hypotheses. Even if their hypotheses are false, managers will have learned and will be able to continuously incorporate new information (Lee 1993).

Respect for Cogs and Wheels. We presently have too little knowledge to understand the value of all the parts and processes in natural systems surrounding and supporting human communities. But it would be foolhardy to dismiss them as unimportant. Leopold long ago mused:

> The last word in ignorance is the man who says of an animal or plant: 'What good is it?' If the land mechanism as a whole is good, then every part is good, whether we understand it or not. If the biota, in the course of aeons, has built something we like but do not understand, then who but a fool would discard seemingly useless parts? To keep every cog and wheel is the first precaution of intelligent tinkering. (Leopold [1953] 1966)

A truly sustainable community would be conservative in its tinkering.

If ranchers and loggers in Plumas County wish to sustain a trout fishery, then it follows that they must also respect the ecosystem of which trout are a part. If foresters aspire to produce an adequate timber supply from an ecologically diverse forest, then the full diversity of species and continuous cover are important. Neither fishermen nor loggers nor even the most knowledgeable resource manager now knows the importance of each organism in every local ecosystem. Indeed, biological scientists have yet to identify—much less understand—their functions and interdependencies of every organism in any ecosystem. In the absence of that knowledge, it must be assumed that even the smallest cogs and wheels play a significant role and therefore must be valued.

A Sense of Place. A sustainable community is deeply attuned to its geographical home. Members of the community possess a sense of harmony, a balance, with their surroundings (W. Berry 1991). Leah Wills, erosion control coordinator for Plumas Corp, added: "If you don't have a sense of place, you don't have a sense of limits. If you don't have a sense of limits, you'll never have a sense of balance" (Wills 1994). When adversaries in Plumas County put aside their differences, they discovered—in addition to their mutual distrust of the Forest Service—they shared a love of the beautiful mountain place they called home and an awareness that it was in grave danger.

Excellent knowledge of local history and geography is the foundation for a sense of place. People must take pride in the triumphant stories and struggles of the past, understand the historical context of their home, know its nooks and crannies, and have a love of local historical and geographical lore. In short, people must become native to their place. They must become "embedded in the ecological realities" of their home; they must learn the limits (W. Jackson 1994).

Acceptance of Change. To manage resources for sustainability, a community must live with ecological change. Change in nature is inevitable and adaptive; nature is replete with "discordant harmonies" (Botkin 1990). To accept the dictum that "the only constant in nature is change" is to recognize that managing natural resource systems will never be static or sure. Natural systems are poorly understood and therefore difficult to predict; we must absolutely expect surprises (Lee 1993, 63).

"The key to a new but wise management of nature is to accept changes that are natural in kind and in frequency. . ." (Botkin 1990) and avoid changes that are unnatural. Resilient communities will aim not to eliminate change but, rather like building for earthquakes, learn to bend with the unpredictable natural world. A sustainable Plumas County, for example, must accept fire, flood and drought, and natural predation. And manage accordingly.

Long-Term Horizon. Aldo Leopold spent his career trying to repair biotic communities and avoid the impacts of overharvesting. He noted that as long as natural resources are viewed only as commodities to be traded in short-term markets, overharvesting is inevitable. More recently, Kai Lee (1993) expressed it this way:

> Converting beavers into pelts and pelts into money permits the money to be invested. In that form, it will grow faster than beavers. This logic faced each trapper. By 1700 beavers had become scarce in New England. . . . Why does this matter to sustainable development? The economic logic that transformed New England is still at work. If resources are economic commodities, their value decreases over time; and overharvest, biologically speaking, can be economically rational. (Kai Lee 1993)

To say that we need a different conception of resources is to understate the challenge. If sustainability means managing resources so that the options of future generations will not be closed, we must realize that a much longer investment horizon is required. It is only when we grasp the essential truth that the capital upon which our life and all life depends is the living infrastructure of the planet, that we will develop an economic system that strives to protect the capital and live modestly on the interest. This will be the ultimate test for a forest-dependent community like Plumas County, and it is obviously too soon to say whether it will rise to the challenge. Thinking not just of children and grandchildren, Plumas County folk must today begin to look ahead to the world they want for great grandchildren, great-great grandchildren, and beyond.

Ability to Set Limits. Ecosystems have tolerances and, as history teaches only too well, ecosystems can collapse if pushed beyond their limits. Witness the collapse in the 1970s of Lake Erie fisheries or the current demise of shell fishing in Chesapeake Bay. Sustainable communities set limits. They recognize that you cannot abuse the natural system with reckless abandon. They discipline themselves to limit consumption. When the Quincy Library Group acknowledged that sensitive areas such as wilderness, scenic river corridors, and riparian margins could not be scheduled for timber harvest, they began the process of setting limits. This is a step toward sustainability.

How to Get There

Of course, Plumas County does not manifest the full combination of these traits. No single community does. Like justice or universal love, these are ideals that will never be fully achieved. In our own search we had to keep reminding ourselves that the journey rather than the destination is our story.

What is necessary to launch a community upon that journey? In our travels, we encountered a curious set of circumstances and personalities that seemed common, like flagstones in a pathway. The more flagstones present, the greater the likelihood a community will set off on a new and enduring journey. Here is what we found:

Visionaries. In every case we found a key person or persons who could see the vital connections between the natural ecosystem and the human community. These people deeply understood the necessity of connecting community to its natural resource base. Plumas Corp resource professionals and planners played this role as did some recent immigrants who could see the region and its problems with new eyes.

Small Successes. Small successes tangibly demonstrate that a piece of the vision can be accomplished. CRM projects on Plumas County's damaged streams had immediate visual, educational, and ecological impacts. They attracted a cross-section of local folk who proved they could work together, provided a base for further collaboration.

Precipitating Crisis. A precipitating crisis galvanizes a community and forces residents to get beyond historic alliances and differences. The collapse of the Northern California timber industry impacted a cross-section of people who, in crisis, began to find common ground. Commissioner Coates lamented: "Our small towns were already endangered. This was going to wipe them out" (Little 1995). And so it has been in our entire sample. Without a crisis and an understanding of its cross-cutting risks, a collaborative forum like the Quincy Library Group is unlikely to emerge.

Collaborative Elements

Leaders. People willing to work in collaborative ways using consensus-based decision making are crucial to success. Respected long-time residents of the community embrace the vision and communicate it to the community. They think long-term, see the big picture, and go beyond emotion. Bill Coates, the county commissioner who first met furtively with other leaders in Quincy, understood that if the community continued to plummet, everyone would lose.

Cooperators. Others in the community then join the leaders, forming partnerships and alliances. These people are good information brokers. They are willing to be on the phone, send out letters and flyers, organize meetings, smooth ruffled feathers, and, through their example and dedication, inspire others. In Plumas County, for example, Susan Baremore, wife of logger Clay Baremore and executive director of the Feather River Alliance for Resources and Environment–a "wise use" organization–was a key collaborative member of the Quincy Library Group (Baremore 1994).

Forum. There must be a regular way of bringing together divergent individuals and groups to participate in real decisions with real outcomes. If successful, this will be a safe place for ideas to flow, and perhaps will become rooted in some neutral turf like the public library.

Decision-making. Ideally, decisions are made by consensus. The group has to be willing to think like Quakers, to accept that everyone has a piece of the truth, to strive for solutions that go beyond the tired legacies of compromise, Robert's Rules, winners and losers, and the politics of conflict where every issue is either right or wrong.

Inclusivity. Whoever is willing to contribute is welcomed to the table. One of the roles of collaborative leaders is to assure that this will happen by using language that makes sense to a broad spectrum of viewpoints. The language, in other words, must "speak" to the community. In Plumas County, the plan was a proposal for "community stability," a situation including environmentalists, loggers, timber executives, and families.

Shared Vision. The community itself begins to divine a new sense of place and a vision for the future of that place. The definition of place possesses knowledge of ecological context. "Here" is distinctive. When community members are asked what their place will look like in twenty years or fifty years, they articulate hopeful views. One resident of Plumas County described "a future in which we have retrieved the environmental integrity of this county, in which we are living off and managing the forests well, in which our children have both a prosperous economy and a high quality environment" (Zone 1994). People may approach the future from different vantage points, but they share similar hopes and dreams. "Sustainability," though not often mentioned per se, is clearly at the heart of these dreams.

Hope. "This can work." "An entirely new ball game. . . ." "We can finally see some light." These statements from our interviews suggest that despair need not rule, even when all else seems gloomy. In spite of a grim short-term economy, the Quincy Library Group infuses the county with optimism and hope. Bill Coates put it this way: "I don't know anywhere in the United States an entire county has gotten environmentalists and people interested in jobs to agree on anything. All at once there are no sides. This is a brand new day" (Little 1995).

Tenacity. Tenacity both draws from this optimism and extends it to another day. Against all odds, the Quincy Library Group keeps meeting, continues to push the Forest Service in new directions, continues to prove wrong skeptics and naysayers. Of the QLG, environmental lawyer Michael Jackson says: "The power we have is the power of an idea we all agree on" (Little 1995).

Capital. New capital is a powerful way of increasing resolve, effectiveness, and attention. But money alone is insufficient. The Appalachian Regional Commission has thrown millions of dollars into environmental and community development projects over the past thirty years, yet both degradation and poverty persist in Appalachia. By the same token, in the absence of community support, money spent on the Feather River watershed would have been fruitless. CRM projects in Plumas County illustrate the importance of other ingredients: a shared vision of success, good working teams and leadership, and a history of small successes enabled CRM capital to make a difference. One of our Plumas County interviews yielded this: "A good solution is the hardest thing to find. Good people to implement the solution. . . second hardest. And money the easiest" (Sheehan 1994).

Conclusion

Leopold wrote that we must change our role from "conquerors" to "plain citizens" of this planet. For at least three million years, humans have evolved with and impacted other life forms, conquering the Earth but never totally losing touch with nature. We are all children of the Pleistocene, says David Orr (1994b), "shaped by a wildness we can scarcely imagine." If we and our natural companions are to survive and thrive, we must grasp this "wild" oneness and we must understand that the "conqueror role is eventually self-defeating" (Leopold [1949] 1987).

We believe this is beginning to happen.

Across the planet, a quiet revolution is underway. It is called many things: sustainability, biophilia, collaborative planning, community-based conservation, ecological restoration, ecosystem management, bioregionalism, new resource management. It is taking people away from a view that the Earth and its resources exist purely for humans to a belief that humans are part of the living Earth. It is born of a new ecological awareness, an understanding of limits, a new respect for all the "cogs and wheels." It is our best hope for a future on an Earth in glowing good health, possessed of diversity, integrity, stability, and wild beauty.

We believe this revolution is happening at the bottom. It tip-toes into communities desperate for ways to escape legacies of bad resource management. What emerges—in the ways we listed above and in much less time than we would have predicted—are partnerships among conventional adversaries, collaboration between government and non-government agencies, engagement of the private sector, deep involvement of ordinary people. Pride in place and confidence in a vision of a biologically and culturally restored region propel a new kind of activism, based not on resisting and finger pointing, but on healing and working together. It takes form in watershed restoration, land trusts, community forestry, clean-up campaigns, recycling, "cottage" and crafts industries, and countless other hopeful ways. It is in communities and neighborhoods, not the halls of Congress or Parliament, that the pulse of this revolution is felt.

What does this have to do with college and university educators? Everything and nothing. What is happening in communities across the globe is immensely important to our future. If it takes hold, it is a light at the end of this dark postmodern tunnel of environmental exploitation and ruin. The story is therefore not just another "case study" in a course or two in the average college or university education. It is *the* course, *the* major, *the* degree of the future. It is everything.

What is surprising and troubling is that this revolution has so far scarcely involved the academy. When one asks the question—What have universities done to foster this quiet revolution?—the simple answer is almost nothing. It has taken place mostly outside the context of formal education. David Orr (1994a) remarks that universities offer only degrees in "upward mobility" and, curiously, people with the best ideas often have little formal education.

What must we do? David Orr argues that the purpose of university education must be turned on its head. Colleges and universities must offer not degrees in upward mobility, but instead degrees in homecoming. Homecoming is about "restoring ecological and human scale to a civilization that has lost its sense of proportion and purpose. . . regenerating roots in particular places and traditions" (Orr 1994a). Our curriculum must draw deeply on our Pleistocene inheritance; it must draw lessons from nature itself.

"Education that builds an affinity for life would lead to a kind of awakening of possibilities and potentials that lie largely dormant and unused in the industrial-utilitarian mind. . . . [T]he good news is that our own nature will help us in the process, if we let it" (Orr 1994a).

Once students understand the stakes, they hunger for this kind of education. As educators, we must ensure that we are not barriers to its implementation. Education for sustainability, for homecoming, for a future infinitely better than the industrial age is a matter of great urgency. At our peril, we have ignored Aldo Leopold too long. It is time to let him teach us again.

[Editor's note. The above chapter and other research studies are thoroughly developed in the authors' book, *The Ecology of Hope: Communities Collaborate for Sustainability,* New Society Publishers, Philadelphia, Pa.]

Literature Cited

Baremore, S. 1994. Executive Director of Feather River Alliance for Resources and Environment. Personal interview. April 13, 1994.

Berry, T. 1991. *Befriending the Earth: A Theology of Reconciliation Between Humans and the Earth.* Mystic, Conn.: Twenty-Third Publications.

Berry, W. 1991. Living With the Land. *Journal of Soil & Water Conservation,* 46: 390–393.

Bernard, T., and J. Young. 1996. *The Ecology of Hope.* Vancouver: New Society Publishers.

Bolling, D. M. 1994. *How to Save a River.* Washington, D.C.: Island Press.

Botkin, D. 1990. *Discordant Harmonies: A New Ecology for the Twenty-First Century.* New York: Oxford University Press.

Cutter, S. 1980. Environmental Management: New Paradigm for Old Commitments. *Resource Management. & Optimization,* 1: 77-87.

Doppelt, B., M. Scurlock, C. Frissell, and J. Karr. 1993. *Entering the Watershed.* Washington, D.C.: Island Press.

Dowd, M. 1991. *Earthspirit: A Handbook for Nurturing an Ecological Community.* Mystic, Conn.: Twenty-Third Publications.

Fernie, J., and A. S. Pitkethly. 1985. *Resources, Environment, and Policy.* London: Harper and Row.

Gore, A. 1992. *Earth in the Balance: Ecology and the Human Spirit.* Boston: Houghton Mifflin.

Greenland, D. 1983. *Guidelines for Modern Resource Management.* Columbus: Merrill.

Hamilton, J. 1993. Streams of Hope. *Sierra* (Sept.–Oct.), 98-104, 120, 122.

Hays, S. P. 1959. *Conservation and the Gospel of Efficiency: The Progressive Conservation Movement, 1890-1920.* Cambridge: Harvard University Press.

———. 1987. *Beauty, Health and Permanence: Environmental Politics in the United States, 1955-1985.* Cambridge: Cambridge University Press.

Helvaarg, D. 1994. *The War Against the Greens.* San Francisco: Sierra Club.

Jackson, M. 1994. Practicing attorney, Quincy, Calif. Personal interview. April 13, 1994.

Jackson, W. 1994. *Becoming Native to this Place.* Lexington: University of Kentucky Press.

Lee, K. 1993. *Compass and Gyroscope: Integrating Science and Politics for the Environment.* Washington, D.C.: Island Press.

Leopold, A. [1953] 1966. *The Round River.* New York: Oxford University Press.

———. [1949] 1987. *A Sand County Almanac.* New York: Oxford University Press.

Little, J. B. 1995. The Quincy library group. *American. Forests,* 101: 22-24, 56.

Lowenthal, D. 1990. Awareness of Human Impacts: Changing Attitudes and Emphases. In *The Earth as Transformed by Human Action,* edited by B. L. Turner et al. Cambridge: Cambridge University Press, 121-136.

Massey, M. 1989. *Seeking the Kingdom.* Argenta, BC: Argenta Friends Press.

Mitchell, B. 1989. *Geography and Resource Analysis.* 2d ed. London: Longman.

Orr, D. 1994a. *Earth in Mind: on Education, Environment, and the Human Prospect.* Washington, D.C.: Island Press.

———. 1994b. Love It or Lose It: The Coming Biophilia Revolution. *Orion,* 13: 8-15.

Pinchot, Gifford. 1947. *Breaking New Ground.* New York: Harcourt Brace.

Pister, E. P. 1987. A Pilgrim's Progress From Group A to Group B. In *Companion to a Sand County Almanac,* edited by J. B. Callicott, 221-232. Madison: University of Wisconsin Press.

Plumas National Forest. 1994. *Forest Statistics: 1991-1994.* Quincy, Calif.: Plumas National Forest Supervisor.

Quincy Library Group. 1993. Community Stability Proposal. Quincy, Calif.: Quincy Library Group.

Sale, K. 1986. The Forest for the Trees: Can Today's Environmentalists tell the Difference? *Mother Jones,* 11: 25-26, 28-29, 32-33, 58.

Schneider, P. 1992. When a Whistle Blows in the Forest. *Audubon* (January-February): 42-49.

Sheehan, John. 1993. Riparian Restoration Equals Economic Development. *Bulletin of the California Association of Local Development,* 14:1, 11.

———. 1994. Executive Director, the Plumas Corporation. Personal interview. April 11, 1994.

———. 1995. Testimony on ecosystem management. U.S. Senate Committee on Agriculture, Agricultural Research, Conservation, Forestry, and General Legislative Subcommittee, April 14, 1994. Washington, D.C.: U.S. Senate Committee on Agriculture.

Stegner, W. 1987. The Legacy of Aldo Leopold. In *Companion to A Sand County Almanac*, edited by J. B. Callicott, 233-245. Madison: University of Wisconsin Press.

Stevens, W. K. 1995. *Miracle Under the Oaks: The Revival of Nature in America*. New York: Pocket Books.

Stine, R. 1995. Chief Forester, California Department of Forestry, Quincy, Calif.. Personal interview. April 1995.

Thornton, Wayne. 1995. Plumas National Forest Supervisor. Personal interview. April 16, 1995.

Williams, T. 1995. Only You Can Postpone Forest Fires. *Sierra* (July-August). 36-43, 67-69.

Wills, L. 1994. Erosion Control Coordinator, the Plumas Corporation. Personal interview. April 15, 1994.

Zone, M. 1994. Executive Director, Plumas County Community Development Commission and Housing Authority. Personal interview. April 11, 1994.

8. Live Richly and Simply
Learning from Kerala

William M. Alexander[1]

Materialism simply cannot survive the transition to a sustainable world.
—Lester Brown, *State of the World*, 1990

Abstract

A search among the large human populations with well-defined characteristics led scientists into the Indian sub-continent and the Malayalam-speaking state of Kerala. At very low consumption levels, the twenty-nine million Malayalees have achieved high life quality and sustainable fertility standard—two children in the lifetime of each female, zero population growth. This study shows that human equity is the necessary public policy to achieve desirable conditions of human survival through the twenty-first century.

The examination of the exceptional human behavior in Kerala was initiated by the Institute for Food and Development Policy in 1989 and sponsored by Earthwatch Expeditions two years later. The contributions of eighty-one North American and European participant-observers and the Kerala research staff headed by Drs. P. K. Nambiar and C. R. Soman (1992) are gratefully acknowledged.

Why Study Kerala?

The *Earthwatch Report* (Alexander 1994) as a whole validates and illustrates the conclusion of Berkeley health scientist John Ratcliffe. Kerala, write Ratcliff in 1978, refutes "the common thesis that high levels of social development cannot be achieved in the absence of high rates of economic growth. . . . Indeed, the Kerala experience demonstrates that high levels of social development—evaluated in terms of such quality of life measures as mortality rates and levels of life expectancy,

---

[1] **William M. Alexander** is emeritus professor of world food politics, California Polytechnic State University (1958-88). At CPSU he taught both development administration to graduates preparing to serve in less developed countries and world food politics to undergraduates. For three years he served in the African nations of Kenya and Lesotho, working directly with farmers on fruit and vegetable production. Since retirement Alexander has researched the use of Earth resources in Kerala as consultant for the Institute for Food and Development Policy and as principal investigator for Earthwatch Expeditions.

Kerala, India—a Model for Sustainability?

At very low consumption levels, the twenty-nine million Malayalees have achieved high life quality and sustainable fertility standard—two children in the lifetime of each female, zero population growth.

education and literacy, and political participation–are consequences of public policies and strategies based not on economic growth considerations but, instead, on equity considerations" (Ratcliffe 1978).

A small matrix of behavioral alternatives (figure 1) directs our attention to the urgent need to study Kerala. The two human behavioral patterns which are critical in relationship to our home called the Earth are *the amount of consumption* and *large families,* represented by the upper right box. For modern times, the first world is defined by high consumption and small families, shown in the lower left box:

Figure 1. Human Behavior Alternatives

Family Size	Standard of Living	
	High Consumption	**Low Consumption**
Large Families	Saudi Arabia	World Norm of the Past, Current 3rd World Norm
Small Families	Current First World Norm	Kerala—Possible Future World Norm

The upper left box has a short-time anomaly, Saudi Arabia, with both large families and high consumption. Low consumption and small-family choices are the quality-of-life possibility in the near future of the whole Earth. In addition to Kerala, China and Sri Lanka have been nominated (Murdock 1980) as containing sustainable human behavior patterns. Kerala was chosen as the outstanding exception in the current world pattern of high consumption on simple criteria—both the family sizes and the consumption levels are smaller in Kerala than in either China or Sri Lanka.

Comparative Data. The current comparative data establishes Kerala as a true exception by offering a possibility of a satisfactory human species survival in the twenty-first century. To display this exceptional behavior, the subject of this report, Kerala, is compared with those other nations (with sufficient statistical measurements) closest to Kerala in population size. The sixteen nations selected for comparision are the eight nations with the next larger populations and the eight nations with the next smaller populations.

In column 1 of table 1a, Kerala occurs in the middle of the population range for the sixteen world nations selected for similar size. All-India data (including Kerala) is shown separately for local comparison. In column 2, Kerala is within this set of size mates ordered by per-capita gross national product. The per-capita product measured for Kerala is actually lower than the all-India figure. However, since Kerala receives more repatriated income (not included in state product figures)

Table 1a. Kerala Data Compared with Sixteen Nations[1]

Ordered by Population (millions)		Ordered by GNP per Capita (U.S. Dollars)		Total Fertility Rate (Completed Family Size per Female)	
Column 1		*Column 2*		*Column 3*	
Nepal	19	Canada	$20,470	Spain	1.2
Peru	22	France	$19,490	Romania	1.4
Romania	23	Spain	$11,020	S. Korea	1.6
Kenya	24			France	1.7
Algeria	25	S. Korea	$5.400	Canada	1.8
Morocco	25	Algeria	$2,060	Poland	1.8
Tanzania	25	Poland	$1.690	**Kerala**	**1.9**
Canada	27	Romania	$1,640		
		Colombia	$1,260		
Kerala	**29**	Peru	$1,160	Colombia	2.7
		Morocco	$950	Peru	3.5
Colombia	32	Egypt	$600	Egypt	3.9
Zaire	37			Morocco	4.0
Poland	38	Kenya	$370	Algeria	4.2
Spain	39	**Kerala**	**$350**	Nepal	5.5
S. Korea	43	Zaire	$220	Kenya	6.3
Ethiopia	51	Nepal	$170	Tanzania	6.3
Egypt	52	Ethiopia	$120	Zaire	6.7
France	56	Tanzania	$110	Ethiopia	6.9
India	850	India	$350	India	3.6

[1] Data in the six columns of table 1 is drawn from *1994 World Population Data Sheet* (Population Reference Bureau), *The Environmental Data Book* 1993 (World Bank), and the *Economic Review* 1993 (Government of Kerala).

Table 1b. Kerala Data Compared with Sixteen Nations

Infant Mortality (No. of Deaths per 1,000 Live Births)		H.S. Enrollment of Females (Pct. of Age Group)		Life Expectancy (Years of a Child Born Today)	
Column 4		*Column 5*		*Column 6*	
Canada	7	Spain	110%	Canada	77
France	7	Canada	105%	France	76
Spain	8	France	100%	Spain	76
				Romania	76
Kerala	**16**	**Kerala**	**93%**		
Poland	16	Romania	92%	**Kerala**	**72**
S. Korea	17	S. Korea	84%	S. Korea	71
Romania	27	Poland	83%	Poland	71
Colombia	37	Egypt	71%	Colombia	69
Egypt	66	Colombia	53%	Algeria	65
Algeria	67	Algeria	43%	Peru	63
Morocco	67	Peru	34%	Morocco	62
Kenya	67	Morocco	30%	Egypt	60
Peru	69			Kenya	59
		Kenya	19%		
Zaire	94	Nepal	17%	Nepal	52
Nepal	106	Zaire	16%	Zaire	52
Tanzania	115	Ethiopia	12%	Tanzania	48
Ethiopia	132	Tanzania	4%	Ethiopia	48
India	92	India	31%	India	59

than other states, the per-capita income for all India is used. The highest Kerala per-capita income estimates is chosen for display in these comparisons.

Beginning with column 2, the three nations with very high income figures are grouped at the top, and distinctly low income countries are grouped at the bottom. These groupings are repeated in table 1b, columns 4, 5, and 6, showing the commonly anticipated relationship of wellness and education to incomes in all nations in each set (excepting only Kerala). Column 3, Total Fertility Rate, clearly divides into two categories, populations with and without sustainable fertility behavior. The exceptional performance of Kerala on crucial measures of wellness and education is displayed in columns 4 to 6. Infant Mortality, Female Education, and Life Expectancy are among the equity factors explaining the modest fertility of Kerala.

If income level (and inferred consumption of Earth resources) determine the Kerala wellness and educational behavior as it evidently does for other nations, Kerala should remain in the lowest income set as established in column 2. An additional comparison, geographically and historically similar populations, all-India data, is shown separately at the foot of each column. Holding per-capita income measures constant, Kerala is shown to be two to five times more efficient. If the wellness and educational measures are compared to GNP per-capita measurements, even larger Kerala efficiency ratios appear.

Efficiency. Attention is also called to those populations which do not have wellness measures equal to or better than Kerala. They lack either the necessary resources and/or the efficiency in the use of these resources to attain a self-actualization threshold. Given that the relative shortage of natural resources in Kerala precludes a material economic growth solution, the use of the other resources must be considered. Is human time being used efficiently? Anticipating the conclusion of the Kerala story that follows, a matrix, figure 2, displays the strategies for applying human time.

Figure 2. Applying Human Time to Produce High Life Quality
Variable: Declining Amounts of Resources Available Per Capita

Skill in the Application of Human Time	Availability of Resources	
	Large Amounts Available	**Small Amounts Available**
Low Skill	Produce and Waste More Goods	Produce More Goods
High Skill	Produce and Waste More Goods	Distribute Equitably

The Society and Politics of Kerala

Background. As India freed herself from the British empire, the three Malayalam-speaking areas, Malabar and the former princely provinces of Travancore and Cochin, were merged into the state of Kerala. Kerala made international headlines when a communist-dominated coalition romped into power in the state's first parliamentary elections in 1957. The chairman of the Kerala Communist Party, E. M. S. Namboodiripad, became the chief minister, the first major success for communism in a free and democratic country.

The forty-year Stalinist record of suppression of free democratic processes elsewhere did make the communist electoral success in the Kerala an exception. Even more amazing was a second exception. There was no dictatorship of the proletariat; the proletarian majorities of Kerala retained power over their communist leadership. The electoral majority in Kerala enthusiastically adopted the communist ideology–the proletariat should overcome the bourgeois in order to level the playing field, opening to themselves an opportunity to participate in the markets and free exchange of their goods and services.

Visitors may find Kerala's lush vegetation, supported by the frequent rains, refreshing. The rains, the breezes, and the warm sunshine give Kerala the ambiance of the island states of Fiji and Seychelles. The streets are hot, but most people live in rural Kerala under the shade of coconut trees. The form and appearance of human institutions–shops, banks, police, government, schools, universities, media, telephone and postal service, railroads, airlines, temples, churches, mosques–are very much Indian.

Thoughtful visitors to Kerala, especially those familiar with lifestyles throughout India and the south, do notice Kerala lifestyle differences. Except in areas customary for foreign tourists, such as Kovalam Beach, visitors appreciate the absence of beggars and hustlers. Visitors notice the better quality of the homes and their distribution throughout the countryside, as contrasted to the bunching of houses in village India. As they encounter the people, the strength and the independence of the women is noted. Contrasted to their experience in high consumption societies, visitors notice the slow, infuriatingly deliberate pace of task completion. In spite of repeated assurances of best intentions, those tasks requiring resources not readily available to all (or not preallocated for visitor use) probably will not happen.

Religion. Our search for the causes of the Kerala efficiency to produce wellness leads to the rest of India. Kerala, like the rest of India, is a Hindu culture. At the same time it is different. Perhaps the unusual proportion of other major religions present in the Kerala mix offers a clue:

Figure 3. Religious Identification in India and Kerala

India		Kerala	
Hindus	88%	Hindus	60%
Muslims	10%	Muslims	20%
Christians	2%	Christians	20%

Outside of Kerala there is no pattern showing that either Muslims or Christians are more modest consumers and have smaller families as compared to Hindus. Still one might argue that somehow the mix is synergistic. That is to say, perhaps a Hindu culture with a large admixture of Muslims and Christians is different from the Hindu culture of India at large. For another clue, let us glance at the near neighbor of Kerala, Sri Lanka (figure 4). The agricultural base and climate of Sri Lanka is much like Kerala. More important, the lifestyle and wellness measures are similar, although a little less efficient.

Figure 4. Kerala Compared with Sri Lanka

	Popula-tion (Millions)	GNP Per Capita	Female H.S. Enroll-ment	Infant Mortality Rate	Total Fertility Rate	Life Expec-tancy
Kerala	29	$350	93%	16.0	1.9	72
Sri Lanka	17	$470	76%	19.0	2.5	71

What is different about Sri Lanka compared to India, particularly in seeking efficiency in the production of human needs, not higher GNP per capita? Buddhist culture and practice is dominant in Sri Lanka. Buddhist and Hindu teachings have many parallels and similar origins; to the unsophisticated the teachings seem alike. Given the lifestyle similarities of Sri Lanka and Kerala, is there a difference between the Buddhist experience in Sri

Lanka and Hindu life in India? The striking difference is the absence of the Hindu institution of caste in Buddhism.

Accordingly, the behavioral difference in the influence of caste in Kerala and all India became an organizing hypothesis explaining the high life-quality found in Kerala as contrasted to India. Perhaps the unusual Kerala mix of Muslim, Christian, and Hindu faiths acted with synergistic strength to overcome the economic impediment of caste identification in Kerala, making Kerala different from all India.

Gender Equality. The status of women within the Hindu culture of Kerala is slightly different from India as a whole. Matrilineal customs within the powerful Nayar caste either preexisted or have permeated practices of the entire society (including Christian and Muslim families). In Kerala the status of female deities from earlier times has survived a Hindu patriarchal transformation in India.

The patrilineality of the Brahmins, ritually dominant Hindu caste in Kerala, was newer than the matrilineality of the large, powerful Nayar caste. This background certainly contributed to the maintenance of female status. Gender equality adds strength to the movement which has united people across former caste boundaries in Kerala.

Caste in Kerala. In the nineteenth century the caste system in Kerala was the most restrictive in all India. Not only were there untouchablilty restrictions, but also unapproachability and unseeability. Referring to Kerala, Mahatma Gandhi observed in 1925,

> Socially the Untouchables are lepers; economically they are worse; and religiously they are denied entrance to places which we miscall houses of God. They are denied the use, on the same terms as caste Hindus, of public roads, public schools, public hospitals, public taps, public parks, and the like. And in some cases their approach within a measured distance is a social crime. They are relegated for their residence to the worst quarters of the cities and villages, where they get no social service. They are too downtrodden to rise in revolt against their suppression.

Struggle. The "revolt against their suppression" was underway as Gandhi wrote. As early as 1820 a protest was organized by Untouchable women seeking the right to fully cover their bodies in public. By 1898 a low-caste social reformer, Ayyankali, was organizing strikes of field workers seeking permission to use the public roads and market places, and demanding an opportunity for their children to attend school. Most significant of all was the organization of caste improvement associations among the Hindus and parallel improvement efforts among the Muslims and Christians.

The Ezhavas, a very large lower caste, were organized into the Ezhava Social Reform Movement by the famous Kerala social reformer Sri Narayan Guru. In addition to extensive effort for improvement within castes came the privilege of worship in Hindu temples. These temple entry marches were huge protests extending over years, some led by Mahatma Gandhi. Their fervent and non-violent pressure produced the Temple Entry Act of 1936, legally opening all Hindu temples within the jurisdiction of Travancore. Opening the temples to all Hindus was an event of epic importance for the future Kerala. The oppressed had succeeded at the highest levels, religious and political. By their own action the lower castes and Untouchables empowered themselves.

At first glance the creation of caste associations might seem a retrograde step in a process of abolishing caste boundaries. The caste associations brought together hundreds of sub-castes. Those experiencing fellowship across sub-caste boundaries found it easier to reach across caste boundaries. Economic barriers for the oppressed were breached along with the religious barriers.

As India moved toward independence from Britain in 1945 into the process of restructuring a renewed Indian nation, several otherwise disparate forces joined into a synergistic movement for unity and equality within Kerala. This was a union of democratic forces organizing and leading the downtrodden of Kerala. The leadership contributions of Christians, Muslims, Gandhians, and Communists deserve special note.

Christians. Some Christians date themselves from the visit of the apostle, Saint Thomas, in A.D. 52. These Christians built for themselves a niche as farmers and traders in the larger Hindu culture, rather like a middle level caste. The Portuguese brought Catholic rites in the sixteenth century with successful conversions in the fishing communities. As throughout India, the Christians made converts among the numerous Untouchables, who had no caste advantages to lose. The London Missionary Society (LMS), which came to Kerala following the British invasions of the eighteenth century, performed a great service establishing English-speaking Christian schools and colleges. LMS teaching rejected caste as a heathen institution.

As the administrators and trading companies of the British raj arrived in Kerala, they traded with and hired English-speaking Indians as local supervisors. Many of these Indians had been trained in the Christian schools and colleges, which treated Untouchables as equals. In defense of their privileged positions in the economy of Kerala, the high caste groups accelerated the educational opportunity of their children by adding English, mathematics, and the sciences to the curriculum. Christian leadership built an early demand for universal education in Kerala. At the same time the Christians infused the idea of "equality before God" among their Untouchable converts.

Muslims. Like the Christians, the Muslims are also largely converts of earlier times from among the Untouchables, who had no caste privileges to lose. Like the Christians, Muslims in Kerala share culture with their Hindu neighbors, yet see themselves as religiously separate. On the criteria of income and education, Muslims have been below the Kerala standard. And like the Christians, they have felt an isolation from the power centers of high caste Hindus. The Muslim League served like a caste improvement association in the past and like a political party today.

Muslim disinterest in the temple entry protests may have added stability to Kerala during the years of the passionate Hindu temple entry struggles. At the same time, they did not experience empowerment until they shared in the Kerala election victory of 1957. Since 1957 the Muslims have fit neatly into winning political coalitions led by communists and have profited much from the alliance.

Gandhians. Mahatma Gandhi returned to India from his adventures in South Africa determined to strike hard at India's great sin, caste. Gandhi and his many faithful disciples in the struggle against caste were caught up in the fight for Indian independence. Gandhi taught that Christians, Muslims, and Hindus of all castes must work together against British oppression, and his followers joined with vigor and enthusiasm in the struggle in Kerala.

Communists. An incidental legacy of British imperialism was the separation of labor from labor's product, which becomes a basis for labor consciousness and communist political organization. Most of the union leaders in the few industries of Kerala were high-caste radicals and communists. While the Congress Party leadership preached an end to untouchability, the communists ate in the homes and tea shops of the oppressed, organized drama clubs among them, undertook legal action on their behalf, and agitated for higher wages and a share of the land.

An Untouchable villager recalled events of 1951: "The influence of Communism brought a new shape to the life of my village. Some of the high caste Nairs became the spokesmen for this new ideology. My father and uncles also joined them. They, the leaders of all castes, conducted meetings in Pulaya houses and slept in Pulaya houses. This phenomenon actually swept away caste feeling in my village, especially untouchability" (Mencher 1980).

In their analysis of the sustained assault on the caste system of Kerala, Franke and Chasin (1989) give special credit to the militant, organized, progressive forces, "A particularly central role was played in the land reform and anti-caste struggle by the cadres of communist parties, who developed a reputation, even among their opponents, of being relatively honest and uncorrupt. Communist parties have, in fact, been voted into offices and become vital pillars of reformist governing coalitions several times in the last thirty years."

Democracy. An evident quality-of-life factor in Kerala is the vigorous democracy maintained by a politically sophisticated and active electorate, more than ninety percent of those old enough to vote. Keralans see democracy as an attempt to reconcile the natural phenomena of human diversity and the belief in human equality before God. Given that an electoral majority should have the power, and given that poor majorities everywhere see themselves as victims of unfair market rules, it logically follows that democratic majorities would seize power, rewrite the rules, and level the economic playing field. In Kerala, they did.

In a vision of democracy, the Earth is seen as a human habitat owned by all humans on an equal-share basis. A primary entitlement allows each a share of the resources, which may allow the basis for life quality, wellness needs. The secondary democratic entitlement offers each a fair opportunity to compete for the use of the balance of the available resources satisfying psyche needs. Democratic processes can create and maintain fair opportunities for this competition. This level playing field is the simple story of Kerala politics, beginning with the empowering election of 1957.

Empowerment. Communists won political leadership for the first Kerala election in 1957. They assembled a huge proletarian majority, the Untouchables, the lowest caste groups, the Muslims, and a large part of the Christians. The formerly oppressed were empowered.

Empowerment of a suppressed majority has two important political consequences. First, the winners are motivated to vote again to maintain and reinforce their victory. Second, any political opposition wanting to win in a subsequent election must support the winning issues. Names of candidates and party labels may change, but the fundamental purpose of the government has been set—to serve the interest of the electoral majority, in this case the formerly oppressed.

The winning platform of the first communist government of Kerala (1957) was elimination of caste restrictions, especially economic discrimination and disabilities. In telling this story it is crucial to emphasize that the legislative processes of democratic governments provide a focus for the public dialogue led by public sentiment. Adjustments and reassignments of provider status occurred as families and neighborhoods reached across former caste boundaries supporting each other's needs. The Kerala governments offered visible institutional support for these dramatic social and economic changes. Notable were the efforts supporting land reform, food distribution, health care, and education.

Land Reform. An issue on which Muslims and Christians joined low-caste Hindus was land tenancy. In an agrarian society, land is a reality of life. Before 1969, eight percent of the landowning households controlled forty-four percent of all rented land and sixty-two percent of the best irrigated lands. The actual cultivators were in a most difficult position. Despite some British and state legislation to protect them, their leases could be arbitrarily terminated by a class of middlemen tenants or by the titled landowners above them. Exorbitant rents were the order of the day. In Cochin, for example, the cultivators paid at least fifty percent and sometimes seventy-five percent of the gross product of the land to landlords and their middlemen.

When the new state of Kerala elected a communist majority to the state legislature in 1957, the government included cabinet members who were seasoned militants of peasant and worker movements. They were set on a course of radical land reform. In reaction, the landlords organized demonstrations and within two years persuaded the New Delhi government to dismiss the communist state government. In the late 1960s, the tenants with communist leadership took matters into their own hands, planting red flags on their tenancies and claiming the right to farm the land without paying rent. Pressure organized by the communists and their allies became so great that India's then ruling Congress Party enacted the land reform law in 1969.

The reform compensated the landlords. For rice fields, they received sixteen times one year's fair rent. The compensation for house-compound land was twenty-five percent of market value, half paid by the tenant and half from a government trust. For the new owners of the rice paddies, half or more of their families' food needs were now assured. For their part, former landlords transformed themselves into teachers, government administrators, and mid-sized farmers and continued their contribution to the Kerala economy (Franke and Chasin 1989).

Food Equity. A system of ration shops established under the British in 1941, now called "fair price shops," has been vastly expanded. This system offers rice, wheat, sugar, palm oil, and kerosene at controlled prices. The location of the 13,000 fair price shops within walking distance of every Kerala home contrasts with the assistance offered in the other progressive Indian states which only began to extend ration shops into rural areas in 1980. Each household receives a ration card allowing the purchase of limited amounts of basic commodities at fixed prices. Although all households buy some items through this distribution system, the poorest one-third of the households buy two-thirds of their cereals through the fair price shops. Some shops are cooperatives, but most are privately owned. The parallel private market provides a full range of food stuffs. The equitable distribution of food is only part of the story. Studies carried out by the National Nutritional Monitoring Bureau of the Indian Council of Medical Research have consistently ranked Kerala lowest in food intake among Indian states.

These low levels of per-capita nutrient consumption might be associated with severe growth retardation and nutritional disorders. However, the opposite prevails for two deficiency diseases: *kwashiorkor* has virtually disappeared, and the prevalence of *marasmus* has declined dramatically in recent years. Compared with other Indian states, Kerala has the highest proportion of normally nourished children and the lowest proportion of severely undernourished children under five years of age. The three comparisons states in table 2 are Kerala's close neighbors with equal or better per-capita incomes and higher food intakes.

Table 2. Malnutrition of Preschool Girls in Selected Indian States

Four Categories, Normal to Severe (Soman 1990, 86)

State	Normal	Mild	Moderate	Severe
Kerala	14.5%	38.9%	34.4%	2.2%
Tamilnadu	7.0%	38.5%	47.7%	4.8%
Karnataka	2.7%	33.6%	53.4%	10.4%
Andrapradesh	5.8%	32.1%	52.7%	9.4%

The combination of low food intake and better growth performance is offered to substantiate the claim of food equity in Kerala. Since more food is not the cause of the superior child growth patterns, other causes must be examined. Of all the explanations of healthy children, female education is the most powerful. The following two-part graph, figure 5, clearly illustrates the association of increasing female literacy and our most important wellness measure, declining infant mortality.

A description of the many factors causing high female literacy would provide a more complete explanation for Kerala food equity. The significance of female literacy as an important indicator can be further illustrated by pointing to the comparisons of female literacy—thirty-nine percent for all India contrasted to eighty-six percent for Kerala. Female literacy is the one single most significant indicator of declining fertility in all low-income populations. The two summary explanations for the nutritional success of Kerala despite the meager food input are: (1) equitable food distribution and (2) more efficient utilization of the available nutrients in a positive interaction with effective health care. Females are the principal family managers for both.

Health Care. The governments of Kerala have supported the ayurvedic and homeopathic health systems while enthusiastically adopting the best of western medical practice. Smallpox vaccination was undertaken in 1879, and by 1936 nearly everyone in southern Kerala was protected. By 1970, Kerala was the first Indian state to have entirely eradicated smallpox. Successful health and education measures have wiped out cholera and malaria, and in contrast to many parts of India, there has been no recurrence.

A lively private health care sector is backed by a comprehensive public sector—health care centers within four kilometers of every home throughout Kerala. The high female education level is related to the excellent maternal understanding of health care services. As evidence of prenatal care in the state, ninety-two percent of births take place in public and private health care institutions, and breast feeding is nearly always practiced for the first six months. The visiting nurses make regular checks of every household for good health practices, ensuring the ill get adequate treatment and monitoring recovery.

Figure 5. Relation Between the Rise in Female Literacy and the Decline of Infant Mortality in Kerala (Soman 1990, 89)

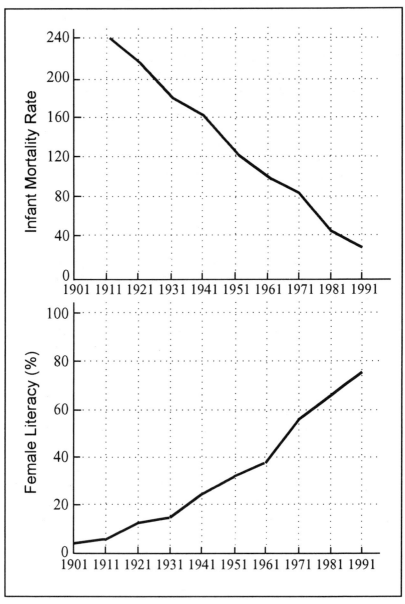

Education. In order to explain the successes of food distribution and health care systems, it is necessary to refer to the high education levels. In figure 5, the curve showing the increase in female literacy also shows that literacy was less than forty percent in 1951. Ninety-three percent of the females of high school age are now attending high school. The current generation is more than literate; it is well educated.

As contrasted to many low-income countries which have lavished their public funds on university training, the funding in Kerala has been directed to primary and secondary education, but does not neglect higher education. There are forty-one arts and sciences colleges with government support and 133 privately financed, for a total of 174. In addition there are nine engineering colleges, four in the government sector and five private, and a host of polytechnic training institutes. More women than men enroll in the colleges and universities, even in the engineering programs.

Kerala's citizens make great use of education. They boast a high newspaper and journal consumption in both Malayalam and English. For those who cannot afford books or a newspaper, there are nearly 5,000 village libraries—more libraries than in all of the other Indian states combined. Educated professionals and skilled workers are exported to employment opportunities in Bombay, Delhi, and the Gulf states. Remittances from this well-paid employment are significant in Kerala income.

Eschewing both political party connections and foreign funding, the Kerala Sastra Sahitya Parishad (KSSP), an educational institution, involves hundreds of thousands of people. The KSSP popularizes science to serve the needs of society by innovative and colorful methods, including environmental protection campaigns.

Contrasts.

In Kerala, a premium is placed on the correct decisions and on efficient distribution of resources, not on quick decisions. The delay in making the correct decision is a time investment by which the information system is cross-checked. Nearly all humans in Kerala serve as store houses and rapid transmitters of necessary information. In organizational terms, each Keralan is on a network receiving and sending messages by direct and indirect routes to and from all others.

Organization refers to the decision system, that is, who listens to whom and who tells whom what to do. Organization in Kerala may be called intense community—everyone making decisions in full knowledge of the interests and preferences of everyone else. In contrast, the first-world decision organization is frequently a hierarchy of executives making rapid decisions for subordinates. Many goods and services are allocated to serve the psyche wants of executives.

Executive hierarchical decisions work well as long as the total product of goods and services is great and sufficient resources are available. Under these conditions, all may meet their wellness needs. On the other hand, observed disparities in the distribution of goods and services create anxiety of imagined needs, known as the "Keeping up with the Joneses." There is reason to be pessimistic about the future if leaders seek to maintain the customs, rules, regulations, and laws fixing the materially wealthy humans in their high-consumption status.

On the other hand, if customs, regulations, rules, and laws shift in the direction of human equity, there is reason for optimism. The potential for human equity is evident given the enormous disparity in economic power worldwide, measured in income as currently distributed. Eighty-five percent of the world population subsists on average incomes of $1,000 a year; the remaining fifteen percent utilize an average of $21,000 per year.

Three remaining contrasts observed between the first world and Kerala are important, although only indirectly connected to the use of Earth resources. Placing an individual on a higher pedestal than importance of family or tribes and communities means that needs and wants should be satisfied separately. In contrast, joint satisfaction of wellness needs can occur in large family groups; water and housing are examples.

In Kerala, as contrasted to the first world, there is less confusion about whether work is an unpleasant exchange of human time for wellness needs or whether work itself serves important psyche wants. The large "love economy" (Henderson 1991) of Kerala is motivated by the fulfillment of psyche wants, not payment. In addition, the pay associated with work in Kerala is accepted more as a sinecure—payment for the wellness needs of their families, not so much an obligation to perform assigned tasks. Approved task performance, paid or not, fulfills psyche wants. Leisure choices, usually thought of as fulfilling psyche wants, may use more or less Earth resources. Choice of leisure toys like automobiles and audio-visual systems use more Earth resources than visiting and playing. Visiting yields information about the wants and needs of friends and neighbors that in turn, supports the deliberate decision systems within the Kerala experience.

Kerala Lessons Learned

Dominguez and Robin (1993) describe the choice for modest consumption learned in North America, living lightly on the Earth, in a best-selling book, *Your Money or Your Life.* This study offered Kerala as an analogy for successful human behavior in 2050. What are we able to report? The lessons learned on the Earthwatch-sponsored research in Kerala for 1991, 1992, and 1993 direct attention to standard of living and lifestyles.

The lessons reported are a straightforward assessment of relationships of humans to each other in community on a finite Earth. The people of Kerala enjoy a good life beyond the fading North American dream of endless material wealth. The people of Kerala have set a high standard of efficiency—careful use of small amounts of resources to produce high life quality. The explanation for the high efficiency is like the innocence of the child crying, "The emperor has no clothes." Kerala efficiency is easily understood by some. Others, addicted to high-consumption status, are in denial like the emperor's yes-men. Surely a good life opportunity is more than a right to consume the Earth.

Community.

The habitual practice of community best explains the Kerala good life success. Community may be properly defined as human relationships within our families, among our friends, and in our neighborhoods. Large numbers of interlocking and overlapping relationships make a group of humans into an intense community. Given skillful application of human time, human community can be expanded to the whole Earth. An important motivation for the millions of inter-relationships which make up community is the need for services and goods which can be provided each other, as in Kerala.

A society which consumes Earth resources far beyond wellness needs, seeks privacy and individualism. In a society short on Earth resources, humans accept the discipline of community as a means to share goods and services. Although community does impinge on privacy and individualism, community provides compensations of its own—family, friends, neighborhood, and self-actualizing tasks.

The lessons learned by the ten Earthwatch research teams, first background statements and then current evaluation, are summarized in the following twenty-two statements:

Background

1. Within the gigantic entity of India, Kerala is a small state with uncommonly high quality of life.
2. Kerala is a lush green place with a dense rural population.

3. The per-capita incomes are very low in Kerala but not the lowest in the world.
4. The Kerala mix of religious traditions has a majority of Hindus but includes more Muslims and more Christians than the rest of India.
5. Some matrilineal traditions persist in Kerala.
6. Beginning in the nineteenth century there was an epic and successful struggle against the division of human communities formerly enforced by Hindu religious practice, caste.
7. Life quality improvements were initiated within caste associations (i.e., Ezhava Social Reform Movement) and the processes of improvement were maintained by across-caste organizations (i.e., Kerala Science for Social Revolution).
8. Christians led the way to universal education.
9. Muslims supported the struggle against oppression.
10. Gandhians provided anti-caste leadership.
11. Communists forged the Untouchables and lower castes into an effective political majority against inhumane caste discrimination and economic disabilities.
12. Communists accepted democracy by majority rule. In Kerala they did not create a dictatorship of the proletariat.
13. Effective land reform, land to the tillers, was instituted.
14. Food, health care, and education were equitably distributed.

Evaluation

15. The above successes empowered the former Untouchables and lower castes into a powerful democratic majority, a durable defense within Kerala maintaining an agenda of economic democracy.
16. As caste boundaries were destroyed, a very large community was created, fostering and nourishing life quality improvements for all in Kerala.
17. Human time can be utilized to create and maintain organization and information systems which efficiently distribute scarce Earth resources filling human needs.
18. This empathic and sympathetic use of human time satisfies psyche wants, adding more efficiency to these processes.
19. The enormous disparity in income distribution under current customs, rules, regulations, and laws worldwide shows latitude for redistribution in our future—plenty for all wellness needs plus enough for psyche wants.

20. Numbers 16 and 17 above were the most difficult lessons for the Earthwatch researchers to learn.
21. Kerala strategies based on equity considerations noted by John Ratcliffe (1978) are the limited equality conditions delineated in Herman Daly's steady-state economics (1991).
22. Improvement in life quality allows some (particularly those with higher caste origins) to wander away from strong community into individualism, a basis for hierarchy and class. This erosion may lead to a decline in Kerala life quality.

Teaching Sustainability in Higher Education.

The writer would be pleased to share his experience of teaching sustainability to sections of architecture students, based on the Kerala experience. In this teaching the following questions were examined:

1. What is quality of life (different from standard of living)?
2. How high must quality of life be to motivate moms and dads to choose small families?
3. How high must the consumption of Earth resources be to motivate moms and dads to choose small families?
4. How may we distinguish between needs and wants?
5. How can the opportunity to share the Earth resources be distributed to allow the minimum conditions to motivate moms and dads to choose small families?
6. How should the remaining Earth resources (beyond satisfying the minimum conditions motivating choosing small families) be distributed?

Research Note. Longer Kerala stories have been told by others. The two most readable accounts are by Richard Franke and Barbara Chasin (1989); and Venessa Baird (1993).

Perceiving and explaining the positive contributions of Kerala to human life in the twenty-first century has been a difficult and uncertain task. The researchers found problems integral to their social science research tools. Cultural values (such as "more is better" and "poor is bad") growing out of the successes of western resource exploitation during the past two centuries are particularly imbedded in Keynesian and Marxian economics. These problems and the researcher's adaptations have been explained in a section called "How to Study Kerala" in the complete report (Alexander 1994). More detailed information is also available in "The Kerala Phenomenon" (Alexander 1996).

Literature Cited

Alexander, William M. 1994. Exceptional Kerala: Efficient Use of Resources and Life Quality in a Non-Affluent Society. *GAIA: Ecological Perspectives in Science, Humanities, and Economics,* 3: 4.

———. 1995a. Defining Efficient Human Behavior on Planet Earth. *Hunger Notes,* 20(4).

———. 1995b. The Kerala Exception: Limited Equality. *Hunger Notes,* 20(4).

———. 1996. The Kerala Phenomenon, a report prepared for the International System Dynamics Society meeting, Cambridge, Mass., July 1996. Offprint available from the author at 30 El Mirador Ct., San Luis Obispo, CA 93401; (805) 594-1839; e-mail: walexand@oboe.calpoly.edu.

Baird, Venessa. 1993. Paradox in Paradise: Kerala, India's Radical Success. *New Internationalist* 241 (whole issue).

Brown, L. 1990. *State of the World.* New York: W. W. Norton Co.

Daly, Herman E. 1991. *Steady-State Economics.* Washington, D.C.: Island Press.

Dominguez, Joe, and Vicki Robin. 1992. *Your Money or Your Life.* New York: Penguin Books.

Franke, Richard, and Barbara Chasin. 1989. *Kerala: Radical Reform as Development in an Indian State.* San Francisco: Institute for Food and Development Policy.

Government of Kerala. 1993. The *Economic Review.*

Henderson, Hazel. 1991. *Paradigms in Progress: Life Beyond Economics.* Indianapolis: Knowledge Systems.

Mencher, Joan. 1980. On Being Untouchable in India: A Materialist Perspective. In *Beyond the Myths of Culture.* New York: Academic Press.

Murdoch, W. M. 1980. *The Poverty of Nations: The Political Economy of Hunger and Population.* Baltimore: Johns Hopkins University Press, 69–82.

Population Reference Bureau. 1993. *World Population Data Sheet.*

Ratcliffe, John. 1978. Social Justice and the Demographic Transition: Lessons from India's Kerala State. *International Journal of Health Services.* 8(1): 140.

Soman, C. R. 1992. Nutrition and Health Development—Lessons from Kerala. *Proceedings of the Nutrition Society,* 51.

World Bank. 1993. The *Environmental Data Book.*

9. Integrated Rural Development and Sustainability
Lessons from Honduras for Liberal Arts Colleges

Leonard Brown[1]

A growth process that benefits only the wealthiest minority and maintains or even increases the disparities between and within countries is not development.
—The Cocoyoc Declaration

Abstract

This report describes a rural development organization in Honduras, a program both integrative in design and oriented toward sustainability in its approach to development. The organization's goal is to "reconstruct" the existing social/economic structure of the poor with whom they work. Working at and through the center has proven beneficial to our university and its students.

Introduction

This report is based on the premise that the "sustainability" of development programs and their accomplishments are enhanced by using an "integrated development" approach. The first concept has been defined as "balancing our human activities, social/cultural and especially economic, with the resource base provided by our Earth ecosystem" (Kadekodi 1992). The "time frame" for that balance is an integral aspect of the concept of sustainability. Ultimately the materials involved in the "throughput" on a short-term or daily basis must be balanced. In general, the longer the imbalance is extended, the

---

[1] **Leonard Brown** is a professor of geography at Wittenburg University. His research interests are social change in rural societies and his research area has been Mexico and Central America. Much of his research has been with post-disaster communities and has been conducted following the occurrence of major natural hazards.

134

harder it is to "pay up." In this brief definition, human activities are not always negative, nor damaging, nor is the resource base fixed. Changes in our technological capabilities can alter our resource base dramatically. We live in a finite system, however, and that reality must be recognized and accepted to achieve sustainability.

Integrated development is based on the recognition that "to help people achieve meaningful social change the development programs must be holistic in nature, and not narrowly focused or unconnected." For example, to deliver high quality medical care without providing access to safe, clean drinking water will not solve the health problems of the recipients. In the following description some examples of multi-goal, integrated programming will be presented.

Organization

The NGO Program for Rural Reconstruction (PRR) is involved in "grassroots" development and presently assists some twenty villages and "aldeas" (hamlets). Most of these are located in the state of Santa Barbara, in northern Honduras (see map). Offices for the staff and housing for a few staff members, as well as a health clinic and warehouse, are maintained at La Buena Fe headquarters. In addition, there is a dormitory, a kitchen-dining building, and a classroom-educational building. These three buildings are used by PRR to offer short-term workshops to members of the villages with whom they are working, and to house the North American medical brigades when they are in Honduras. The buildings are rustic, constructed of cement block with concrete floors and tin roofs. The center is not connected to the national electricity "grid," but does have a small generator for limited power production. Potable water is obtained from an adjacent village where PRR has helped install a water system and septic tanks. In addition to their buildings, they own an adequate amount of land for agricultural test plots and the pasturing of milk goats on a short-term basis.

Conditions

All the villages with which PRR is involved are in the mountains surrounding Lake Yojoa and occupy land that was not traditionally farmed. Most of the families lack sufficient land to qualify for government assistance programs, a problem common to the national agricultural programs in many Third-World countries. As Roland Bunch (1982) has written, there are two reasons the poorest are rarely helped by official governmental programs: "Poor people often lack both the self-confidence needed to approach large organizations and the knowledge to know what to ask them once they do. . . and large programs are reluctant to work with them. . . because they are afraid their cost-benefit ratios will be lowered."

During the pre-European period, the mountain slopes around Lake Yojoa were covered with forests. The forests have been and are being cut by the growing number of displaced rural poor, as they are forced off the more fertile land and move up the mountain slopes and into less accessible areas often unserved by any roads. One of the more pressing environmental problems is erosion, which is severe due to the slope of the fields and the removal of the original tree cover. Pressure to cut more trees is exacerbated by the shortage of wood for building and fuel. That resource shortage stresses the remnant forest which was left on slopes that were too steep to till, and which, until recently, were tree covered. By adding coarse, sandy material to the surface of the existing fields, erosion decreases the fields' fertility.

It is important to recognize the links between the poor and their environment. In general, the environment is degraded by poverty, just as a degraded environment creates/sustains poverty. As W. M. Adams (1990) observes, the rural poor do not farm such poor land out of perversity but out of necessity. They know that the slope in their "milpa" is too severe and that while the soil in the valley is of higher quality, they farm the only land they have any hope of owning. The biological reality of this microregion of Honduras reflects the larger aspects of the need for sustainability discussed in this book.

Programs

Development work at PRR is divided into four administrative areas, but all programs are considered supportive and integrative. Health-medical care is the oldest program, the one with which PPR has been working since the organization was formed in the early 1960s. Prior to the formation of PRR, a physician who moved from the U.S. to Honduras during the 1950s arranged the first health clinics at La Buena Fe to provide free medical help to the poor.

Medical and health activities range from staff "health providers," who conduct village clinics, to visiting medical teams or "brigades." The latter are composed of medical professionals from the U.S. and Canada who come as volunteers. On the PRR staff are two nursing/health providers and a dental aide. The nurses provide basic health checks for infants and children, deliver babies for those women in the nearby villages, and distribute simple medications and health care information. Their staff "dentist" is trained to extract broken and decayed teeth but is not able to do fillings. In addition to maintaining a daily clinic at La Buena Fe, these three visit those villages with PRR programs.

PRR is also involved in educational programming, one aspect of which is the operation of health and first-aid workshops for volunteers. In those two-day workshops, the focus is on training the village volunteers to provide basic health care and first aid for the other members of their village. The PPR approach follows the guidelines of the book, *Donde Hay No Doctor*. These workshops illustrate the integration of health programming and education. Such locally provided health care also benefits the villagers' economic condition, as it can save them the money they would spend on traveling to visit a clinic.

In addition, PRR has been certified by the Honduras national educational office to direct and administer tests for adult elementary education. This program allows adults living in rural villages an opportunity to study and be tested in their own village by the PRR representative. They can be certified for the equivalent of a sixth grade graduation, which is the minimal requirement for most employment opportunities in urban areas.

One of the four aspects of PRR assistance is that of "organization" within the village communities. Organizational help is offered beginning with the first stage of formalization of relations between PRR and a particular village. An important goal is to increase the group members' level of social concern and interest in social justice for other families. PPR also provides the villagers with skills which will be useful in continuing the development process after the original project has been completed (Bunch 1982).

It is generally agreed that if improvement in the quality of life is to be sustainable, the villagers must become competent in running their own organizations and must acquire the ability to present their own needs and concerns to external organizations such as agencies from their own government.

Economic development programs are focused on simple, non-mechanized agriculture, as that is the most important single economic activity of their members. Again, these programs are integrative in that they also address other needs and concerns in addition to the strictly economic aspect. Fairly new is the Alpine milk goat program, which distributes female milk goats to families who agree to both learn how to care for the goats and to return the first female offspring to PRR. The returned goats are kept at La Buena Fe until old enough to breed, at which time they are distributed to new families. The return of a female for the next round of distribution provides an important level of sustainability.

Males for breeding are maintained at La Buena Fe to guarantee the quality of the offspring. This program has strong health/nutrition aspects, making available high protein/calcium dietary material to the participating families, as well as the potential for income from the sale of the offspring.

Husbandry skills such as "ditching" and "contour planting" are an important economic focus, particularly in their effort to control erosion. Such skills will not only increase income due to increased yields, they also address ecological degradation. Not as obviously connected with the erosion control effort is a program in adopting and building "Lorena" cooking stoves. The use of such stoves has a direct health benefit in that the stoves remove the smoke from within the house, reducing eye and respiratory tract infections; they also reduce the amount of wood needed for cooking by forty to sixty percent. That saving reduces the pressure to cut trees for fire wood, which aids in the struggle to reduce erosion. As the stoves are made almost entirely from local indigenous material, they and the benefits that come from using them are very sustainable.

In their economic programs PRR does not encourage or support the adoption of machinery for agricultural work. Because of their need for fuel and parts, tractors are not considered sustainable. PRR has used mules and oxen for draft animals in some of their economic projects. They have been careful not to create dependency on items/materials which would be problematic after the development funds are expended. In general, their programs fit the new guidelines for agricultural development in poor countries by "using technologies and modes of organization that achieve sustainable high levels of production" (Gran 1983).

Within each of the above four areas, the goal of PRR is:

- To respond to needs articulated by the villages
- To help the villagers develop sustainable neighborhood/village organizations
- To help them acquire the knowledge to "provide for themselves."

The latter concern is commonly referred to as "empowerment" and should be an active component in any development activity that hopes to be sustainable. Guy Gran (1983) observes that a shift from passive to active mode is important to the long-term success of development projects. "The individual must move from a position as subject to one as an actor." This empowerment is perhaps the most important aspect of sustainable development. Development organizations and agencies which fail to address this goal risk merely creating a different form of dependency rather than sustainability.

Educational Benefits for University Students

Those of us in the social sciences in universities or colleges face a serious educational problem in teaching about the Third World. The conditions facing the poor often seem insurmountable to our students, and it is easy for them to feel overwhelmed. Students frequently come to believe that there is no hope for improvement and that aid programs are simply a continuous outflow of funds without any chance for real social improvement in the lives of the recipients.

The first benefit of my contact with PRR was for the students in my geography courses dealing with the developing world. For the instructor to be in regular contact with one rural development agency that is concerned with sustainability is far more beneficial than continually "visiting" different institutions. That benefit is reflected in the nature of the material I present in courses about the Third World and/or development issues, material both more realistic concerning the operational problems and more hopeful regarding the possibilities for social change. Sustainability emerges as one of the most critical issues.

In addition, the connection of our university to the PRR development center in Honduras has allowed more than twenty-five of our undergraduate students the opportunity for service learning at PRR. They are usually majors in one of the social science disciplines and often return feeling that they want to re-order their academic focus. They develop an appreciation for the necessity of a holistic approach to development and the need to use sustainable measures when evaluating development programs.

A formal educational experience, including course credit, has been supplemented by an informal experience for students from our campus chapter of Habitat for Humanity. Twelve of our university students spent two weeks during winter break of 1994 helping build a house near the health clinic at La Buena Fe, so that families from distant villages having members in the clinic would have a place to stay. Those families need housing so they can provide the meals and care for their family members who are patients in the clinic. Because some thirty-five to forty-five percent of the adult villagers working with PRR are functional illiterates and because many desire the opportunity to learn to read, we are also starting a volunteer program for some of our Spanish-speaking students in which they will serve as adult literacy teachers.

Even though the total number of students that will participate may be small, it is important for the university to facilitate those students who wish to actually observe development performed with an integrative and sustainable focus. Their experiences will in the years to come have a major positive contribution to our overall understanding of the Third World and its struggle to achieve sustainable development.

Literature Cited

Adams, W. M. 1990. Development and Environmental Degradation. *Green Development,* 87–112.

Asian NGO Coalition, IRED & PRD Forum. 1993. Economy, Ecology and Spirituality: Toward a Theory and Practice of Sustainability. *Development,* 4:74–80.

Bunch, Roland. 1982. *Two Ears of Corn: A Guide to People-Centered Agricultural Improvement.* Oklahoma City: World Neighbors, v–vi.

Gran, Guy. 1983. *Development by People: Citizen Construction of a Just World.* New York: Praeger, 146.

Kadekodi, Gopal K. 1992. Paradigms of Sustainable Development. *Development,* 3, 72–76.

Korten, David C. 1992. A Not So Radical Agenda for a Sustainable Global Future. *Development,* 4:72.

10. Global Change from the Grassroots Up

Kathryn W. Hansen

When spider webs unite, they can stop a lion.
—Ethiopian proverb

Abstract

The relationship between academia and the wider community is sometimes tenuous and rocky. The academic community bristles at suggestions that the wider community has anything to say about its dominion, values, and research. The wider community, on the other hand, resents intrusion by those in an "ivory tower," saying, "You don't know what the real world is all about." Interaction is absolutely necessary, however, and each has something to say to the other. This essay considers the importance of the United Nations Earth Summit and principles formulated by the NGO community to the academic community.

Academia and Society at Large

To academics—as investigators, observers, and teachers—scholars are supposed to minimize the influence they have on their surroundings and cause as little change as possible. Theoretical scientists, in particular, tend to minimize the influence and responsibility they have on the practical results of their work. Academicians cannot, however, separate themselves from society.

---

[1] **Kathryn W. Hansen,** Orange City, Iowa, received a B.A. from Alfred University in 1962, an M.S. in chemistry from Iowa State University in 1965, and an M.Ed. from Arizona State University in 1981. After joining the Peace Corps and teaching chemistry and mathematics in Nigeria from 1967 to 1968, she became involved in the Returning Peace Corps Volunteers movement, serving as president of the National Peace Corps Association from 1986 to 1989. In 1991 she helped to found the Returning Peace Corps Volunteers for Environment and Development. The organization's theme, "Bring the World Back Home" led to her involvement in the 1992 UN Conference on Environment and Development (UNCED). After serving as president of the Iowa Division of the United Nations Association., she began work as associate director of that organization in the fall of 1996.

In this day and age where changes occur rapidly and issues critical to our very survival are considered on a day-to-day basis, the work of the scientist and teacher is crucial to the discussion of the problems and possible solutions. At the same time, the discussions of values and principles by society need to have a significant impact on how academia conducts its own affairs.

By choosing not to deal with social problems, some scientists may be limiting their science. How do we combine the responsibility that is inherent in our academic endeavors and at the same time exercise our responsibility as a member of society? How do the two work together?

If academia responds to society, I believe academia will also do better in its academic endeavors. To illustrate, I will focus on the concept of "sustainable development" and the work that is ongoing worldwide. Sustainable development has been defined by the Brundtland Commission (1987) as "meeting the needs of the present without compromising the ability of future generations to meet their own needs." At the Earth Summit, the world community developed a set of basic values to use in working for sustainable development.

Basic Values from Government and NGO Treaties

The United Nations Conference on Environment and Development, known as UNCED or the Earth Summit, was held the first two weeks of June, 1992 in Rio de Janeiro, Brazil. Two major events happened at the Earth Summit: the first was the official government conference that ended with more than 100 heads of state addressing the world community. The second was a parallel conference called the Global Forum attended by over a thousand nonprofit groups (NGOs or non-governmental organizations) from around the world. Both conferences wrote treaties and negotiated agreements. Both sets of treaties have relevance as to how we go about looking at our responsibilities toward sustainable development (see appendices B and C).

The government conference produced:

1. The Rio Declaration, a statement of principles for guiding states in sustainable development
2. The Convention on Climate Change
3. The Convention on Biodiversity
4. A Statement of Principles of the World's Forests
5. *Agenda 21* (United Nations 1993), a work plan for national and international action on environment and development issues. [*Note.* See chapter 2, table 4.]

All of these are agreements between governments about what governments can and should do in order to work towards sustainable development. Within these documents, and especially in the Rio Declaration, are the principles by which governments are directed to act. These are not written in stone; all documents can change with time as new understandings arise. They do represent a lowest common denominator to which everyone could agree at the time.

The Global Forum also had negotiations and produced treaties and agreements known as "The People's Treaties," which were published in the United States by Commonweal (1993). Forty-six treaties were negotiated. They list basic principles while at the same time presenting plans for action to be carried out by NGOs working at the grassroots level.

Both sets of documents—one by governments, the other by NGOs—should be considered by academia in revising its own set of values. How does academia help with society's problems, the problems of sustainable development? What must be its own set of values if it is to contribute to the discussions of the wider society?

A Set of Values

The forty-six NGO treaties go further than the government treaties in laying down guiding principles for sustainable development, reflecting the experiences of people working in local communities around the world (Hansen 1993). Five basic themes arise from the NGO treaties (Commonweal Sustainable Futures Group 1993):

Reverence for Life, Diversity, Equity. This theme runs through all the NGO treaties, discerning the need for respect for all individual beings and all human beings. Some examples follow:

- We agree to respect, encourage, protect and restore Earth's ecosystems to ensure biological and cultural diversity. (from "The Earth Charter," *Commonweal* 1993, 17)
- We emphasize the creation of an international code of ethics for biodiversity studies that will underline the researcher's commitment to fully respect the intrinsic value of the living organism to be studied. (Draft Protocol on Scientific Research components for the Conservation of Biodiversity, in *Commonweal* 1993, 194)
- We accept a shared responsibility to protect and restore Earth and to allow wise and equitable use of resources. (from "The Earth Charter," in *Commonweal* 1993, 17)

This is the first basic principle from the Earth Summit, which academia must consider as its own: respect for life, diversity, and equity.

Participation, Accessibility, Transparency. The solution to problems require a holistic vision to be obtained through people's participation and cooperation (Fresh Water Treaty in *Commonweal* 1993, 119).

This theme challenges all institutions, including academia. A basic value espoused by NGO groups, it demands active recruiting of groups not currently well-represented as a necessary step to achieving sustainable development.

Although accessibility and transparency are values of academic investigation, I believe academia has some difficulty with participation. Unless academia opens its doors to full participation, its work will never achieve what it might. We need the participation of a full range of viewpoints.

Alternative Structures. The NGO treaties clearly see present economic structures as detrimental. They demand alternatives based on decentralization, diversity, local control, and equity. Academia in the western world is intimately connected with western economic systems. Most scientific investigations are financed by government, foundations, or industry, industries whose main concern is profit. I believe academia needs to reexamine its connections with the established economic systems, and understand clearly the degree of control and limitations these systems place on academic research and pursuits. Is academia ready to seek alternatives?

Basic Human Needs. "The fundamental purpose of economic organization is to provide for the basic needs of a community. . ." (Treaty on Alternative Economic Models, in *Commonweal* 1993, 59).

Much science and academic work already deals with basic human needs. It may be time, however, for the academic world to focus more closely on these needs if humanity is to survive.

Education, Information, Networking. "Access to information is essential for informed decision making at all levels" (Communication, Information, Media and Networking Treaty, in *Commonweal* 1993, 35). This important value is clearly within the present value system of science and the academic community.

These, then, are five values expressed through the forty-six NGO treaties. They represent a set of values developed by wider society. Some, such as education, information and networking, are clearly already an integral part of the academic community's value system. Others need to be considered more thoroughly; for example, "participation" is critical to quality academic investigations, yet often investigations are far from inclusive.

An Earth Charter and Agenda 21 for Iowa

Earth Charters are also being formulated at the state level. *An Earth Charter and Agenda 21 for Iowa* (Iowa Division United Nations Association 1994) is a document resulting from grassroots meetings across the state, conducted by the Iowa Division of the United Nations Association. It states that "[Iowans] seek to make an effective contribution to solving the environmental problems of our community, our state, our nation, and our world. [They] want the opportunity to participate in guiding our world toward sustainable development in a cooperative and inclusive way."

The document lists the issues of concern to Iowans and presents the key elements to make it possible for Iowans to participate in solving the problems. These are:

Education. "Education is viewed by Iowans as key to addressing our environment and development problems" (Iowa Division United Nations Association 1994).

There is a realization among the grassroots that more information is needed. People know that they do not know enough. They know they want to know more in order to act on the problems and issues affecting them.

Here is a challenge to academia, for while academicians often deal with very theoretical aspects of issues, they are also educators. It is their responsibility to translate information so that it can be understood and used in the life of the common person. This is, of course, done for students. But we lack a widespread structure where the majority of adults continue to learn throughout their lives. People outside academia want more information, but do not readily see where to find it.

Opportunities. "Citizens want to be heard, and they want to act. The opportunity to be involved in the discussion of these issues and in developing the answers will help individuals create solutions on the local level" (Iowa Division United Nations Association 1994). The grassroots want to be involved. They want the opportunity to act. With education, people will have the information they need to act in ways that are meaningful and productive.

Summary

I believe that it is ultimately ordinary people who will effect change. At the Earth Summit in Rio, the NGOs discovered that governments could establish the lowest common denominator, but would not and could not make the innovative decisions necessary for long-term solutions to problems of environment and development. The NGOs know that it is up to the local community to bring real change, the kind of change that will solve problems.

The same challenge applies to academia: it can provide information, but that information needs to be used by the local community in order to make the changes that will solve the problems. No matter the brilliant discoveries or the myriad details revealed from research, the academic community cannot by itself effect the needed changes. The grassroots organizations will make governments raise their lowest common denominator. The academic community needs to help in that process by making information available and understandable.

Literature Cited

Brundtland, Gro. 1987. *Our Common Future.* New York: Oxford University Press.

Commonweal Sustainable Futures Group. 1993. *The People's Treaties from the Earth Summit.* Bolinas, Calif.: Common Knowledge Press.

Hansen, K. W. 1993. What the People's Treaties Say about Development and Development Projects. Paper presented at the International Conference on Sustainable Village-based Development, September 25–October 1, 1993. Fort Collins: Colorado State University.

Iowa Division United Nations Association. 1994. *An Earth Charter and Agenda 21 for Iowa.* Iowa City: Iowa Division United Nations Association.

United Nations Department of Public Information. 1993. Earth Summit. *Agenda 21,* New York: The United Nations Programme of Action from Rio.

11. Reaching Students on Sustainable Development
Inside and beyond the Classroom

Robert L. Wixom[1]

To transform the essence of Our Common Future (and Agenda 21 [1993]) into reality will require broad participation. Every person can make a difference. Changes are the sum of individual actions based on common goals. A particular challenge goes to youth. More than ever before, we need a new generation—today's young people—that can use their energy and dedication to transform ideas into reality. Many of today's decision makers have yet to realize the peril in which the Earth has been placed.

–Gro Brundtland

The creativity, ideals and courage of the youth of the world should be mobilized to forge a global partnership in order to achieve sustainable development and ensure a better future for all.

–Principle 21, *Earth Charter, Agenda 21,* United Nations 1993

Abstract

Agenda 21, produced by the United Nations Conference on Environment and Development, has a message for the members and the institutions of higher education. In this chapter, I will present some resources, student achievements, sources of commitment, and approaches to achieve these goals—within the academic framework of classes and outside the formal classroom.

---

[1] **Robert L. Wixom,** a graduate of Earlham College and University of Illinois, has taught and conducted research on amino acid and protein metabolism/nutrition and biomedical information retrieval in the departments of biochemistry, the University of Arkansas, School of Medicine; and the University of Missouri, School of Medicine and College of Agriculture. Currently he is professor emeritus of biochemistry. His lifelong interests in environmental concerns, hiking, camping, and canoeing have been expressed for the past six years (1990–1995) as advisor or co-advisor for the University of Missouri Earth Week Coalition (some ten to twelve student organizations each year). These activities were recognized when he received the 1995 Conservation Educator of the Year Award of the Conservation Federation of Missouri, an affiliate of the National Wildlife Federation.

Introduction

*A*genda 21 (United Nations 1993) is a compact, 294-page book; it takes intellectual work and persistent study to understand its comprehensiveness and interrelationships (see outline of *Agenda 21* in appendix C). It has relevance for every person on this planet In this chapter, we are concerned with the necessity of higher education—whether as students, professors, administrators, trustees, or curators—to meet the challenges within *Agenda 21.*

Agenda 21 has five figures, each of which is two to three pages long. They illustrate and simplify (maybe oversimplify) the multiple connections among four Driving Forces, five Natural Resources, nine areas of Production, seven facets of Consumption, seven related Environmental Effects, and Human Welfare. These six common denominators are found in each of the five figures and are also related to Priority Actions (which vary from two to eleven) and Essential Means (nine avenues described). One of these five figures is shown here as figure 1. The Driving Forces are "value systems and lifestyles, population, socio-economic system and knowledge" (United Nations 1993). Knowledge is not clearly defined herein, but seems to include both scientific observation and education. "The Nine Essential Means" are both exciting to read and particularly meritorious to suggest how higher education relates to the other identified Means, processes, or routes to achieve the Priority Actions; one of the nine Essential Means is "Strengthening the Role of Major Groups." In our figure 1, items 1 and 2-b of Priority Actions relate to this book and this chapter.

The role of higher education is delineated most clearly in chapter 7.1 (education, public awareness, and training) and 7.2 (strengthening the role of twelve major groups—women, children, and youth; indigenous people; non-governmental organizations; farmers; local authority initiatives; trade unions; business and industry; and the scientific and technological community) (see appendix C).

> Education is the social institution entrusted with the main responsibility for passing on to succeeding generations the wisdom, knowledge and experience from the past. . . . Education is perhaps the single most important influence in changing human attitudes and behavior. . . . It equips people for meeting contemporary needs. . . . A major priority is to reorient education towards sustainable development by improving each country's capacity to address environment and development in its educational programmes, particularly

148

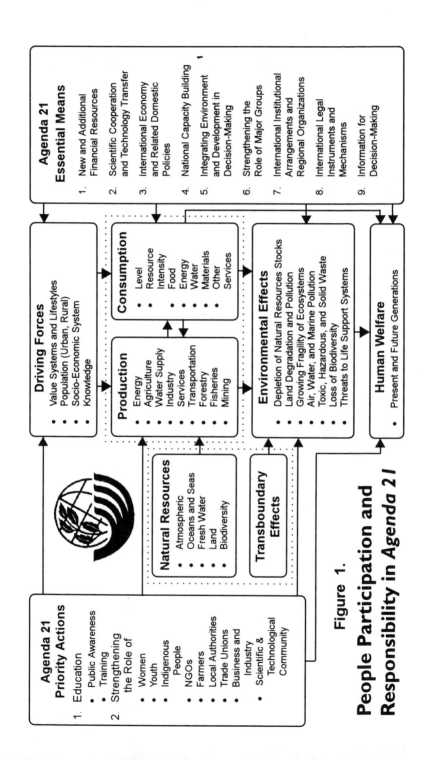

Figure 1.

People Participation and Responsibility in *Agenda 21*

in basic learning. . . . Education should, in all disciplines, address the dynamics of the physical, biological and socio-economic development, and human development, including spiritual development. (United Nations 1993, chap. 7.1)

The text discusses both the promotion of public awareness and the promotion of training. Again, education has a crucial role to strengthen the role of the ten major groups listed above (United Nations 1993; see appendix C). *"Agenda 21* is based on the premise that sustainable development is not just an option, but an imperative, in both environmental and economic terms. . . . *Agenda 21* is a realistic action programme to chart a new course for the sustainable future of the human family. . ." (United Nations 1993).

To summarize, one should remember that *Agenda 21* was written mainly prior to the UNCED Conference (June 1992) and primarily by the numerous interactions of scientists, government delegates and the United Nations Secretariat, with some input by NGOs and not necessarily educators. As indicated above, they have provided some clear messages to those of us in higher education.

Query/Question: *Have we, as educators and/or leaders of academic institutions, heard the above challenges? Have we modified our courses, majors, departments, and educational programs to respond to these so-called "imperatives"? If we have been critics of the UNCED process or its results, do we have alternative(s) to provide an improved response over those suggested to date?*

Resources for Students, Faculty, and Administrators

Campus Outreach Program. A well-known campus environment program for students is the National Wildlife Federation's Campus Outreach Program, called "Cool It!", which started in 1989 to support Earth Day 1990 on college campuses. The mission of Cool It! was to motivate college leaders to establish national campus and community models of environmentally sound practices through a culturally-inclusive process. Cool It! underwent a transformation in 1994 to be NWF's Campus Ecology Program. It continues to provide students, faculty, and administrators with resources (nine issue packets—from tree planting and energy efficiency to cultural diversity and organizing), organizing tools (a newsletter, speakers bureau, directory, EcoNet, etc.), plus individual consultations and site visits. The Campus Ecology Program has a central administrator, Nick Keller, and four geographically distributed regional coordinators, most of whom are recent college graduates. This invaluable program has the resources of the National Wildlife Federation with its staff of about

800, budget of $90 million, 6,500 local groups and 4.4 million members. For more information, see Smith (1993) or Keniry (1995), or write to Campus Ecology Program, National Wildlife Federation, 1400 16th St. NW, Washington, D.C. 20036.

Student Environmental Action Coalition. Students at the University of North Carolina began in 1989 to network with student environmentalists across the country to develop a national student environmental movement, called Student Environmental Action Coalition (SEAC). By 1993, it had grown to have members at 2,200 colleges, universities and high schools in all fifty states. "SEAC is a grassroots network working for environmental protection and social justice, and is guided solely by the needs and efforts of students and youth. . ." (Smith 1993). SEAC has a monthly magazine (*Threshold*, about thirty-six pages), national and regional student gatherings, field organizers, and seventeen regional networks, and belongs to A SEED (Action in Solidarity, Equality in Environment and Development), a worldwide youth environmental network (see Smith, 1993, or write to SEAC, P.O. Box 1168, Chapel Hill, NC 27514). SEAC has an *Organizing Guide*, an *Action Guide*, a *Directory* and several books. Similarly, Zero Population Growth (ZPG) has a Campus Program and a *Campus Organizer's Newsletter*, which reaches 700 student organizations. The Sierra Club has a Sierra Student Coalition with 18,000 members and a newsletter, *Generation E.*

Campus Earth Summit. Students at Yale University organized a national student conference, called "Campus Earth Summit" to draft a *Campus Blueprint for a Sustainable Future* (Feb. 18-20, 1994; Yale University). The Yale Student Environmental Coalition organized this excellent conference for about 400 students and invited faculty and administrators. Three students and two faculty members from the University of Missouri-Columbia attended and thanks to support from the Heinz Family Foundation, appreciated the thoroughness and creativity in the planning for speakers, workshops, roundtables, low-cost food, housing, and, of course, social activities. We had the benefit of shared expertise from leaders of the Campus Ecology Program (NWF), SEAC, and other environmental groups, as well as Yale and Harvard professors on the same campus. This conference developed specific recommendations to :

1. Make environmental education a top priority
2. Improve campus environmental practices
3. Organize campuses for a sustainable future.

Their many concrete ideas are available for students and educators in the final report, *Blueprint for a Green Campus* (Heinz Family Foundation 1995), which is partially included in Keniry (1995). Read it; digest it; apply appropriate ideas for your campuses!

Pugwash—Recent Recognition and New Directions. Science, scientists, and society have undergone major changes in recent years. Linus Pauling, 1901–1995, Nobel Prize in chemistry, 1954, was a unique scientist in many ways, but is mentioned here for his long campaign to ban nuclear testing in the late 1950s and 1960s. This ban is accepted by many countries around the world, with France and China being the main exceptions. For his early recognition of this issue, Pauling received the 1963 Nobel Prize for peace. In mid-October 1995, the Nobel Prize Committee announced that Joseph Rotblatt, a British physicist, would be the 1995 recipient of the Nobel Peace Prize. Rotblatt was a participant in the World War II Manhattan Project to build an atomic bomb, but left before the bombs were dropped in 1945. In 1955 Rotblatt started the Pugwash Conference on Science and World Affairs at Pugwash, a small village in Nova Scotia. Under Rotblatt's presidency, Pugwash has grown in scope (over 200 conferences by mid-1994, with groups and individuals in seventy countries), stature (by contacting levels of official policy making), publication (newsletters, annuals, many books and monographs) and significance (i.e. the 1995 Nobel Peace Prize). Some of their conferences have focused on the adverse environmental effects of nuclear weapons and their continued testing, and aid to developing countries (Marshall et al. 1995).

While the parent Pugwash has offices in London and Geneva, they have a strong offspring in the United States, the Student Pugwash USA, born in 1979. By 1995 Student Pugwash had grown to 6,000 members, a staff of six and a $300,000 budget. They have active chapters on fifty U.S. campuses and contacts with 175 more. They sponsor many educational projects in the fields of science, technology, and society at the campus and national levels. They plan student conferences, symposia, and workshops (similar to their parent's International Pugwash Conferences). They have a New Careers program; a monthly newsletter, *Pugwatch*; and a quarterly magazine, *Tough Questions*. Like their parent, they have gradually developed to include environmental issues. Members have a pledge:

> I promise to work for a better world, where science and technology are used in socially responsible ways. I will not use my education for any purpose intended to harm human beings *or the environment* (emphasis added). Throughout my career, I will consider the ethical implications of my work before I

take action. While the demands placed upon me may be great, I sign this declaration because I recognize that individual responsibility is the first step on the path to peace.

Between the announcement of Rotblatt's award on October 13, 1995 and its presentation on December 10, 1995, Student Pugwash developed a campaign "to get a million for the millennium"—a commitment from one million students and young professionals to the responsible use of science and technology. They delivered the initial 2,042 pledges to Rotblatt at the December award ceremonies! Then eighty-six years old, Rotblatt sent a Plea to Young People, saying, "We scientists, young and old, must nurture a vision for a better world in the next century, a world without war, a society based on care and equity, a community *that will protect the environment* [emphasis added]. And we should make it our task to turn this vision into reality."

Query/Question: *Has your campus student or faculty adviser explored mutual interests with Student Pugwash? Have you helped one of your students to attend a Pugwash conference? Have you considered a Pugwash chapter on your campus?* (From earlier experience, I know their office staff will be eager to respond.)

Resources in Print

Korten (1990) has a potent chapter to clarify how voluntary organizations, which build on integrative power, are different from governments that use threat power and business organizations that rely on economic power. They:

> . . . depend primarily on appeals to shared values as the basis for mobilizing human and financial resources. Citizens [or students] contribute their time, money, and other resources because they believe in what it is contributing to society. They share in a commitment to the organization's vision of a better world. . . . While recognizing the complementary roles of all sectors, the central role of the decade of the 1990s is one of innovation and change: in values, institutions, and technologies. Such change is the realm of civil society, but most particularly of the voluntary sector. . . . Within the past three decades, peoples' movements have reshaped thought and action on the environment, human rights, women, peace, and population. Though these are all wars yet to be won, the progress has been rapid and pervasive. . . . (Korten 1990)

The students I have met may not know these descriptions, but Korten, with former years at Harvard University, has described the Missouri students that I have observed. An older but still timely book, *Environmental Leadership*, edited by Stuart Langton (1984), has valuable chapters on the dilemmas of leadership, fund raising, public hearings and media utilization for both student and adult groups. Langton (1984) mentions that environmental groups need networking processes and structures, since they are frequently limited in resources, may have crises in issues faced and may require institutional interdependence. Network analysis facilitates the environmentalist's influence in a community, recognizes the variation in intensity and spontaneity of networks, identifies patterns of linkage between organizations, and enhances the work of individuals functioning as social catalysts or facilitators. Networks may focus on training, exchange, advocacy, or some combination thereof. "Shared values . . . and trust . . . (are) essential in networking" (Langton 1984).

Newsletters are great for prompt news, fresh ideas, and networking, but unless one is fastidious and has extensive file space, they become mislaid or forgotten. However, April Smith (*Campus Ecology* 1993) and Julian Keniry (*Ecodemia* 1995) have provided an invaluable service by bringing together in their respective books the many available, but scattered, resources; Keniry's list of resources at the end of each chapter (bibliography and outreach by networking on campus or regional and national levels) and index at the end are particularly valuable. For instance, you may want to know about the Student Environmental Action Coalition (SEAC), the Center for Environmental Citizenship, the Campus Green Buying Guide, the Campus Green Vote, the Green Corps, the Greenlights Program (EPA), and similar information. Turn to Smith (1993) and/or Keniry (1995) for names, addresses, phone numbers, mission, etc. Essentially all environmental organizations (about 2,390 in 124 categories) are briefly described in the *Encyclopedia of Associations* and/or the *Conservation Directory* produced by the National Wildlife Federation (40th ed. 1995). Other organized information may be found in the *Environmental Encyclopedia* (1994). With this wealth of available information, this section can be brief and serve to refer the reader to the above sources. Furthermore, their copious detail and helpful organization may end the response, "I don't have the time to dig out the needed information to organize an environmental program."

A major resource for the educational enterprise in the United States is *Our Living Resources—A Report to the Nation*, a recent comprehensive report of the National Biological Service, U.S. Department of the Interior (LaRoe et al., eds. 1995). One might inspect the section on Distribution, Abundance and Health of Species (six groups), four ecosystems and four ecoregions; but keen interest builds when they are tied to global climate change, human influences, non-native species, and habitat assessments. A Program has been developed to protect biodiversity and to prevent species from proceeding from endangered status to extinction is described therein. Satellite imagery has been developed by the cooperation of the National Aeronautics and Space Administration (NASA), the U.S. Geological Survey (USGS), the U.S. Environmental Protection Agency (EPA), the National Oceanographic and Atmospheric Administration (NOAA), the National Biological Service (NBS), and their respective subagencies and research groups to provide detailed information on vegetation patterns and changes over the decades, land management status, and the loss of wetlands. "The areas with the highest percentage of land modified from its natural condition are in the central United States. . ." (LaRoe et al. 1995). The challenge for educators is to bring such specialized knowledge and its implications to the attention of students and, perhaps, citizens at large.

Faculty and students have learned rapidly the merits of electronic communication and databases for almost every conceivable subject area, whether the Internet or the World Wide Web. "EcoNet" is an electronic network with information from the United Nations, the United States government and its agencies, many universities, and other organizations. "EE-Link" is an environmental education service by the National Consortium for Environmental Education. "EnvironLink" was started by a student at Carnegie-Mellon University and serves as a clearinghouse for information, a directory of environmentally sensitive products, and a source of environmental teaching materials; the aforementioned *Blueprint for a Green Campus* can be downloaded from EnvironLink. *Earth Negotiations Bulletin* is a periodic newspaper covering inter-governmental environment and development negotiations, and is published by the International Institute for Sustainable Development, Winnipeg, Canada (a core staff of twenty-eight and a budget of $5 million); *Earth Negotiations Bulletin* can also be accessed through Linkages and EcoNet.

The scholar knows that the best comprehensive and original, professional articles are usually integrated into reviews, books, monographs, and, later, encyclopedias. However, not everyone can wait for the encyclopedia or wade through multi-volume treatises. The environmental movement is blessed with many careful, comprehensive, and timely books, which have been cited in other chapters. Among serials, the senior staff of the Worldwatch Institute have been producing *State of the World–A Report on Progress Toward a Sustainable Society from 1984 to Date* (L. R. Brown et al. 1995). *The Earth Summit* (United Nations 1993) mentions the need for indicators, tools to follow and measure social, economic, and environmental trends over time. L. R. Brown et al. (*Vital Signs* 1992 to date) has now fifty-four key indicators in nine chapters (trends in food, agricultural resources, energy, atmospheric, economic, transportation, environmental, social, and military trends), followed by summaries (environmental, economic, social, and military features). These annual publications are highly recommended for the student beginning a term paper, or for the professor searching for the latest information to insert into next week's lecture. The lucid quality of their respective writings make interesting reading for all citizens of the United States and others around the world (they are translated into twenty-seven languages!). To conclude, the main practical books and organizational resources have been indicated, but can be supplemented by many other references.

Query/Question: Do our liberal arts colleges teach the nature of major social movements, the leaders therein, and the nature of networking as a part of our complex modern world?

Non-Governmental Organizations and Networking as Resources

The social development of Non-Governmental Organizations (NGOs) was introduced in chapter 2. Students and faculty should be informed on the nature of NGOs as a focus of change in our present-day world.

Elise Boulding (1990, chap. 3) describes the considerable depth and character of the International Non-Governmental Organizations (INGOs). Their number has grown from 176 in 1909 to 18,000 by 1985, which is clearly beyond the 2,000 International Government Organizations (IGOs). In the decade since her 1985 figures were compiled, the number has grown. INGOs, a transnational network, has looked at longer time horizons and security concepts, lobbied for constructive foreign policies of nation-states, provided education for world citizenship, expanded conceptual innovations and state-of-the-art expertise, created opportunities for the North to learn from the South, maintained information channels, and offered activity as an antidote to despair (Boulding 1988). "The people's associations have learned to provide coalitions to provide just that horizontal flow of information to each other that is so lacking through formal communication channels. . . ." Local branches coalesce to form national sections, which in turn organize international NGOs. "The networks of international people's associations thus reach directly from individual households to world forums; no other diplomatic activity has this capability. . . ."

Boulding (1990) presents cogently the known limitations in communication for the present world, leading to the summary thought:

> The recovery of all our ways of knowing involves understanding the socialization situation in which learning takes place. This means attending to settings, agents of socialization, and the kinds of faculties involved in the more complex knowing in which we are interested. The balanced development of cognitive/analytic, emotional/affective, and intuitive ways of knowing depends on stepping outside the technological shield for primary data about the empirical world, as well as for the utilization of secondary data. That balanced development can bring about the recovery of image literacy, or imagination, and lead to a wide range of solutions to the problems society faces. (Boulding 1990)

Boulding's comments in 1990 are applicable to the hustle and bustle of NGO activity in the pre- and post-UNCED conference (1992), the present CNSD, and the Earth Council.

Sometimes relationships are clearer by holding up a mirror to make comparison(s); such is the case of reading the intimate details and comparison of thirty NGOs in Peru, Costa Rica, Chile, and several other Latin-American countries, as described by Thomas F. Carroll's penetrating study *Intermediary NGOs—the Supporting Link in a Grassroots Development* (1992). Carroll's detailed examination leads to "Six Performance Indicators: Service Delivery, Poverty Reach, Participation, Group-Capacity Building, Innovation, and Policy Reach" (see pp. 252-4 for further details). Since students (and others) like to use the term "grassroots organizations" loosely, these six indicators may be useful to students as they reflect on their own organizational strengths and weaknesses.

The writer has heard the depth of student concerns for the present environment and their own future. All interested students are encouraged to join a pertinent campus group, or if none exists, find several similar friends and start one. The early organizing steps are known and have been described. Help is available when they request from a knowledgeable faculty member, or from the Campus Ecology Program (National Wildlife Federation), SEAC, or the Sierra Club's Student Coalition program. At an early date, learn the skills of networking and the role of volunteer NGOs. The adult NGOs need the vigor, ideas, and contributions of college students; students can, in turn, learn much from NGOs for their own work on or off campus (see Boulding 1988, chaps. 3 and 6), Smith (1993, chaps. 20 and 21), Savitt (1993, chap. by K. M. Wiegert), Boulding and Boulding

(1995, chap. 9 for women's NGOs), and Caldwell (1990). Caldwell, a political science professor at Indiana University, wrote, "These organizations are the divisions and battalions of the environmental movement in Western Europe and North America, are significant sources of influence on environmental policy, and are among the more effective transmitters of information from science to policymaking..." (Caldwell 1990, 26-28).

Question (Query): *Do educators include this ever-growing role of NGOs, INGOs and people's movements in the appropriate curricular place, along with the constitutions and structure of governments?*

Environmental Ethics among College Students

Students have responded to a clear call and a moral message, if not a religious message. Many students have responded to the moral challenge of the Earth Summit, although they may be unaware of the contemporary writing that followed in the 1990-95 period, or that cited in chapter 14. Students know and use the terms of environmental ethics, environmental justice, concern, and commitment.

Callicott (1989) wrote that environmental ethics began in the early 1970s as a distinct subject of disciplined inquiry, partly due to the environmental crises of the 1960s engendered by our western industrial civilization. He states, "we may have a one world view and related environmental ethic . . . (or) we may also have a plurality of revived and renewed traditional world views and associated environmental ethics. . . . Each of the many world views and associated environmental ethics may crystallize the international ecological environmental ethic in the local cultural tradition. . . ." (Callicott 1994). This summary is amply documented in his two books, *In Defense of the Land Ethics* (1989) and *Earth Insights: A Survey of Ecological Ethics from the Mediterranean Basin to the Australian Outback* (1994).

The vast area between chapter 2 (Environmental Principles of the Garden) and chapter 14 (Synthesis of Religious Faith and Sustainable Development) is the subject of an outstanding book, *Ethics and Agenda 21*, edited by Noel J. Brown, the vigorous director of the UN Environment Programme. Brown (1994) wrote, "*Agenda 21* lays out the tasks. It is now up to the world community to move beyond the Rio consensus to the commitment necessary for implementation. And a commitment is a moral act, perhaps the missing element in the global equation. . ." The scientific observations have alerted the world to the continuing dangers. The political debate has started and will continue in UNCSD and national capitals. The economic debate has begun and requires serious wrestling with the

$600 billion a year estimated costs to restore, care, and maintain our planetary home (N. J. Brown 1994). The social debate has commenced; however, "still to begin is the official debate on the moral implications of *Agenda 21*" (N. J. Brown 1994).

Brown (1994) has brief chapters by Hazel Henderson, "Ethical Implications of *Agenda 21*" (see her chapter 3 in this book); Dieter T. Hessel, "For the Sake of Earth and People" (see our chapter 14); McFague, "A Theological/Ethical Response to *Agenda 21*"; and fifteen other scholars. Sallie McFague notes that the growing worldwide movement related to the Earth Summit leads to the question, "What can I do? Is the Earth merely a hotel, or is it our home? Is it a place where we use its resources. . . or a place that we cherish and need to protect? . . . Is the Earth a machine . . . or a living body? . . . If we learn to live in and think about our Earth as a body and (not a machine), a body like other bodies that we love and care for, our answer may be yes. The yeses of millions of us could make a difference—all the difference" (McFague, in Brown 1994).

Earth Day Manifesto and Its Sequel at the University of Missouri

Among the many events planned for April 1990, the student environmentalists at the University of Missouri wanted to send a five-point written message to their fellow students. I suggested adding a message to the faculty; the students added six points. Since the Earth Week speaker, an outstanding biological scientist, was also then a university curator, the students added two points for the curators. (Read their manifesto in appendix F; are some of the suggestions applicable to your college/ university?) Soon thereafter, the administration appointed a Campus Recycling Committee of staff, students, and faculty that has grown in strength and accomplishments in each succeeding year. As then chair of the Biological Sciences Sector of the Graduate Faculty Senate, I, along with another faculty member, sparkplugged the effort to develop an MU Environmental Affairs Council. Our initial objective was "to promote policies and programs to enable the University of Missouri to become a model institution for environmental sensitivity." Finally, we persuaded the chancellor to appoint this council composed of nominated faculty, students, and staff. The council's objectives are in table I. Students, with their refreshing initiative, skepticism, and ideas have had an invaluable, constructive role in each.

Another expression of student environmental concerns beyond the classroom is in the preparation, planning, and presenting of Earth Week for the past six years (1990-95) (see table 2). Students selected the overall themes (see table 3) and then implemented them each year by their choices of the keynote speaker (see table 2), panels, and ten to twelve library displays (see table 3). Note the grand scope of these titles and closeness of titles to world-wide concerns. Considering that students have classes, term papers, exams, jobs, etc., it is amazing to me how much their volunteer and creative efforts accomplished. Some readers know that Francis Hole, Stephen Collett, and Stan Becker are Quaker scholars. Jim Enote is a Zuni Indian leader who went to UNCED and is a dedicated environmental leader on the Zuni reservation in New Mexico. Deidre Hirner, the new director of the Missouri Conservation Federation, warmed students' hearts and minds with her emphasis on "involvement."

Table 1. Objectives of Environmental Affairs Council, University of Missouri-Columbia (MU)
(Approved April 1, 1992)

General Objectives:

A. To advise on the development of policies that will enable MU to become a model institution to address environmental issues and to recommend environmentally sound practices and mechanisms and facilitate their implementation

B. To advise on policies and to develop formal and informal mechanisms for improved education to enhance environmental awareness

Specific objectives: The council was divided into three working committees—the Campus Environmental Awareness Committee, the Environmental Practices Committee, and the Environmental Curriculum Committee. Their more specific objectives follow:

1. Improve communication and interaction between students, faculty and staff
2. Promote and initiate selected campus environmental program(s)
3. Review and make recommendations about the university's environmental practices, in the following areas: the university's physical environment, possible pollution-generating activities, energy consumption/conservation practices, enhancement of university—city environmental cooperation, and evaluation of selected campus environmental proposals and their alternatives
4. Enhance the university's curriculum in environmental areas: assess student and faculty interest in multidisciplinary, environmentally related courses; publish environmental-related course lists on a periodic basis; encourage or co-sponsor environmental seminars and lectures; and work toward an interdisciplinary program in environmental undergraduate and graduate studies.

Note. Some specific objectives have been completed in subsequent years and are deleted here; others are currently being developed.

Table 2. Keynote Speakers for Earth Week at the University of Missouri (1990–1995)
by Earth Week Student Coalition and Environmental Affairs Council

Date	Speaker	Title of Lectures	Other Events for Speakers
4/16/90	**Dr. Peter H. Raven,** director, Missouri Botanical Garden, St. Louis, Mo.	"Global Sustainability—A New Responsibility"	Discussion with student environmental leaders and talk with Biol. Sciences Sector graduate faculty
4/15–15/91	**Dr. Francis D. Hole** professor of soil science, University. of Wisconsin, Madison, Wis.	"Walking Gently on the Earth—An Exploration in Community"	Talks with three soil science classes; "Opportunities in Biology" seminar and dinner; interviews
4/21–22/92	**Dr. Stephen Collett** executive director, Quaker United Nations Office, New York	"The Goals and Processes of the Earth Summit"— Rio de Janeiro June 1–12, 1992	Talks with two classes, Honor Society; luncheon on Internat'l Affairs; breakfast with MU Peace Studies Committee; media interviews
4/22/93	**James Enote** Zuni chief/ environmental leader, participant in Earth Summit, Zuni, N.M.	"Zuni Perspectives on Sustainability"	Talks to religion and anthropology classes; four informal meetings with students
4/22/93	**Dr. David Shorr,** director, Missouri Department of Natural Resources	"Missouri and the Environment — DNR Goals"	Invited dinner and reception
4/22/93	**Dr. John Faaborg** professor of ornithology, Univ. of Missouri	"Migrant Birds from Missouri to the Tropics"	Invited dinner and reception

4/21/94	**Dr. Deidre Hirner** executive director, Conservation Federation of Missouri	"Goals and Motivations on Environmental Concerns"	Invited dinner and reception
4/18–19/95	**Dr. Stanley Becker** professor of population dynamics, Johns Hopkins University	"Research and Politics Prior to the Cairo Population Conference"; "Population, Sex, and the Cairo Conference"	Journalism school class; medicine seminar; PSR student meeting; pizza party; media interviews

The candor of students is refreshing; I can hear now one MU student telling me, "I have seen windows open in the hot summer and air conditioners running, windows open in the winter, and yet the heat is turned on . . . an incredible abuse of paper use. . . . I see hypocrisy and apathy in my MU faculty. . . . I am disillusioned."

Query/Question : *What is the situation on your campus? Is it feasible for faculty to encourage a shift from "a significant number" to "many students"? Remember–Principle No. 21 of the* Earth Charter *suggests that the present college environmental leaders will affect the lives of our grandchildren!*

Most students are serious about their advanced education; many of them struggle with a full class load plus off-campus jobs and summer jobs. With this background, it is remarkable that two MU students traveled with me to be NGOs at Prep Con 4 at the United Nations in March 1992. Three MU students traveled a long weekend to attend the Yale "Campus Earth Summit" in February 1994, and six MU students traveled to Michigan State University for a conference organized by CNSD in a van supported by a friendly dean and scholarships from the CNSD (Porter et al. 1992). Another six students traveled to the next CNSD-related conference at Louisville, Ky., sponsored by the governor of Kentucky (Taylor et al. 1993); summer jobs prevented their attendance at the Davenport, Iowa, conference of CNSD (Hansen and Steinmaus 1994). At each of these five conferences, students were active participants in the workshops, roundtables, question-and-answer periods, mealtime conversations, exhibits, and informal networking.

Table 3. Additional Events Planned for Earth Week
at the University of Missouri (1990–1995)
by the Earth Week Student Coalition and
the Environmental Affairs Council

Dates	Theme/ Displays	Planned Events in Addition to Speakers and Displays	No. of Student Orgs
4/23–29/90	**"Earth Week 1990,"** Nine displays	Earth March; tree planting; talk on Mo. Stream Teams; talk on Mo. natural history	9
4/15–22/91	**"One Earth, One Future,"** Ten displays	Panel on campus environmental issues; panel on tropical rainforests; environmental education fair; clean up of MKT Trail	12
4/20–23/92	**"The Earth—In Our Hands,"** Nine displays	Videotape and panel on tropical rain forests; speakers on local natural food systems	11
4/19–23/93	**"Achieving Sustainable Development,"** Nine displays	Panel on Indigenous peoples; panel on sustainable agriculture; panel on "The Earth: Ethics, Religion, and Minorities"; panel on energy efficiency and alternatives	11
4/16–23/94	**"Environmental Justice,"** Seven displays	Teleconference on popula-tion; panel on Mo. flood of 1993; panel on public land use issues; tree planting ceremony by a Native American, Jake Swamp; bicycle rally; ecological restoration of roadsides	11
4/17–20/95	**"It's About Respect"; "Free the Earth,"** Ten displays	Transportation rally; vegetarian giveaway; adverse technology impact; campus cleanup; MU—Crimes/Earth	13

They grew in educational perception and were stretched by their experience. While my comment might be prejudiced, I heard many favorable evaluations from other attenders on the students' contributions. Their MU education was "internationalized" by these relatively short off-campus experiences.

For the Yale "Campus Earth Summit" (see earlier in this chapter), I was invited to speak at one of the roundtables. After some preliminary remarks, I showed two summary tables, which are derived from conversations with the environmental student leaders at the University of Missouri (see table 4).

Education is a two-way street, hopefully a broad and creative one. University of Missouri students have suggested to me what they believe faculty should know; a condensation that includes some ideas heard at the Yale "Campus Earth Summit" appears in table 5.

Table 4. Messages for University/College Students

A. Welcome to the struggle for:

- A Sustainable Environment
- Sustainable Institutions
- A Sustainable World Community

B. Promote student environmental organizations:

- Work with others, keep plugging.
- Invite a concerned faculty member as advisor.

C. Learn and practice organizational skills:

- Student leadership; networking
- Identification of goals, strategies, timetables, etc.
- Democratic decision-making, clear communication

D. Join (or initiate) appropriate university/faculty committees:

- Present your ideas, keep plugging.
- Identify concerned faculty members.
- Include them in your planning.
- Be prepared for seemingly endless meetings.
- Be ready to compensate for cynicism and lethargy.

(P.S.: Faculty need your insights, critiques, and vision.)

Table 5. Message to Professors

A. Our college students have heard the earlier environmental messages:

 • "Earth Day, Every Day"
 • "Think Globally, Act Locally"
 • "We All Live Downstream"
 • Earth Summit's "In Our Hands," etc.

B. Explore/expand the voluntary, environmental learning experiences: Earth Week speakers and panels, seminars, environmental clubs, affiliation with national student environmental organizations, etc.

C. Encourage student leaders to draw in younger students, thus promoting responsibility, developing continuity and leadership, and practicing networking in creative ways.

D. Relate the specifics of "Reduce, Reuse, and Recycle" to values of simplicity and sharing of finite resources.

E. Invite selected students to serve on faculty and administrative environmental committees—a real learning experience—such as the Campus Recycling Committee, the Environmental Affairs Council, or equivalent.

F. Recognize the competition for students' attention: classes, exams, term papers, part-time jobs, sports, social life, etc.

G. Endeavor to be a student organization adviser who is extra flexible and extra patient, who will listen continuously and facilitate creatively, and who will return for evening hours.

H. Encourage development of student leaders interested in conservation, sustainability, and peace. (See *Earth Charter's* principles 21, 24, and 25.)

I. Nurture your spiritual resources. Express the underlying spiritual values, as well as the practical aspects, of conservation and your vision of a sustainable world in order to share with student seekers.

J. Recognize that advanced students can teach younger students in creative ways (e.g., student organizations, networking, library environmental displays, etc.).

K. Request department chairs, deans, and presidents to recognize that being a student organization adviser is a demanding role that should be recognized as a key part of teaching and service with respect to salary, promotion, and tenure decisions.

L. Expand campus funding, programs, and outreach so that students and faculty may have a week-long sponsored visit at the United Nations—CNSD, church organizations or other. Being present at the working United Nations is a stirring experience.

M. A new generation of leaders is incubating in academia:
- Wake up, adults!
- Encourage these students with a decisive role in the shared tasks ahead!
- Provide space for them to participate in the global partnership that is underway!

One student, Christine, encouraged me to share with you the message, *"Walk the walk, talk the talk, act the act!"* These words are close to the older adage, "Practice what you preach." She also admonished me, "Be insistent, Bob—students learn by example." Wow, what a closing message!

To conclude, these remarks are not the final answer; they were designed to provoke discussion, modification, and adoption of complementary educational approaches on sustainable development outside the formal classroom.

Environmental Leadership on Campus

I have had the good fortune to be associated with many outstanding, environmentally concerned students. Some are creative leaders, some are workers, almost all of them are team players. Did they learn these personal skills at home, high school, churches, or in voluntary groups? I do not know. I suspect they have missed the scrutiny of the political scientists, sociologists or social psychologists who examine the roles of leaders, organizations, and institutions. Smith (1993, chaps. 20 and 21), Keniry (1995, chap. 9), the Campus Ecology Program (National Wildlife Federation), and the Students for Environmental Action Coalition (SEAC) have helpful insights for this subtheme.

To recognize and encourage future student creativity and leadership, the Environmental Affairs Council at the University of Missouri has recently approved an annual awards program, entitled "the Peter H. Raven Environmental Leadership Award" and its three-page detailed description. The idea may have merit on other college/university campuses.

However, students and faculty interested in environmental concerns would find considerable merit in examining the known aspects of *Environmental Leadership Developing Effective Skills and Styles* (Berry and Gordon 1993). Leadership—"the ability to cause and guide positive change toward a vision of a better future"—is crucial in light of the environmental problems discussed elsewhere in this book. Yes, "leaders tend to be individuals. . . . [L]eaders must have followers. . . . [S]uccessful leadership has some kind of end results, . . . and the thought or action, whatever it may be, must be deemed useful. . ." (Berry and Gordon 1993). While leadership is usually collective, is causative and at its best, is morally purposeful, environmental leadership has a strong traditional mix of amateurs, volunteers, part-timers, scientists, and professionals. The book delineates the needed skills for environmental leadership—ethics, communications, conflict resolution, policy and legislation, and fundraising, whether in state agencies, national and international government, voluntary organizations, corporations, or foundations. James E. Crowfoot, professor of natural resources and planning, University of Michigan, and author of the chapter on Academic Leadership, provides a beautiful elaboration of cardinal features: be compassionate, discover what is and what could be, act interdependently, share power, honor resources, and promote change. Many other helpful features are present to be utilized by the reader, whether student, faculty, or volunteer activist (see chaps. 1, 2, 12, 14, and 16 of Berry and Gordon 1993).

Talloires Declaration and Educational Approaches

In 1990, a group of college and university presidents met at Talloires, France, under the aegis of Tufts University "to encourage, facilitate, and promote an environmentally sustainable future" (Kelly 1994). They drafted "a declaration of actions to define the role of universities and their leaders in global environmental management and sustainable development" (Kelly 1994) (see appendix G). The twenty-two original university signatories have increased to more than 236 additional universities and institutions in forty different countries. A Secretariat for the University Presidents for a Sustainable Future (UPSF) was started in 1993 and "promotes institutional leadership by universities in pursuing sustainable development at the local, regional, and global level. This leadership begins with each university's mission, curriculum and operations, and radiates into the community, the nation, and the international sphere. . . . The Secretariat provides a clear structural framework for these efforts, unifying them in a university education and operations strategy reflecting a commitment to the knowledge and practices of environmental literacy. . ." (Kelly 1994). Recently the UPSF underwent a transformation to be the University Leaders for a Sustainable Future (ULSF) and an address change.

Thus, for students, faculty, or administration, the Talloires Declaration (appendix G) becomes a yardstick to evaluate one's academic institution. Similar to the principles of UNCED, ICPD, and PCSD (see appendices B, D, and E), the Talloires Declaration proposes academic institutional goals to which we educators may strive. By signing the declaration and joining the ULSF, one receives valuable information to implement the stated goals.

Possible Sources of Concern and Commitment among College Students

The authors of earlier chapters in this book know firsthand the environmental concerns of many students in today's college generation. The growing number of related books (Orr 1992; Smith 1993; Keniry 1995; Collett and Karakashian 1996, etc.) testify to the same deduction.

The origins of such present-day student concerns are probably diverse and, for many, began before entering higher education. Their words to the author provide evidence for the effectiveness of K–12 environmental education programs, the lasting value of school recycling events and environmental clubs in schools, and the power of television (such as wildlife shows, beautiful wilderness America themes, or anthropological-based shows that illustrate the connectedness of all life). Other students support the rippling effect from astronauts who imaginatively described our planet from outer space. Some students mention the strong and lasting appeal of youth movements that emphasize outdoor activities (Boy Scouts, Girl Scouts, 4H Clubs, summer camps, etc.).

Last but not least, some college students mention their parents or grandparents, whose love of nature led them to take family hikes in nearby woods and parks and/or to participate in longer family outings to regional and national parks. Such youth remember the first-hand experience of the grandeur of Grand Canyon National Park or similar inspiring surroundings. Our national and state forests have similar hiking trails and campgrounds that students, as youth, may have experienced with their parents. Some students mentioned picnics near wild, free-flowing streams rather than the manicured city parks. Other students recall swimming in one or more of our clear streams and rivers, or standing under a waterfall, as contrasted with their neighborhood swimming pool. Some families with children go on canoe trips on such beautiful rivers as the upper Delaware and Brandywine in Pennsylvania, the Kickapoo in Wisconsin, the Current in Missouri, the Buffalo in Arkansas, the connecting lake systems in the Boundary Waters of northern Minnesota, or the Adirondack region of northern New York. Teenagers that I have observed prefer to join ten or twelve of their friends in an eight-passenger rubber raft and float down a spring-fed river in the southern Missouri Ozarks region! Families with older adolescents may have experienced the power of rushing water, the excitement of seeing wild animals in their own habitat, and the overall oneness of nature by white water rafting on the Kennebec River in Maine, the Lehigh River in Pennsylvania, the Colorado River at the bottom of the Grand Canyon in Utah and New Mexico, or the Rogue River in Oregon. Other nearer-to-home rivers could be added. Wintertime provides opportunities to go on family snow hikes, to observe wild animal tracks and puzzle about their behavior, to admire rows of glistening icicles, or to listen to the tingling sound of ice floes scurrying down a major river.

Recently my two sons taught me and their families a powerful lesson of geography, imagination, and spiritual oneness. My sons and three grandchildren (six to nine years) worked together to construct a crude wood raft with a keel, sail and flag from driftwood on the banks of the Missouri River. They inscribed on the deck the first names of all of us, plus the names of two adult dogs, seven new-born puppies, and two phone numbers! The raft was christened the USS *Columbia* and launched with the family singing "God Bless America" and "Jingle Bells." All watched as it moved into the main current and passed around a curve a mile away, bound for St. Louis, New Orleans, and the Gulf of Mexico! Regardless of whether it reached this destination, the kids will remember for a lifetime the imaginative geography lesson, the states passed enroute, and the possible hardships to be encountered. To summarize, parents have values to share with their children; they can make a choice between using family resources for family outdoor adventures, or relying on glittering theme parks or arcades with their acquisitive games. College professors are encouraged to recognize these earlier contributions of parents as teachers.

Consistent with the above comments, Elise Boulding, a respected Quaker sociologist, writes, "When we talk of 'making history,' we often think of dramatic public acts, yet, history is really made by the painstaking accumulation of different kinds of experiences and skills in private and public settings. We can never really act 'on the national scene' or 'on the international scene'. We can only act in specific geographical and social space which may serve as metaphors for larger scenes. . . ." Thus Boulding (1989) regards the family as a practice ground in making history. We are encouraged to do likewise with respect to teaching the values, the beauty, and the diversity of our natural world.

While an ever-increasing number of families live in large and small cities, several college students have described to me their earlier life growing up in a farm, knowing first-hand the rhythm of daily life and the unity of nature expressed with such variety during four seasons. They want this rural closeness to nature to continue in their later adult lives. The riches, weaknesses and the future options of life in rural America have been vividly portrayed by David Orr (1994, chap. 23).

The arousal of environmental concerns in students may lead to a commitment to be responsible for their actions and to be active in some campus environmental activity. They may not know the writings of the religious scholars, but they use "commitment" and "connectedness" in their vocabulary when they slow down to be reflective. The equivalent phrase from the aura of the Earth Summit participants was "willingness to act." Some college students in the post-1970 decades have clearly expressed their disgust with older members of society for their apathy, delays, double-dealing and rationalizations on environmental issues, whether in academia or the larger society; some students are disappointed that their commitments have not been adequately heard in their respective academic institutions. To conclude, faculty are encouraged to recognize the depth of student concerns and to respond creatively in appropriate avenues.

Visioning the Future of University/College Education

The thoughtful observer Thomas Berry notes that higher education has become:

> . . . more an external conditioning than an internal discipline, more a training in manipulative techniques than initiation into religious rituals. The skills to be mastered were not the contemplative skills or imaginative capacities . . . but were rather the skills needed by industry to bring forth the natural resources from the hidden depths of the planet, the skills to shape them in the manufacturing establishments and to make them available to a consumer-oriented society. . . . After generations of analytical preoccupation with taking the Earth apart, the sciences begin a new phase of synthesis. . . . This integration of the human with an organic functional world, after detaching the hu-

man from the mechanistic world, can be considered among the most difficult of all historical transitions. The feel for life, the skills for creative interaction with the Earth processes have been suppressed over a series of generations. . . . (Berry 1988)

Then Berry proceeds to describe his dream of the American college in the ecological age.

William Savitt, director of the Office on Education of the Interfaith Hunger Appeal, a non-profit, sectarian educational agency, has edited an invaluable book for the academic community, *Teaching Global Development—A Curriculum Guide* (1993). The book has many relevant chapters for faculty interested in teaching global issues and Third World development. The same book is excellent for students who want to explore the stated areas on their own. Initial essays concern education for the global citizen, ethics and development, paradigms for development, humanities and development and development education via the mass media. The second reason to praise this book is the presence of seven course outlines, with candid notes on objectives, texts, group projects, assigned readings, exams and evaluation, etc. The third reason to recommend this book is the final section of a selective bibliography, which lists about 177 books (1983 to 1993) in eight subject categories (development/theory, economics, environment, food and hunger, gender, democracy/grass roots power, interdependence and refugeeism); each book has one or two paragraphs of evaluation. Each of the above subject areas overlaps with sustainable development. "The concept of global citizenship provides a means of fusing multiculturalism and internationalization in common cause for increasing the curricular visibility and viability of what is called, more often in the informal than the formal education section, 'development education'. . . . The idea of global citizenship, like global education and international aid itself, has been resisted and sometimes criticized on the grounds that engagement represents a failure of commitment to this country and its needs. . ." (Savitt 1993). Savitt then cites several reasons, including the one that the "transformation of the globe has created a similar need for transformation of the curriculum, without which students will arrive in any realm of endeavor lamentably unprepared to achieve" (Savitt 1993).

Dr. Marvin L. Rogers, a professor of political science at the University of Missouri, has visited some twenty countries in Southeast Asia and Africa; his special research interest is Malaysia and Thailand. From the depths of his expertise, Dr. Rogers summarizes his paper:

Malaysia, like most nations on the world, is committed to industrialization as a means of developing the country, raising the standard of living, and as a means of "becoming modern." As Malaysia continues to industrialize, her economy will become increasingly interconnected with those of other countries. Further industrialization will also accelerate the pace of social change and create new challenges for those responsible for educating future generations. While many national leaders stress the importance of human resource development in order to reach the goals of 2020, few address the imperative need to internationalize undergraduate education in order to equip students to confront the challenges of the twenty-first century. (Rogers 1995)

Based on his extensive overseas observations, Rogers (1995) has clear recommendations for American higher education. He concludes:

As we approach the start of the twenty-first century, it is imperative that we recognize the need to internationalize our undergraduate programs in order to better equip our students to handle the challenges they will face in the future. We need to nurture the development of our students, to challenge them to achieve their very best, and to offer instruction and experiences that enable them to master a foreign language and to gain a well-grounded understanding of at least one other country or global region. An internationalized education in chemistry, history, business or civil engineering ought to equip graduates to work with others from different parts of the world. The goal is excellence. Either we internationalize our undergraduate curriculum or we will marginalize our students. . . . (Rogers 1995)

The students and participants at the Yale "Campus Earth Summit" (Heinz Family Foundation 1995) made a clear recommendation to integrate "environmental knowledge into all relevant disciplines." A variety of academic models are known—an overall college or school, a strong department with considerable outreach, a research institute with a teaching component, or a spread within a wide variety of departments and courses. The merit of each approach may vary with the nature of the institution; the strength and vitality of each approach may be related to both the leadership provided and the resources brought to bear. For instance, the MU Environmental Affairs Council is developing several "environmental cluster courses" that may be combined with one or more traditional majors. Thus, a comparison and an evaluation of these approaches at this date is probably premature.

The dean of thinking about environmental education in academia is David W. Orr, professor of environmental studies, Oberlin College, who has no less than three books on various aspects of the subject (*Ecological Literacy—Education and the Transition to a Post-Modern World*, 1992; *The*

Campus and Environmental Responsibility, 1992; and *Earth in Mind–On Education, Environment and the Human Prospect*, 1994). Rooted in a strong liberal arts college, Orr knows the woof and warp of a liberal education. He has a clear vision of a revised college education based on an ecological literacy.

Orr suggests that "the crisis of the biosphere is symptomatic of a prior crisis of mind, perception, and heart. It is not a problem in education, but a problem of education. . . . " This crisis is unsettling with respect to beliefs on the purposes of education, the routine institutional and operational procedures, our perception of being creative educators and our commitment to the truth. Orr observes that "the crisis of sustainability, the fit between humanity and its habitat, is manifest in varying ways and degrees everywhere on Earth. It is not only a permanent feature on the public agenda; for all practical purposes it *is* the agenda. . . . Yet we still educate at all levels as if no such crisis existed. . ." (Orr 1992). He develops the case for ecological literacy, which, beyond reading and mathematical skills, "requires the more demanding capacity to observe nature with insight, a merger of landscape and mindscape. . . ." While ecological literacy is nurtured by a sense of wonder in our beautiful, yet mysterious, world, this viewpoint is difficult for Western culture with its emphasis on specialization and book learning (an indoor activity), its decline in aesthetic appreciation, and its increase in fragmented lives, with minimal direct experience of the Garden.

In his third book (1994), Orr examines in greater detail the purposes, dangers, problems, business, and destinations of education; his depth is too great to outline here. With his liberal arts background, Orr makes a crucial distinction between a career and a calling: "A calling has to do with one's larger purpose, personhood, deepest values, and the gift one wishes to give to the world. A calling is about the use one makes of a career. A career is about specific attitudes (a job, a way to earn one's keep, a way to build a long resume, a ticket to somewhere else); a calling is about purpose . . . and comes out of an inner conversation. . . " (Orr 1994). To summarize, Orr is a critic of many facets of current society and its practices. His comprehensiveness, inclusiveness of other scholars, and lucid writing set the stage for future thinking and planning in environmental literacy. Academia must wrestle with his viewpoint and recommendations.

Island Press, the publisher of many environmental books, has announced the 1996 publication of Collett and Karakashian's book, *Greening the College Curriculum–A Guide to Environmental Teaching in the Liberal Arts*. The advance description states that the book provides "tools for college and university faculty to meet personal and institutional goals for integrating environmental issues into the curriculum" for eleven subject areas from anthropology to religion. The presence of guidelines for course units, plans for upper-level courses, and annotated resources will make this book a valuable asset.

Conclusions

Reaching students and educators on the subject of sustainable development may be difficult due to the many meanings of the term, the gaps in public communication, the growing awareness of the richness implicit in the term, and its derived sociological, economic, and political implications. However, the challenge has been delivered to those in education to teach their subject creatively. Furthermore, academia has the intelligence to understand the subject, and skills to serve as catalysts for outreach to students and the larger society.

Many resources within and outside the classroom have been identified in this chapter. The motivation to proceed and the vision ahead are depicted here and in chapters 1 and 14. A variety of educational approaches has commenced in recent years. What remains? The message for students, faculty, and academic administrators, in the words of a student, is *"Walk the walk, talk the talk, act the act!"*

Literature Cited

Berry, Joyce K., and John L. Gordon, eds. 1993. *Environmental Leadership–Developing Effective Skills and Styles.* Covelo, Calif.: Island Press and Rainforest Alliance.

Berry, Thomas. 1988. *The Dream of the Earth.* San Francisco: Sierra Club Books.

Boulding, Elise. 1990. *Building a Global Civic Culture–Education for an Independent World.* Syracuse, N.Y.: Syracuse University Press.

Boulding, Elise, and Kenneth E. Boulding. 1995. *The Future–Images and Processes.* Thousand Oaks, Calif.: Sage Publications.

Brown, Lester R., Christopher Flavin, Hilary F. French, and Linda Starke, eds. 1984-1995. *State of the World–A Worldwatch Institute Report on Progress Toward a Sustainable Society.* New York: W. W. Norton & Co.

Brown, Lester R., Hal Kane, David M. Roodman, and Linda Starke, eds. 1992-1995. *Vital Signs–The Trends That are Shaping Our Future.* New York: W. W. Norton and Co.

Brown, Noel J., and Pierre Quiblier. 1994. *Ethics and Agenda 21–Moral Implications of a Global Consensus.* New York: UN Environment Programme, United Nations Publications.

Brundtland, Gro. 1990. In *One Earth, One Future–Our Changing Global Environment,* edited by Cheryl S. Silver and Ruth S. De Fries. Washington, D.C.: National Academy Press.

Caldwell, Lynton K. 1990. *Between Two Worlds–Science, the Environmental Movement and Policy Choice.* New York: Cambridge University Press.

Callicott, J. Baird. 1989. *In Defense of the Land Ethic–Essays in Environmental Philosophy.* Albany: State University of New York Press.

———. 1994. *Earth's Insights: A Survey of Ecological Ethics from the Mediterranean Basin to the Australian Outback.* Berkeley: University of California Press.

———. 1994. Towards a Global Environment Ethic. In Brown and Quiblier, 1994. Loc. cit.

Carroll, Thomas F. 1992. *Intermediary NGOs–The Supporting Link in Grassroots Development.* West Hartford, Conn.: Kumarian Press (an Inter-American Foundation).

Collett, Jonathan, and S. Karakashian, eds., 1996. *Greening the College Curriculum–A Guide to Environmental Teaching in the Liberal Arts.* Covelo, Calif.: Island Press.

Cunningham, William P., et al., eds. 1994. *Environmental Encyclopedia.* Detroit: Gale Research, Inc.

Eagan, David J., and David W. Orr, eds. 1992. *The Campus and Environmental Responsibility,* In the series, *New Directions for Higher Education,* No. 77, Vol. XX, No. 1. San Francisco: Jossey-Bass Higher and Adult Education Series, Jossey-Bass Inc., Publishers.

Gordon, Rue E., ed. 1995. *Conservation Directory,* 40th ed. Washington, D.C.: National Wildlife Federation,

Hansen, Kathryn W., and Mary Steinmaus, eds. 1994. *Two Years After UNCED– Exploring Partnerships for Sustainable Development.* Proceedings of the July 20-24, 1994, conference. Citizens Network for Sustainable Development, the Stanley Foundation, and Iowa Division United Nations Association-USA. University of Northern Iowa Press.

Heinz Family Foundation and Yale Student Environment Coalition. 1995. *Blueprint for a Green Campus: The Campus Earth Summit Initiatives for Higher Education.* Pittsburgh: Heinz Family Foundation, (412) 497-5775; also available from the Center for Environmental Leadership, Washington, D.C., (202) 234-5990.

The *Independent* (London), Oct. 15, 1995.

Kelly, Thomas H. 1994. The Talloires Declaration and the University Leaders (formerly Presidents for a Sustainable Future). Letter and brochures. Medford, Mass.: Center for Environmental Management, Tufts University.

Keniry, Julian. 1995. *Ecodemia–Campus Environmental Stewardship at the Turn of the 21st Century.* Washington, D.C.: National Wildlife Federation.

Korten, David C. 1990. *Getting to the 21st Century–Voluntary Action and the Global Agenda.* West Hartford, Conn.: Kumarian Press.

Langton, Stuart, ed. 1984. *Environmental Leadership–A Sourcebook for Staff and Volunteer Leaders of Environmental Organizations.* Lexington, Mass.: Lexington Books/D.C. Heath & Co.

LaRoe, Edward T., *et al.*, eds. 1995. *Our Living Resources–A Report to the Nation on the Distribution, Abundance and Health of U.S. Plants, Animals, and Ecosystems.* Washington, D.C.: U.S. Dept. of Interior, National Biological Service.

McCoy, Michael, and Patrick McCully. 1993. *Road From Rio– An NGO Action Guide to Environment and Development.* Utrecht, Netherlands: International Books and World Information Service on Energy.

McFague, Sallie. 1994. A Theological Ethical Response to *Agenda 21.* In Brown and Quiblier. 1994. Loc. cit.

McKay, Beth. Letter and enclosure from Student Pugwash.

Marshall, Eliot. 1995. Physicist Wins Nobel Peace Prize. *Science.* 220, #5235, 372 (1995);

Orr, David W. 1992. *Ecological Literacy–Education and the Transition to a Postmodern World.* Albany: State University of New York Press,.

———. 1994. *Earth in Mind–On Education, Environment and the Human Prospect.* Covelo, Calif.: Island Press.

Peterson's Guides. 1995. *Education for the Earth–A Guide to Top Environmental Studies Programs,* 2d ed. Princeton, N. J.: Alliance for Environmental Education and Peterson's Guide,

Porter, Catherine, Tom W. Carroll, and Tracy A. Dobson, eds. 1992. *The Citizens Respond–The Earth Summit and Beyond: Convergence of Knowledge and Action for Change.* Proceedings of the September 25–27, 1992 conference. Bolinas, Calif.: Citizens Network for Sustainable Development; and East Lansing: Michigan State University (CASID and ISP).

Pugwash Conferences, *Yearbook of International Organizations,* 32d ed. 1995-96.

Rogers, Marvin L. 1995. Internationalizing Education to Meet the Challenges of the 21st Century. *Jurnal Antropblogi dan Sociologi (Journal of Anthropology and Sociology,* published by the National University of Malaysia), in press.

Savitt, William, ed. 1993. *Teaching Global Development–A Curriculum Guide.* Notre Dame: University of Notre Dame Press and Interfaith Hunger Appeal.

Schwartz, Carol A., and Rebecca L. Turner, eds. 1995. *Encyclopedia of Associations,* 29th ed., 4 vols. Detroit: Gale Research, Inc.

Smith, April A. 1993. *Campus Ecology–A Guide To Assessing Environmental Quality and Creating Strategies for Change.* Los Angeles: Student Environmental Action Coalition and Living Planet Press.

Stevenson, Richard W. 1995. Peace Prize Goes to A-Bomb Scientist Who Turned Critic. The *New York Times,* Oct. 14, 1995.

Student Pugwash, *Encyclopedia of Associations,* 29th ed. 1995, 218.

Taylor, Diana, Rebecca Stutsman, et al., eds. 1993. *From Rio to the Capitols–State Strategies for Sustainable Development. Citizens Network for Sustainable Development and President's Council on Sustainable Development.* Proceedings of the May 25-28, 1993 conference, Louisville, Ky.

United Nations. 1993. *Agenda 21–The Programme for Sustainable Development.* New York: United Nations.

IV. From the Humanities

12. The Spiritual Basis for Sustainable Development

Sally B. Merrill[1]

> *Hell is now technologically feasible.*
> —Wes Jackson, *Altars of Unhewn Stone*

Abstract

This article clarifies the concept of sustainability with a view toward its spiritual components and cross-cultural presence, especially in traditional medicinal and agricultural practices informed by spiritual wisdom. Some key cultural works are cited which refer to sustainability as a practical and spiritual problem, e.g., in Judaic traditions, in Shakespeare's work, and in Native American traditions among others. Some of the most important and spiritually focused work on the topic of sustainability is occurring in ecofeminist circles. Diverse sources are cited for use in teaching and research.

Defining "Sustainability" by Holding Its Spiritual Foundations in the Light

"Sustainability" is the long-term goal or steady state of the many fields of study and social movements now known as sustainable socio-economic development: sustainable agriculture, sustainable technologies, and sustainable communities. Sustainability can be defined as the balance between entropy and care, between the second law of thermodynamics and the energy to love and renew with the finite resources that are also sources. Things which are

---

[1] **Sally B. Merrill**, an associate professor at Purdue University-Calumet, works mainly in the fields of applied and professional ethics, feminism, and the history and philosophy of education. She is finishing a book on personhood in clinical care and the first-ever book on ethical challenges in construction engineering and contracting. Interested in Lucretia Mott as a moral development theorist, she has performed Mott's speeches and sermons among Friends and elsewhere. She taught at Kansas State University, earned her M.S. in linguistics at Georgetown University, and received a Ph.D. in philosophy at the State University of New York-Albany, with an emphasis on bio-medical ethics. She was a fellow on women and public policy through the Center for Women in Government.

"sources," not merely resources, are intrinsically or even aesthetically valuable. Sustainability demands the impossible, it seems, representing a variety of agapic love for all Creation, or at least for the fragile but enduring creations and ecosystems as we know them, in which we are already enmeshed and nested.

Sustainability is science and love in dialectical tension, creating an enduring order or process which at least seems to security-craving humans to be something that will endure. Wes Jackson, co-founder of the Land Institute for research on sustainability, says that "sustainable" is a complex political word (1987). It is a simple, profound spiritual concept, if one has the discipline to see humans as something other than the center of the universe. Each of us is related to the sacredness of personhood in all other creatures and perhaps in what we see as the living planet itself. This connection can be seen in Judaic, Eastern, Anglo, and Native American spiritual practices, which express a unity with nature, and sustainability.

The concept of sustainability is at the core of most Buddhist philosophies. In the ancient Hindu roots of Buddhism, as well, is the concept of "maya," or illusion, which is usually represented as a self-deceptive and temporary human belief that "permanence can be achieved." This belief is as ridiculous in the positive sense as is Wes Jackson's warning phrase in *Altars of Unhewn Stone* that "Hell is now technologically feasible." So we know that a sustainable hell is possible. But what of sustainability in a positive spiritual sense? Are love and faith enough? Will God provide an enduringly fruitful Earth to us, the wasteful, high-input sinners who remain deliberately ignorant of the effects of our lifestyle, see no choices, and think we have no power to do otherwise?

Perhaps the new seeking, both spiritual and material, for sustainability is a vain search, like the considerations in Shakespeare's Sonnet 15 concerning "every thing that grows." Things that do not grow are covered by this philosophy, too, wearing away or decaying in some way or other. The ones that grow, the living, are no more sustainable, without love or care or a supportive community, than rocks. Even these may increase, as when, after hundreds of years, tophaceous mosses deposit minerals on rocks that "grow" on the prairie, in places held to be sacred for centuries by Native Americans impressed with the sustainability of the stone.

Sonnet 15

When I consider every thing that grows
Holds in perfection but a little moment,
That this huge stage presenteth nought but shows
Whereon the stars in secret influence comment;
When I perceive that men as plants increase,
Cheered and check'd even by the self-same sky,
Vaunt in their youthful sap, at height decrease,
And wear their brave state out of memory;
then the conceit of this inconstant stay
Sets you most rich in youth before my sight,
Where wasteful Time debateth with Decay,
To change your day of youth to sullied night;
And all in war with Time for love of you,
As he takes from you, I engraft you new.

On the Anglo-Shakespearean model, sustainability is a constant battle against Time and Decay. But love has a certain staying power in this model, constantly "engrafting" the loved one anew and so in a sense renewing the energy.

Let's go back to the roots of the earliest Western Judaic and Christian traditions of stewarding the Earth and of conceiving time: the roots of anthropocentrism are in the Gospel of John, in *Koine,* or common spoken Greek, even if the Greek "logos" is translated as "the way" in a Taoist mode, rather than "the word" *En arche en o logos, kai o logos en pros ton theon, kai theos en o logos.* (In the beginning was the word, and the word was with God; God was the Word.)

Here the human, the word made flesh in the Christ figure, is still the beginning and the end of what seems important. But today, we need a Copernican revolution of the spirit, away from anthropocentrism, or at least away from treating the human race like an isolated only child in an otherwise empty, dead mechanistic space. There *are* spiritual roots of sustainability, of seeing nature as source, not resource, and *not just* a place for our *use*-based stewardship. Psalm 65, an instance of the undercurrent of sustainability in Judaic culture, does not rest upon the "this is your place to use" approach, which is not sustainable. Even stewardship has limits, and implies the steward's agency. Psalm 65 makes it clear that there is another approach, which is more ultimate, more viable, and sustainable, but not through our own power or control:

Psalm 65

O thou that hearest prayer, unto thee shall all flesh come. . .

By terrible things in righteousness wilt thou answer us, O God of our salvation. . .

Thou visiteth the earth, and waterest it: thou greatly enrichest it with the river of God, which is full of water; thou preparest them corn (grain), when thou has so provided for it.

Thou waterest the ridges thereof abundantly: thou settlest the furrows thereof: thou makest it soft with showers: thou blessest the springing thereof.

Thou crownest the year with thy goodness; and thy paths drop fatness.

They drop upon the pastures of the wilderness; and the little hills rejoice on every side.

The pastures are clothed with flocks; the valleys also are covered with corn (grains and grasses); they shout for joy. They also sing.

Thus Psalm 65 has still some vestige of human-centeredness in collecting the fruits of the Lord's labors with the Earth, but it does recognize an intrinsic value, even rejoicing, in the land itself, the fields that shout for joy and the fruitful valleys that "also sing." The Earth here is source and not mere resources. And God does the real work, not human hands. Rosemary Radford Ruether points out that the model here is not one of domination, but of what appears to be interdependence, although she would show us how the pre-Hebraic, Hebraic, Christian, and Medieval roots also set up a patriarchal model of nature. As she tells us, the "dark side of Medieval thought saw nature as possessed by demonic powers that draw us down in sin and death through sexual temptation" (in Adams 1993). Woman is "temptress." So our work with nature on sustainability must resolve a gender problem at its roots and must clarify key concepts before we can agree to proceed with sustainable activities. Basic spiritual concepts will have to be overhauled: God, soul, body, woman, and salvation. I would add: family, nature, love, and death. Ruether continues:

> The western flight from mortality is a flight from the disintegration side of the life cycle, from accepting ourselves as part of that process. By pretending that we can immortalize ourselves, souls, and bodies, we are immortalizing our garbage and polluting the Earth. In order to learn to recycle our garbage as fertilizer for new life, as matter for new artifacts, we need to accept our selfhood as participating in the same process. Humans are finite organisms, centers of experience in a life cycle that must disintegrate back into the nexus of life and arise again in new forms (in Adams 1993).

Sustainability is love, justice, and care for the Earth, combined with the very best interdisciplinary science that we can invent. It is as teachable as the model of exploitation was.

Sustainability Requires Changes in Us

Sustainability requires what Ruether calls "a conversion from alienated, hierarchical dualism to life-sustaining mutuality," a new urgency "about the untenability of present patterns of life, and compassionate solidarity with those who are its victims" (in Adams 1993).

Sustainability is being able to put oneself in the place of a profoundly "other" in the nature which seems not part of ourselves, to "think like a mountain" and to flow like a river, to dip into Aldo Leopold's practical, direct metaphors. Sustainability is beyond, before word and flesh. It is the source of word and flesh, and their renewal.

Sustainability is not human-centered. The eighteenth century philosopher David Hume wrote in a pre-nuclear era that the life of a human being is "of as much importance to the universe as the life of an oyster." Humans are still just as important to each other, but we have not yet learned to show this importance in sustainable ways. We kill and threaten to kill any and all species that obstruct our human projects. We (over) reproduce to please each other, or someone, or no-one, just not thinking about the ecological effects of each high-consuming human. We build things, loving to construct and solve engineering problems, but not seeing the eventual pollution they may cause, not demanding a science that is sustainable and far-reaching enough to show us more of the future. Sustainability is whatever transcends and is immanent in the imagined boundary between "mankind" and the "rest" of nature, i.e., nothing is sustainable which insists on a separation between humans and nature. . . and thus we are already "in unity with nature."

The sources of traditional Judeo-Christian traditions are helpful, but not as soul-lifting and constructive, I think, as the sources of spiritual sustainability in what has been left to us from Native American cultures. The famous, even if controversial, message of Chief Seattle is now taught to most schoolchildren, with its admonishment that we consider the seventh generation in our wake, that we be aware of the sin of the White Man in destroying natural balance, and that we are in fact "brothers" or kin to other creatures. This concept is catching on only incompletely, since humans tend to be attracted to only "cute" species or animals. Though many do not yet see their kinship to slime molds, mosses, lichens, liverworts, invertebrates, or phytoplankton, the idea of deep spiritual kinship with, and familial duty toward, all the rest of creation has a terrifically uplifting effect. In my old family home on an island in Lake Erie, we no longer spray for spiders, respecting their helpful role, and my nephews and nieces are no longer, like my brother years ago, deathly afraid of spiders and snakes, since we frequently express reverence at a spiritual level for the rare Lake Erie water snake. Reverence is expressed in Native American and Eastern Indian traditions as two complex sets of spiritual approaches to an ecological way of living in this life and the next. Serious scholarly work in both the "Indian" spiritualities and in a reviving Buddhism has taken us well ahead on the path Chief Seattle mapped out.

In her paper "Acting with Compassion," Stephanie Kaza has written a great deal of spiritual value (in Adams 1993). Kaza, who teaches Environmental Ethics at the University of Vermont and is a student of Zen, of Vietnamese Buddhist Thich Nhat Hanh, and of despair-fighting Joanna Macy, addresses the freeing of the individual spirit from its obsession with being individual, rather than essentially related or merged with a whole—a move into sustainable consciousness which is necessary if we are to make progress. Kaza has also gathered interesting reflections on anger—a mysterious emotion seen from a spiritual point of view. At first blush, anger is often not felt as spiritual by most of us. But we are asked to reconsider; it becomes necessary to know how we feel in order to act morally. As Beverly Harrison asserts, "The failure to live deeply in our bodies, ourselves, destroys the possibility for moral relations between us." Anger is for her "a feeling signal that all is not well in our relation to others or the world around us. . . . Anger is a wake-up call to look more deeply into the situation at hand, and create a world of moral relations—a basically spiritual task" (Kaza quoting Harrison in Adams 1993).

Presumably, being angry at polluters is the "wake-up call"; we must attempt a moral relationship with them in order to work out a solution, either inside law or outside it. The combination of Buddhist mindfulness practice and feminist moral responses is a powerful antidote to widespread despair and depression over the possibility of nuclear annihilation, environmental catastrophe, or out-of-control corporate greed—all of which are distinct signals of unsustainability. The spiritual practices she recommends do not, Kaza notes, remove the threats, but they "help to generate the tremendous energy needed to address the complexities of the global environmental situation" (in Adams 1993). Perhaps some Eastern spiritual sources can begin to help where Western peacemaking has either failed or not been tried, e.g., in the Korean and Bosnian situations. Constant contemplation and action are needed to creatively resolve conflicts which have brewed for millennia, and to sustain the prevention of nuclear holocaust.

Except for the many-personed aspects of ultimate reality for the Eastern spiritualities (as in many diverse goddesses of the Earth, e.g., the vegetable goddess, and Corn Mother, Thought Woman, etc.), the Eastern and

Native American spiritual responses highlighted above are remarkably similar to some early Quaker views. For example, there is a real similarity between the cosmology of the Quaker scientist and philosopher Anne Finch Conway, who prefigured Leibniz's "monads" in word and concept, and the Mahayana Buddhist image of the Jewel Net of Indra, in which a multidimensional net stretches through all time and space, "connecting an infinite number of jewels (monads), each of which is multifaceted and reflects every other jewel in the net" (Kaza, in Adams 1993). "There is nothing outside the net, and nothing which does not reverberate its presence throughout the web of relationships."

How is this approach to nature do-able? The very question belies the spiritual task at hand—just to be, not necessarily to *do* anything! One could say we humans have already "done" enough. Does this Being in the Net speak to the condition of the unemployed spouse whose family depends on her for food and medical care? Does this sort of spiritual interdependence and Being, not Doing, speak to the condition of the small rural Quaker Meeting that has a problem with wild creatures damaging the Meeting house, and that must, indeed, *do* something? It might, in fact, affect practices in this more trivial sense, since among Friends, as among relatives, often the unimportant is important.

I recently saw the invasion of my father's house and barn by raccoons after my brother chopped down a beautiful huge dead cottonwood tree that housed the coons' nest. While family members on the front porch were discussing extermination by drowning in Lake Erie, my brave son Noah climbed up onto the rafters to determine what and how many they were, and to let them know that we lived there too. When the mother raccoon threatened him with hissing and bared teeth, he drew back respectfully, saying in his kindest soft voice, "It's okay, guys, I'm not gonna hurt you!" While he bore the news to the front porch, I left a trail of chicken leftovers from the barn to the field out back of the barn. By morning, all three raccoons had vacated and did not return until the next spring, when they invaded the chimney and slid down the banister. No victory is forever, except extinction. The comforting thing about the raccoon problem, or—from their point of view—the human problem, is that neither short-term survival and protection nor a strict exclusion strategy is sustainable. Eventually, for raccoons, as for human sustainability, balanced populations in harmony with available resources and appropriate habitat are needed. This aspect of deep ecology deepens spiritual virtues such as the awareness of interdependence, gratitude and humility.

For those who are interested in finding moral, spiritual and political support to awaken others to sustainability, there are already many groups which can help: the Buddhist Perception of Nature project, the Buddhist Peace Fellowship, the Nuclear Guardianship Project, and Buddhists Concerned for Animals. Other sorts of groups, like the Green Gulch Zen Center in California, teach mindfulness in gardening. The Quaker environmental group, Friends Committee on Unity with Nature, has a spiritual base and an active though small global network.

Numerous writers and activists—Karen Warren, Jim Cheney, Dana Jackson, and others in the United States; Maria Mies in Germany; and Vandana Shiva in India—have focused on ecofeminist approaches to spirituality and ecology. Shiva's book, *Staying Alive* (1989), has awakened many of my students to the practical complex needs of women as healers and traditional practitioners of agriculture. These women, not thinking themselves to be God, but wisely interdependent in their powers, are being replaced by men who think themselves chosen by the gods of Western marketing or grantors of technologies, who give the immense, "godlike" tractors and large tools of non-sustainable agriculture to the men, not the women formerly in charge. Thus, in India, whole forests of diverse species of trees with healing powers for the numerous diarrheal illnesses of infants, for instance, are replaced with cash monocrops of, for example, eucalyptus trees, which are of unsustainable market value and are destructive of the natural health and spiritual connectedness of the people with the forests and their universe. In a brilliant chapter, Shiva details "Chipko" and the sustainable forestry struggle.

I want to close with a directive from Black Elk, from the Lakota spirituality that places humans appropriately in, not over, our environment. Carol Lee Sanchez, a Lakotan, Laguna Pueblo, and Lebanese who recently moved to central Missouri after years of teaching in New Mexico, explains that the Lakota use the phrase *"Mitakuye Oyas'in"* at the end of a formal voicing to the spirits. It means, loosely translated, "all my relations or relatives." Black Elk (in Black Elk and Lyon 1990) says:

> This Chanupa (Sacred Pipe) is your relative. The Powers of the Four Winds are your relatives. Pray to them. Talk to them. They are your relatives. To the west—the Thunder Beings, they are your relatives. Send a voice out there. These are your relatives. Look to the north, the Buffalo Nation—White Buffalo Calf Maiden—The Chanupa—these are your relatives. To the east, the Elk Nation and the Elk Nation Woman, that brings joy and happiness, these are your relatives. To the south, the Swan, two legged spirits that bring joy and happiness. The medicine people that bring joy and health come from there.

These are your relatives. Above you is the Eagle Nation. They watch, control, govern. These are your relatives. Down to Earth—the Stone People [and the green] are your relatives.

Mitakuye Oyas'in

Literature Cited

Adams, Carol J., ed. 1993. *Ecofeminism and the Sacred.* New York: Continuum Books.

Black Elk, Wallace (Lakota), and William S. Lyon. 1990. Black Elk: The Sacred Ways of a Lakota. New York: Harper and Row.

Jackson, Wes. *Altars of Unhewn Stone.* 1987. New York: Farrar, Straus, and Giroux.

Mies, Maria, and Vandana Shiva. 1993. *Ecofeminism.* London: Zed Books.

Plant, Judith, ed. 1989. *Healing the Wounds: The Promise of Ecofeminism.* Philadelphia: New Society Publishers.

Ruether, Rosemary Radford. 1994. *Gaia and God: Toward an Ecofeminist Theology of Earth Healing.* San Francisco: Harper and Row.

———. 1972, 1979. Motherearth and the Megamachine: A Theology of Liberation in a Feminine, Somatic, and Ecological Perspective. In *Christianity and Crisis* (April 12). Reprinted in *Womanspirit Rising: A Feminist Reader in Religion,* edited by Carol P. Christ and Judith Plaskow. San Francisco: Harper and Row, 1979.

Shiva, Vandana. 1989. *Staying Alive: Women, Ecology, and Development.* London: Zed Books Limited.

Warren, Karen J., ed. 1994. *Ecological Feminism.* New York: Routledge.

Warren, Karen J., and Jim Cheney. 1995. Ecological Feminism: A Philosophical Perspective on What It Is and Why It Matters. Boulder, Colo.: Westview Press.

13. Sustainability Models in Two Novels and Other Literature

Susan Schmidt[1]

*There are more things in heaven and earth,
Horatio, than dreamed of in your philosophy.*
—Hamlet

Abstract

A 1987 UN Commission defined sustainable development as "meeting the needs of the present without compromising the ability of future generations to meet their own needs." In two novels and one story, full of land and water images, the second generation struggles to survive as farmers or fishermen, but the third generation must move away from natural territory and natural professions. In Jane Smiley's A Thousand Acres, *because of incest and groundwater pollution, the two sisters' Iowa farming corporation fails, and their marriages collapse. In John Casey's* Spartina, *a deep-sea fisherman off Rhode Island outlasts unemployment, developers, hurricane, class rage, and extramarital temptation. In Christopher Tilghman's "On the Rivershore," a farmer kills a crabber. Tenant farmers own no land, and watermen bring in smaller catches. Local focus has merit in literature and in action.*

[1] **Susan Schmidt** is an assistant professor at Brevard College, where she teaches wilderness literature, environmental policy, and environmental journalism. She also edits for the U.S. Forest Service in Asheville, N.C. She has a doctorate in American literature from the University of South Carolina and masters degrees from the University of Virginia in environmental sciences and English. She did research in literature at Oxford University and postdoctoral study of bioethics at Duke University. She recently had a fellowship from the National Endowment for the Humanities to study environmental literature and ecological criticism. She has worked as environmental journalist, policy scientist, and sailboat captain. She is finishing a spiritual autobiography of wilderness adventures to be published by Lyons and Burford. She is a member of Asheville Friends Meeting.

Introduction

Discussing literature in the classroom can serve as grounding in an interdisciplinary environmental course. By offering realistic examples that bring concepts to life, fiction leads students to examine their own real lives. The definition of sustainable development, according to the United Nations' Brundtland Commission (1987) is, "meeting the needs of the present without compromising the ability of future generations to meet their own needs." In three stories, the sons and daughters struggle to survive as farmers or fishermen, but grandchildren must meet their needs away from family land and outdoor work. I will discuss ecological images where land and water meet in two novels, Jane Smiley's *A Thousand Acres* and John Casey's *Spartina*, and in Christopher Tilghman's short story "On the Rivershore."

Ecological criticism, using concepts of the science of ecology to address literature, has flourished in the last decade (Grumbling 1996; Schmidt 1994a,1994b,1990; Parini 1995; Winkler 1996). Scholars and writers have formed the Association for the Study of Literature and Environment (ASLE). To join ASLE or subscribe to Interdisciplinary Studies in Literature and the Environment (ISLE), contact Cheryll Glotfelty, Professor of English, University of Nevada, Reno, NV 89507. To join an active ASLE e-mail discussion group, contact asle@unr.edu. Regional stories, fiction, and nonfiction, may show cultural values of people in a place, based on the geography and climate that create history. My students use a wide range of ideas and tools—anthropology, hydrology, soil science, engineering, psychology, economics, critical thinking, and policy seminars. As we examine causes and consequences, we see that plenty of technological fixes have been invented but are not applied. Many solutions rely on social skills of negotiation, which is based on cultural understanding; that's why reading regional literature helps. The ultimate solution, my students determine, is communication of existing information, and they want to learn an English major's skills.

Nature Writing

Nature writing is about sense of self, sense of place, and sense of self in place. Local focus has merit both in literature and in action. Useful to opening discussions of sustainability practices in courses on agriculture or oceans policy, Jane Smiley's *A Thousand Acres*, John Casey's *Spartina*, and "On the Rivershore" by Christopher Tilghman all mix land and water images. *A Thousand Acres* unfolds as a story of hydrology, chemistry, and epidemiology. Understanding marsh ecology and meteorology helps the readers of *Spartina* and "On the Rivershore." On the basis of sustainability, I ask in class discussion, how long can each system continue the way it is running? In all three, adults struggle as farmers and fishermen, but children move to cities instead of continuing family professions on land or water. In *A Thousand Acres*, the two sisters' Iowa farming corporation fails, and their marriages collapse. More land, more animals, and bigger machinery cannot pay back the big debt. Abuse and groundwater pollution deplete Ginny's and Rose's health and determination to stay on the family land.

In *Spartina*, Dick Pierce, like his father a deep-sea fisherman off the coast of Rhode Island, outlasts unemployment, real estate developers, a hurricane, class rage, and extramarital temptation. He does need a bigger boat to succeed, whereas the Iowa sisters will not be helped by more land and bigger machinery. Dick ultimately succeeds but does not pass on the family profession. Dick's two sons will go to college, for they will not work on the water.

"On the Rivershore" is the story of a confrontation between fishermen and farmers, but they are both hostage to economic class structure. As tenant farmers on Maryland's Eastern Shore, they own no land; watermen on the Chesapeake Bay are working longer days to bring in smaller catches. This trend away from natural professions on land and water moves people away from connections to family territory and heritage. The city immigrants seem aware and able "to meet their needs" of individual growth, but at what loss to emotional and environmental values?

Iowa Farmers

In each novel the main character maps boundaries of natural territory. Ginny, the older sister in Smiley's novel, gives county road numbers that border her farm. In Casey's book Dick sees upland hills that delimit the watershed of his saltmarsh; at sea he enters Loran coordinates of his lobster traps. In Tilghman's story the boy knows the farm and his house where his mother also grew up, but the landowner's big house and deep water are strange.

Ginny knows the geologic history of their Iowa farm's soil; she says, "our babyhoods perched . . . over layers of rock, Wisconsin till, Mississippian carbonate, Devonian limestone. . . . For millennia water lay over the land, soupy water—leaves, seeds, feather, scales, flesh, bones, petals, pollen— mixed with the saturated soil below and became . . . soil." Ginny knows the family history of draining marsh and installing tile. "However much these acres looked like a gift from God, they were not." Her great-grandparents from England bought land unseen, freshwater wetland. The ancestors dug canals and installed tile drains so they could till rich organic soil. Her father has expanded the acreage, adding a section which is 640 acres, a half section, and a parcel to equal 1,000 acres.

In a game that parallels their debt load, the daughters play a Monopoly tournament with Jess, the neighbor's prodigal son, who wants to convert his father's land to organic farming. Good husbandry absorbs the farmers in *A Thousand Acres:* topsoil, price of gasoline, condition of animals, good breeding line, machinery; the right order of things versus the failure of hope. Ginny limns a catechism: What is a farmer?

> A farmer is a man who feeds the world.
> What is a farmer's first duty?
> To grow more food.
> What is a farmer's second duty?
> To buy more land.
> What is sign of a good farm?
> Clean fields, pretty painted buildings, breakfast at six, no debts, no standing water.
> How will you know a good farmer when you meet him?
> He will not ask you any favors. (Smiley 1991)

Contrasting this code, the family farm fails from their father's fatal pride: his lust to run things, poison the water, destroy the topsoil, buy bigger and bigger machinery. Natural and human systems in both novels are overruled by economic pressures.

A storm rips apart this Iowa family that incest and nitrates have already weakened. After raging as a madman, the father charges into the stormy night, much as King Lear who also divided his kingdom between daughters. Blindness plays too: the adjacent farmer loses his sight in a chemical spill. The father accuses his oldest daughter of barrenness: Ginny has had five miscarriages, the last two hidden from her husband because she wants to keep trying, burying her bloody nightgown and sheets in the barn. Almost like Lady MacBeth, Ginny scrubs her floors and shampoos the carpet; "Dirt is the least of it. There's oil and blood and muck, too." She bathes herself in the farm pond; knows to wash her hands after handling farm chemicals. Ginny's thoughts are full of water images; she says, "I was always aware . . . of the water in the soil. . . , molecules adhering, clustering, evaporation, heating, cooling, freezing, rising to the surface, . . . dissolving this nutrient and that." But Jess surprises her, "It's the . . . water. . . . Have you had your well water tested for nitrates? . . . Didn't your doctor tell you not to drink the well water? . . . People have known for ten years or more that nitrates in well water cause miscarriage and death of infants. Don't *you* know that fertilizer runoff drains into the aquifer?"

Fertilizer drains into the drinking water. Three women on the farm have cancer or miscarriages. The mother has died young of cancer leaving two daughters to be abused by their father. The third daughter, Caroline, shielded from incest by her older sisters, has left the farm early enough to escape the drinking water. Rose also protects her two daughters from their grandfather and polluted water by sending them to "the Quaker boarding school in West Branch," which is Scattergood School. Just like Cordelia, the youngest sister in *King Lear*, Caroline claims to love her madman father better than her sisters and, as a city lawyer, helps her father sue Ginny and Rose to regain the land he has given them. Ginny rages that Iowa farming families ignore what is going on: "They all accept beating as a way of life;" unspoken abuse lies subsurface like polluted groundwater. Ginny becomes aware of the chemical legacy she carries, "Lodged in my every cell, along with the DNA, are molecules of topsoil and atrazine and paraquat and anhydrous ammonia and diesel fuel and plant dust." Ginny escapes to a YWCA room and a job as truck-stop waitress in St. Paul.

Rose dies of breast cancer, after her husband commits suicide in a water reservoir. Before she dies, Rose says: "So all I have is the knowledge that I saw. That I saw without being afraid and without turning away, and that I didn't forgive the unforgivable.'" In *Spartina*, Dick survives because of his better vision. Dick has the skill of "seeing what was distinct before most people could—he could make out the edge of a swordfish fin while the fish was still submerged way off, indistinct in the roll and glimmer of the sea." Dick survives, and Rose, who can see better than her sister Ginny, does not.

Rhode Island Fishing

In *A Thousand Acres* groundwater lies under Iowa farmland; in *Spartina* land meets water in a Rhode Island estuary, black earth richer than any farmland. Dick Pierce recognizes the upland hills that form the watershed of his marsh and salt pond. Like Faulkner's Yoknapatawpha, Casey invents a county and pond superimposed on Charlestown Pond. The plant *Spartina alterniflora* is saltmarsh cordgrass; its niche is the intertidal zone, the strip of half-wet and half-dry land, where tide rises and falls. Dick's income is catching sea creatures whose food chain builds on *Spartina*; he names his boat *Spartina*. On land Dick fumbles and offends; at sea as captain he takes command, explaining how to navigate and how to spear a swordfish.

In *Spartina* Dick is a less-than-noble "comic" hero who survives better than a "tragic" hero with nobler qualities might have, as Joseph Meeker suggests in his *Comedy of Survival* (1974). Ecologically, Dick is an opportunist. The dust jacket notes call *Spartina* a modern *Moby Dick*; Dick Pierce's white-whale obsession as Captain Ahab is "class rage," class distinctions that limit him to one acre of land at the top of the creek after his family used to own the whole point of land in the salt pond. Dick's father sold the land to pay medical bills because he had no insurance. Quick-tempered, Dick quits jobs, gets fired; bankers deny his loan requests. He has a brief fling with Elsie, younger, rich, better educated. Better able than Dick at coping with institutional systems, she works for the new wildlife refuge; Dick calls her a cop. Dick remembers what he has learned from his father, who died too young. Dick judges his own behavior by what he wants his sons to learn. He is unfaithful to his wife, he poaches clams from the new wildlife refuge, but he does not smuggle drugs. Dick has his own code as Yankee—too proud to take welfare, too proud to ask a rich neighbor, Miss Perry, for a loan. He does take $10,000 from his girlfriend to finish building the deep-sea fishing boat that will give him a living.

Dick's attraction to Elsie is natural. Like Dick, Elsie is "rooted in this heap of hills, rockbound ponds, scrub woods creased with streams running to the salt marsh." On the "tag end of a glacier" they too are "fertile. . ., stubborn little forms of life accommodating to the old wreck and spill of rock, . . . at it again in the old accident." He recognizes Elsie, "as quick as a tern skimming the water," and as "a blue heron walking in the marsh on her stilts." Their bodies meet in images of fishing and boat building. "When their bones touched, he felt their weight against each other, as though they were small boats at sea rising on the same swell, jostling, fendered by their flesh." When Dick finally resists sleeping with Elsie, he feels her presence "begin to tug him up from a depth as though he and Elsie were being hauled together, thrashing in the same net, . . . feeling the water bilge upward, . . . all undersea, briny and blind, . . . as though he were a fish." Dick also sees himself as a boat aground or adrift with no rudder: "He'd been stuck. . . . He'd blasted himself loose. . . . Adrift or under way, he was afloat on his own." Dick cannot cope socially; he compares his evasions to "a cloud of ink he squirted so he could slip away" like a squid. However, Dick is a successful altruistic organism, biologically, in that he does pass on his genes. When he ends his affair and confesses to his wife, she insists that Dick support his and Elsie's love-child.

The sea makes Dick more humble. He recognizes his own folly, riding out a hurricane at sea for two days until insurance on his new boat is

194

effective. An older captain advises, "If you do get caught [by the hurricane], don't fight. . . . More power isn't the answer, the shape of your boat is the answer. . . . If you let her yield, she'll move right. The wave is a wall if you run at it. If you move with it, it's a wave."

Ultimately Dick must put faith in the boat he has built rather than his own strength. And his family welcomes him back. As a survivor, Dick is a hero; because his boat is one of few that survives, Dick can earn money to pay back the boat loan, pay birth costs for Elsie's baby, and forestall foreclosure on the family land. The storm washes Dick clean of bitterness. "He'd changed, been breached as wide as the cut from the sea to the salt pond and been washed of the worst of his bitterness."

Both families in *A Thousand Acres* and *Spartina* are tied to their land and water, and lyrical passages in both books describe natural bonds. Dick has little social grace, but keen awareness of the grace in the natural world. Dick, like Ginny in *A Thousand Acres*, finds strength and comfort in the elemental mix of soil and water. Dick's sons are in awe of his natural wisdom; a son "looked at Dick like Dick invented everything they found in water or mud—lobster, fish, clams," but his sons will not follow the water.

For each of his boys' birthdays, the rich neighbor Miss Perry gives them books, "history of New England thought and attitudes": Bowditch, Hawthorne, Alcott, Whittier, Longfellow, Thoreau, Melville, Jewett, Parkman, Prescott. When a rare-book dealer reports the value of first editions, Dick is amazed that "one of [his] kids has some . . . storybook. . . worth five thousand dollars," but he is grateful his sons can afford college if they sell Miss Perry's gift-books.

The moral philosophies of characters in both novels are concerned with the natural order of things. In *A Thousand Acres*, Jess the prodigal who seduces both sisters, says, "I always think that things have to happen the way they do happen, that there are so many inner and outer forces joining at every event that it becomes a kind of fate." Skeptical Rose tells Ginny, "Your own endurance might be a pleasant fiction allowed you by others who've really faced the facts." In *Spartina*, when Elsie recognizes that she must leave the natural territory, *Spartina*'s intertidal zone, where she and Dick wallowed naked in the mud, she chides herself, "I've disturbed the pattern. . . . I haven't been a good ecologist."

Chesapeake Bay Farming and Fishing

A small, apt complement to these two novels is Christopher Tilghman's story, "On the Rivershore," in his collection *In a Father's Place*.

The last word is cordgrass, like Casey's book *Spartina*. The story begins "between the clay banks . . . and the brackish waters of the Chesapeake Bay," where "rolled farmland and mirrored water meet;" the boy Cecil has "dirt on his cheeks. . . and salt on his lips." On the land behind him are corn, hay, and tractors; in the water he can see seine haulers and crab boats. On the rivershore with a crab net Cecil has seen his father shoot a waterman, Tommy Todman, and asks help from Mr. McHugh, the landowner, his father's employer. They load the body into a flat-bottomed duck skiff, built for floating in shallow marshes, not suited for the waves in a deep channel. Soil and water mix as in the novels; the boy watches "as the fresh manure and turned earth still wedged into his father's boot soles make whorls in the clear rainwater in the boat bottom." Crabbers in big workboats arrive where they will dump the body. One says twice, "Ain't no one gonna kill a waterman." Crabbers loyal to each other are angry, but farmers and fishermen agree Todman was bad (apt name since he is dead), and they dump his body.

Mr. McHugh, who himself lives on ancestral land, says twice, "What we're doing is wrong by every standard but one. It's history." A crabber tells him to shut up. Both working-class groups begrudge the landowner, feeble after a stroke, and Cecil suspects "Mr. McHugh . . . caused it all to happen in the first place." Two fathers, farmer and waterman, say, "'The boys is the issue. Not us. . . .' 'It ain't just the boys. . . . It's the water. We got to think what's best for the water. Who's gonna follow the water when we swallow the anchor.'"

Like the Iowa and Rhode Island children, Cecil will not work on the Eastern Shore farm. When Cecil the boy grows, he leaves the land where his father and grandfather farmed as tenants to work in Baltimore and the farmland joins an agricultural conglomerate. The rivershore erodes as the Bay swallows land; siltation and chemical runoff from farming ruin the Bay fisheries. On the Bay "the catch is down and the oystermen go to war with the clam diggers and the seine haulers give up for good." Natural professions decline as the natural systems cannot sustain productivity.

Conclusion

Good writing, like an ecological community, has strong organic connections. We read literature, science, and ethics in my interdisciplinary environmental decision-making courses on agricultural or oceans policy. In a systems approach on the blackboard we draw flow-chart models of world-scale problems. As we examine causes and consequences of environmental problems, like greenhouse effect and global warming, we ask how do suburban sprawl and inadequate mass transit in North America contribute to burning more petroleum. Third-world women burn dung as fuel to cook dinner instead of as fertilizer to enrich garden soil; they do not own the land they till, are not educated in better agricultural practices, and may have no access to birth control. Students conclude that cultural understanding, ecological connections, conflict resolution, and communication are more important than a technological fix.

Discussion of these family stories by Smiley, Casey, and Tilghman about farming and fishing enhance our value discussions in the classroom. Stories and poems are both affective—that is, they pull out feelings—and are effective, practical at opening personal dimensions of environmental issues and giving cultural understanding for negotiation. Students who challenge philosophies and actions of fictional characters will hopefully, in a dialectic comparison, strengthen their own environmental philosophy and resolve to act conscientiously.

Literature Cited

Brundtland, Gro. 1987. *Our Common Future.* New York: Oxford University Press.

Casey, John. 1989. *Spartina.* New York: Avon.

Grumbling, Vernon Owen. 1996. Literature. In *Greening the College Curriculum,* edited by Jonathan Collett and Stephen Karakashian. Washington, D.C.: Island Press, 151-73.

Meeker, Joseph. 1974. *The Comedy of Survival, in Search of an Environmental Ethic.* New York: Scribner's.

Parini, Jay. 1995. The Greening of the Humanities. The *New York Times Magazine.* Oct. 29, 1995, 52-53.

Schmidt, Susan. 1994a. Finding a Home: Rawlings Cross Creek. The *Southern Literature Journal.* 26: 6 48-57 (Spring 1994).

———. 1990. Ecological Renewal Images in "Big Two Hearted River": Jack Pines and Fisher King. *The Hemingway Review.* 9.2: 142-144.

———. 1994b. Walking West: Eco-criticism. Nature Writing and Cultural Values. *NC Humanities.* 2.2: 35-51 (Spring/Summer 1994).

Smiley, Jane. 1991. *A Thousand Acres.* New York: Fawcett Columbine.

Tilghman, Christopher. 1990. On the Rivershore. *In a Father's Place.* New York: Harper Perennial.

Winkler, Karen J. Inventing a New Field: the Study of Literature About the Environment. The *Chronicle of Higher Education.* August 9, 1996: A89-9, 15.

14. Synthesis of Religious Faiths and Sustainable Development

Robert L. Wixom[1]

I looked upon the works of God in its visible creation and an awfulness covered me. . . . The produce of the earth is a gift from our gracious Creator. . . and to impoverish the earth now to support outward greatness appears to be an injury to the succeeding age.

–John Woolman

All things are connected like the blood which unites one family. Whatever befalls the earth befalls the people of the earth. We did not weave the web of life, we are merely a strand in it. Whatever we do to the web we do to ourselves.

–Chief Seattle

Abstract

This article describes numerous organizations and publications concerned with sustainable development. The task is to weave together the strands of religious motivation, environmental concerns, academic endeavors, and scientific observations. Connections are the keys to understanding these facets of our modern, complex, kaleidoscopic world. Choices on values and decisions on the next steps are also at stake. Which choices do we–individuals or society–select and follow?

[1] **Robert L. Wixom**, a graduate of Earlham College and the University of Illinois, has been on the faculty at the University of Arkansas, and the University of Missouri; currently he is professor emeritus of biochemistry. His lifelong membership in the Religious Society of Friends and interest in environmental concerns have been expressed for twenty-three years as clerk of Columbia Monthly Meeting's Environmental Concerns Committee; as member and past clerk of Illinois Yearly Meeting's Environmental Concerns Committee (1987 to date); as a member of Friends Committee on Unity with Nature Steering Committee; and as clerk of FCUN's UNCED Support Committee (1993 to 1996), which has become the Sustainability Committee. He is also a longtime member of Friends Association for Higher Education.

Introduction

The authors of the earlier chapters have brought breadth and depth to their topics. They have developed their subjects from the viewpoint of interaction of a broadly defined academic discipline and an environmental focus. With the exception of Henderson and Hansen in chapters 3 and 10, each author has a deep foundation in his/her spiritual beliefs as a Quaker. Indeed, it would be a serious oversight for this book to overlook the six interlocking triangles in figure 1. Any pair of aspects in figure 1 is incomplete; all four are needed in the search for truth and for the related values of insight, spiritual depth, moral vigor, and expressed justice. A triangle is the strongest mathematical or engineering shape for construction. Thus this final chapter focuses on the growing recognition among Friends and many other religious entities of our religious roots and spiritual power—the top part of the triangles in figure 1.

Figure 1. Four Emphases of Sustainability

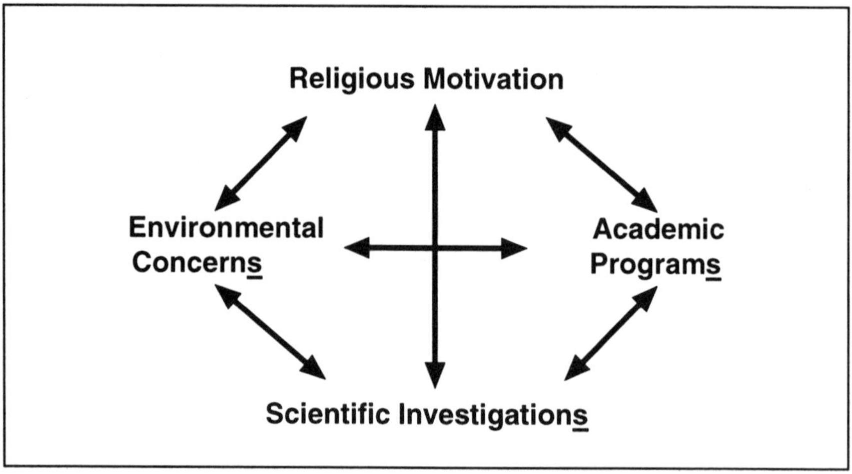

Environmental Concerns within the Religious Society of Friends

Friends Committee on Unity with Nature (FCUN) "is a spiritually-centered organization of North American Quakers and like-minded people seeking ways to integrate their concern for environment with Friends' long-standing testimonies for simplicity, peace, and equality" (FCUN 1987). The goals of FCUN were recorded in 1987 as:

- To search for the life which affirms the unity of all Creation
- To apply Friends' practice to live in deep communion with all life spirit
- To be guided by the Light within us to participate in the healing of the Earth
- To be a reflective and energetic forum within the Religious Society of Friends to strengthen and deepen our spiritual unity with nature.

The publications list of FCUN currently has seven flyers and five pamphlets/books (e.g., Lisa Gould, *Becoming a Friend to the Creation;* Elizabeth Watson, *Healing Ourselves and Our Earth;* Jack Phillips, *Walking Gently on the Earth;* Bill Howenstine, *Loving the Universe;* and Stan Becker and Cynthia Kerman, eds., *On World Population),* plus a variety of leaflets.

FCUN's *Becoming a Friend to the Creation: Earthcare Leaven for Friends and Friends Meetings* (Gould 1994) is an excellent anthology of Quaker environmental writings, including minutes and short testimonials, "Queries on Earthcare," "Other Sources of Inspiration," and "The Earth and the Bible," and a wonderful, thorough section on "Resources for Friends": videos, tapes, poetry, natural history writers, materials for children, bibliographies of scientific and practical books, and directories of environmental organizations. In Gould (1994), Steven Davison has developed an invaluable anthology of Old and New testaments, grouping 153 passages into "9½ Principles of Christian Stewardship," an excellent compilation for Friends and others who are rusty with their Bible sources. Another section compiles the names of beautiful Earth-caring hymns, songs, and singing graces. If singing is not your cup of tea, see the suggested games. In many ways, *Becoming a Friend to the Creation* is a predecessor and an invaluable complementary resource for the present book.

New England Yearly Meeting. Within the Religious Society of Friends is a long-standing practice of spiritual search for Divine guidance, an inner struggle for thoughts and words to express these inspirations, and then recording of the accepted message by one of our Yearly Meetings (a regional gathering) as a corporate minute. The 1991 minute of New England Yearly Meeting states,

> Cultivating a deeper awareness of connectedness with all of Creation enables us to live more Spirit-filled lives. Such awareness brings us great joy, reminds us of God's presence in everything around us, leads to greater clarity and acceptance of ourselves as God's creatures, and helps us avoid the traps of busyness and striving after material things. Failure to respect the sanctity and

interdependence of all Creation is a root of war, social oppression, and environmental destruction. . . .

As we strive to live in the awareness of connectedness, we become more sensitive to the consequences of our words, deeds, and attitudes, and we enter a deeper, more joyous relationship with God. We ask Friends, individually and corporately, to affirm our connectedness with all Creation, and to consider how "the Spirit of Christ, by which we are guided," can help us live in a more loving association with the Earth and its inhabitants. (Gould 1994)

Illinois Yearly Meeting. Illinois Yearly Meeting in 1987 appointed an Ad Hoc Committee on Environmental Concerns:

. . . to seek a harmonious unity with our environment. We see this activity as primarily a matter of sacred and spiritual importance. We have been given only one precious, unique and beautiful world. To assure its continuing life, we must now make very basic changes in the way we humans live on and in it. . . . (Illinois Yearly Meeting Minutes, 1987)

This committee's work led to a set of four environmental queries in the 1988 Illinois Yearly Meeting Minutes and later annual reports.

Gould (1994) reported some twelve other such corporate Minutes from other organized Friends gatherings, as well as devotional writings by individual Friends. In addition to personal expression by these authors, each mentions concerns for the environment by individual Friends over the past 300 years.

The above Minutes and publications imply a greater acceptance of environmental concerns by the Religious Society of Friends than may be warranted at this date. Indeed, the recent past clerk of Friends Committee on Unity with Nature, Ted Bernard (1995) concludes that while there may be an emerging environmental consciousness within Quakerism, he "would not call it a movement. The radical witness which aroused Quakers in the time of other crises (abolition in pre-Civil War days, conscientious objection to war throughout its 300-year lifetime, etc.) is not out there yet." He suggests that the smallness of FCUN has provoked only a tepid response by the larger Religious Society of Friends. Undoubtedly there are strong local or regional areas, as well as weak areas of expression. He quotes two other Friends who suggest that the Society has afflictions of an exclusive (silent) worship and/or becoming comfortably moderate. Then Bernard (1995) makes several suggestions for a Quaker arousal on religion and the environment.

This tepid response may or may not be different from that of other major religious faiths (see next sections). Another possible interpretation is the decentralized nature of the Religious Society of Friends—five separate major national groups that include regional groups ("Yearly Meetings") and local congregations ("Monthly Meetings"). The separations of over a hundred years ago were based on earlier differences in expressions of faith, religious practices, and regional history; the five major groups may understand and tolerate their differences, but they have not healed the gaps to speak with one clear voice on a variety of religious/social issues (some meetings, for instance, belong to the World Council of Churches, but not to the National Council of Churches).

Friends Committee on National Legislation. Friends Committee on National Legislation (FCNL) developed a Policy Statement in 1987, "We seek an Earth restored. . . ." and then revised it in 1994 as one of four parts of their Statement on Legislative Policy:

- We seek a world free of war and the threat of war. . . .
- We seek a society with equity and justice for all. . . .
- We seek a community where every person's potential may be fulfilled. . . .
- We seek an Earth restored. . . .

We recognize the intrinsic value of the natural world as God's creation, beyond its use by humankind. We belong to the intricate web connecting all that is natural. Therefore, we are bound at times to respect purposes not our own. We are also bound to be faithful stewards of the means of human survival and well-being. We are grateful for the blessings of this Earth and make a solemn commitment to protect and restore a sustainable natural environment. To peoples of other nations, we owe a renewed commitment to curb our own excessive consumption and pollution. We are mindful of Friends' historic testimonies regarding simple living and of our obligations for the right sharing of nature's gifts. These are urgent responsibilities, in both local and global settings. (Friends Committee on National Legislation 1994)

This FCNL policy is amplified in later pages to provide the needed specifics.

Quaker Pioneers. Quakers (Religious Society of Friends) were the first settlers in Philadelphia (1682) and were among the first in New Jersey and in North Carolina. As other Americans moved west in the late 1700s and early 1800s, Quakers were pioneers in Ohio, Indiana, Illinois, and Iowa. Thus Quakers in the eighteenth and nineteenth centuries had a long, close reliance on farming, the soil that nurtures crops and farm animals, and the surrounding diversity of life and rural communities in the above states and elsewhere in the 1900s. The nineteenth century shift to urban life, the professions, and white-collar employment affected all rural church groups, including the Quakers.

Rural Life Association. My years at Earlham College (a Quaker college) were influenced by Stanley Hamilton, founder and practical visionary of the Rural Life Movement. For the late 1930s, he and others observed that "for the Ohio Quaker farms, the older people are dying off, the younger people are leaving, and the farms are being bought up and added to larger places. . ." (Hamilton 1968). Such observations led to an invited 1943 conference at Earlham College, Richmond, Indiana, of the rural leaders for the Brethren, Mennonites, and Quakers; several Catholic leaders also had an early influential role. Though only 60 people were expected, 120 came! This conference led to the 1943 formation of the Rural Life Association (RLA). Stanley Hamilton became the executive secretary, with an office at Quaker Hill, Richmond, Ind. Their program emphasized the family farm, rural churches, and small communities; they developed pamphlets and a specialized lending library and grew slowly to about 1,200 members. Their major achievements included a considerable post-World War II food relief program for the devastated areas of Europe, the Heifer Project, CARE, and the Christian Rural Overseas Program. Stanley Hamilton died in the mid-1960s, and RLA was laid down in 1968 (*Rural Life Association Papers* 1968). Though this was a sad demise, some Quakers in the present Friends Committee on Unity with Nature continue the spiritual concern for rural life, farming and a connection to Creation/the Creator.

Environmental Concerns Among Religious Scholars

Prior to the recent writings of the "ecological spirituality" movement stands the devotional message of Liberty Hyde Bailey, professor of horticulture, 1888–1903; dean of the New York State College of Agriculture, Cornell University (1903–1913); and past president of the American Association of the Advancement of Science (1926). Bailey grew up on a farm "cut from the forest" and was surrounded by woodsmen, settlers, pioneers, Indians, and passenger pigeons. He wrote, "Nature repairs and reconstructs itself. It provides its own healing." This inspired agriculture teacher also recorded a lifetime of experience saying,

> The earth is not selfish. It is open and free to all. It invites everywhere. The naturalist is not selfish; he shares all his joys and discoveries. . . . We are to recognize the essential integrity of the farming occupation, when developed constructively, as contrasted with the vast system of improbity and dishonor that arises from depredation and from the taking of booty. . . . The freedom

of the earth is not the freedom of license; there is always the thought of the others that are dependent on it. It is the freedom of utilization for needs and natural desires, without regard to one's place among one's fellows, or even to one's condition of degradation or state of sinfulness. All men are the same when they come back to the meadows, to the hills, and to the deep woods. . . . (Bailey 1943, reprinted 1988)

From this viewpoint, Bailey considers the relationship of the farmer, the neighbor, the daily fare, warfare, industry, the forest, the reformatories, and open spaces, in a practical, but also beautiful rhythm. Thus the reemergence and reliance of Bailey's book in the present day Methodist Rural Life Movement is not a surprise. This writer notes the spiritual kinship in the writings of L. H. Bailey and Stanley Hamilton.

The ferment of environmental concerns (from about 1970 to date) has led religious scholars to examine their faith roots and find relationships. While only five (Kinsley, Berry, DeWitt, Nash, and Hessel) are mentioned in this section, they are representative of other writings.

David Kinsley, a professor at McMaster University, has written a recent book, *Ecology and Religion* (1995), which documents the Bible and Christianity as "constituting primarily negative influences in the advent and development of contemporary ecological crises. . . . " He describes the process where "nature is stripped of its gods, goddesses, and spirits and ceases to be regarded as divine." The domination of nature and anthropocentric emphasis are rooted in the Old Testament (cf. Gen. 1:26–29, Gen. 9:1–3, Ps. 8:5–8 and others). These texts were reinforced by later Christian writers: Origen, Thomas Aquinas, St. Bonaventure, Dante Aligheri, Martin Luther, John Calvin, Francis Bacon, Rene Descartes, and others (see Kinsley 1995). However, this "mastery hypothesis" ignores the respect for the natural world found in Ps. 96:11–13, Ps. 104:8–22, Ps. 121:1–8 or Ps. 148:1–13; the many passages of Augustine and Francis of Assisi; and the views of Albert Schweitzer (Kinsley 1995). Indeed, God "makes Noah the first conservationist by ordering him to save all living things" (Gen. 6:19; 7:14; 8:17; see an extension to every living creature in Gen. 9:9) (Davison 1994). Steven Davison's "9½ Principles of Christian Earth Stewardship" (in Gould 1994) compiles biblical passages that pertain to caring for the Earth.

Western "civilization" for about three hundred years has been preoccupied with the attitude of domination and manipulation of nature for human ends. The myths of gradual progress and evolution of the human species toward perfection, coupled with science and technology, led many in both Christian establishments and mainline sciences to regard the control of nature as a divine imperative. Of course there were early exceptions, such as the lives and written messages of Henry David Thoreau, John Muir, and Aldo Leopold (see Kinsley 1995, chap. 11); in many respects they indirectly stimulated the later synthesis, now known as "ecological spirituality." Though their titles and specific content may vary, there seems to be an underlying major congruence in the writings of Wesley Granberg-Michaelson (*A Worldly Spirituality*, 1984), Sallie McFague (*Models of God*, 1987), Thomas Berry (*The Dream of the Earth*, 1988), Matthew Fox (*The Coming of the Cosmic Christ*, 1988), Douglas John Hall (*The Steward: A Biblical Symbol Comes of Age*, 1990), Michael Lerner (*Jewish Renewal–A Path to Healing and Transformation*, 1994), and others. Traditional cultures, such as Native American and Asian religious expressions, have writers and writings that have contributed to the above relatively recent moral and ethical congruence (Kinsley 1995).

Thomas Berry, director of the Riverdale Center for Religious Research, New York City, is the author of the widely circulated and read book, *The Dream of the Earth* (1988). Berry, a Catholic priest, and John Yungblut, a Quaker scholar, were profoundly influenced by the writings of the Pierre Teilhard de Chardin (1881-1955), the French Jesuit paleontologist and author of *The Divine Milieu* (1960). The pertinent essence of Berry's recent thoughts follows:

> All the human modalities of being that have existed in the past are being proudly altered. We ourselves are being changed. . . . Unfortunately, there is no indication so far that Christians are beginning to think of this scale of change. Just as the planet is changing more than it has changed in such a long period of time, so the human order that brought about this change is being called to alter itself in an equally profound way. That is why I suggest that what is happening now to Christian theology, or any theology or any religious life or any moral code, is the most profound change that has taken place during the past 5,000 years. . . . This includes Christian civilization. It includes the total religious experience of the human. It includes all experiences of the human. We can never do without these accomplishments. They will have a major role in shaping the future. But they have to change on an order in which they have never changed before. Teilhard de Chardin (1881–1955) gave expression to the greatest transformation in Christian thought since the time of St. Paul. . . . (Berry 1988)

Calvin B. DeWitt, a professor of environmental studies at the University of Wisconsin at Madison and director of the AuSable Institute for Environmental Studies, delineates the Seven Degradations of Creation (the familiar ones—species extinction, land abuse, etc.). DeWitt (1944) then describes the "Seven Provisions of the Creator" (energy exchange, soil building, cycling of water and carbon, water purification, creative fruitfulness, global circulating of water and air, and the human ability to learn from Creation). "The Creator, in providing for us and all people, has given us minds and nurturing cultures that allows us to imagine and know how the world works. We human beings have been granted the ability to know Creation and to act upon that knowledge. . . " (DeWitt 1994). For him, the Biblical teachings may be simplified to restoration, fruitfulness, contentment, priority of kingdom, and obedience to God. By observing the steps—awareness, appreciation and stewardship—we can fulfill our ultimate purpose, "to honor God as Creator in such a way that Christian environmental stewardship is part and parcel of everything we do. Our goal is to make tending the garden of Creation, in all of its aspects, an unquestioned and all-pervasive aspect of our service to each other, to our community, and to God's world" (DeWitt 1994). Furthermore, DeWitt ticks off a list of practical environmental ideas that apply not only to churches, but to denominational colleges.

James A. Nash, executive director, Churches' Center for Theology and Public Policy, has written an excellent essay on the urgent need for the ecological reformation of our religious traditions. He stresses that the ecological crisis is a radical challenge to our religious and ethical foundations (Nash 1995). He includes comments on sustainability: "Nevertheless, sustainability seems to me to be critically important. No ecological ethic is adequate or acceptable which does not support sustainability. It expresses our trusteeship for future generations. . ." (Nash 1995).

Such other norms as equity, bioresponsibility, and frugality (Nash 1995) include a new conception of ethics, coherence with contemporary relevant sciences, and an affirmation of the moral functions of civil government. More specifically,

> Christianity's ecological potential is most clearly evident in the elementary and comprehensive affirmation of faith: God is love. This simple but not unrealistic claim has radical implications for ecological ethics. If God the Creator, Christ and Spirit is love, then the process of creation itself is an act of love. And all creatures, human and other kind, are not only gifts of love but products of love and ongoing beneficiaries of love. Since fidelity to God implies respect for divine affections, then Christians are called to be faithful images of God the Lover, to love everyone whom God loves—and that includes all forms of life, along with care for their necessary habitats. . . . (Nash 1995)

Dieter T. Hessel, a member of the Princeton Center on Theological Inquiry and director of an ecumenical program on Ecology, Justice, and

Faith, describes how the program of the World Council of Churches on "justice, peace and the integrity of Creation" has moved to "eco-justice," a new term which has gained acceptance and has been found useful in public discussion. Hessel (1995) describes four basic norms of eco-justice and ethics, namely:

- Solidarity with other people and creatures—companions, victims, and allies—in Earth community, reflective of deep respect for creation
- Ecologically sustainable (environmentally fitting) enterprise that applies appropriate technology on a human scale in the resource-use cycle
- Sufficiency as a standard of organized sharing, which requires basic floors and definite ceilings of equitable or "fair" consumption
- Just participation in decisions about how to obtain sustenance and to manage community life for the good in common and good of the commons ...
- A full-orbed understanding of sustainable society and community encompasses all four eco-justice norms as essential to a healthy future." (Hessel 1995)

Chapter 2 presents several definitions of sustainable development and sustainability. From a religious viewpoint, Hessel (1995) writes, "Sustainability means relating to the natural world so that its stability, integrity and beauty may be maintained. Sustainability also refers, to the stability and healthy functioning of social systems, which depend on natural systems. . . ."

Many people have relied on justice as a major moral value for a long time, both outside and inside the religious community. Hessel (1995) discusses the origin of the relatively new term "eco-justice":

The churches, and other major faith communities, were reluctant to commit to environmental ethics and activism, because the ecological-integrity agenda gained public prominence at a time and in a manner that seemed competitive with the struggle for social justice and peace. In fact, the idea of eco-justice— linking ecological integrity and social-economic equity—first originated in progressive North American religious circles as an ethic to bridge the two. ... Cultural historians looking back at the last half of the 20th century should be able to see that on the one hand, ecumenical theologians and ethicists had to relearn from the ecologists what creation really is, i.e., that nature and not only culture is real. But environmentalism lacked passion for, or adequate principles of, social justice. So it was up to the social ethicists of the ecumenical movement, informed by wise biologists, insightful social ecologists, and grass roots groups demanding environmental equity, to emphasize that we will not have ecological health without social justice, and vice versa. Having come to this realization, the ecumenical movement gradually developed a fulsome understanding of eco-justice. . . . (Hessel 1995)

Interdenominational Ferment on Environmental Concerns

World Council of Churches. The World Council of Churches (WCC) held a major "Conference of Faith, Science and the Future" in July 1979 at Massachusetts Institute of Technology. For this conference the WCC's Working Committee on Church and Society prepared *Faith, Science and the Future* (Albrecht, et al. 1978, 1979), with chapters by scientists, religious leaders, and their committee. The book has comprehensive chapters on the theological and ethical evaluation of science; energy; food and resources; environmental deterioration; population growth and the sustainable society; science and technology as power; and economic issues in the struggle for a just, participatory, and sustainable society. This book was presented to the 900 people participating in the conference. Paul Manglesdorf Jr., professor of physics at Swarthmore College, and two other Quakers attended the two-week conference. He has written a vivid description of the conference (Mangelsdorf 1979) and emphasized that for him and others, "Science and technology are not neutral or value-free, but are instruments of power, and that means political power. . . . How can they avoid being vehicles to perpetuate the structures of injustice and how can they open structures of social control to include all people." Though the word "sustainability" appeared in the chapter titles and text of this book, "the concept of sustainability" received no other discussion—a major contrast to today's prevalent usage.

The WCC Conference book includes the history of a 1974 Bucharest statement on a sustainable society that led to a 1976 WCC link of justice and sustainability, namely:

The twin issues around which the world's future revolves are justice and ecology. "Justice" points to the necessity of correcting maldistribution of the products of the earth and of bridging the gap between rich and poor countries. "Ecology" points to humanity's dependence upon the earth. Society must be so organized as to sustain the earth so that a sufficient quality of material and cultural life for humanity may itself be sustained indefinitely. A sustainable society which is unjust can hardly be worth sustaining. A just society that is unsustainable is self-defeating. Humanity now has the responsibility to make a deliberate transition to a just and sustainable global society. (Albrecht 1978, 1979)

The decade prior to UNCED and the post-UNCED years have seen major changes and activities in the churches and synagogues of the United States (Albrecht 1978, 1979). Five interdenominational environmental associations are working on sustainable development issues:

National Council of Churches of Christ. The member groups of the National Council of Churches of Christ (NCCC) formed in 1983 an Eco-Justice Working Group "to mobilize congregations around eco-justice issues." Jean Sindab provided long and distinguished leadership as program director until her death in January 1996. She was a leader in the Citizens Network on Sustainabile Development and a key planner in the National Black Church Summit on "Environmental and Economic Justice" (Dec. 1-2, 1993), the Orthodox Christian leaders' summit on "The Earth is the Lords" (Nov. 3-4, 1995); and several 1995 regional conferences with a theme close to, "Make Your Church a Creation Awareness Center" (Chicago, Los Angeles, Columbia, Mo., and other cities). NCCC/EJP produced and distributed 10,000 copies of a resource packet, *"God's Earth, Our Home,"* edited by Shantilal Bhagat, Church of the Brethren (see appendix H). EJP working with NRPE has also mobilized congregations and sponsored tours/hearings.

North American Conference on Christianity and Ecology. The North American Conference on Christianity and Ecology (NACCE) started in 1986 as a programmatic organization and changed in 1993 to a networking group with a central clearinghouse for information and interchange. Its board is ecumenical. The current president, Elizabeth Updegraff Dyson, has a Quaker and Presbyterian background. NACCE defines its mission as:

- To encourage churches and faith communities to become centers of creation awareness and to teach reverence for God's creation
- To challenge individuals and congregations to engage their lives on behalf of creation through celebration, reflection and action
- To facilitate the formation of regional faith-based Earthkeeping ministries through conferences, consultations and workshops
- To link Earthkeeping ministries in an empowering network around North America
- To cooperate with all people of good will in the common effort to heal the Earth." (NACCE 1995)

NACCE has sponsored a series of regional networking conferences, has a speakers director, and has a bimonthly newsletter, *Earthkeeping News*, to provide an emphasis on grassroots church organizations.

North American Coalition on Religion and Ecology. The North American Coalition on Religion and Ecology (NACRE) started in 1989 and has the purpose of raising "the awareness of environmental degradation through America's religious communities" (Conroy 1995). They aim "to develop more informed understanding, a deeper commitment, a dynamic sense of environmental mission and to help the wider society understand the essential ethical and value dimension of the environmental movements" (NACRE's *EcoLetter*, 1992 and 1995). The newsletter of NACRE, *EcoLetter*, has a mosaic of articles, such as the "Declaration of Sacred Earth Gathering" (Rio 1992, UNCED), "The 1992 Global Forum," "A Celebration of Native American Survival," "The History of Earth Day," and "Energy Sufficiency, Technology and Sustainable Values." They have developed publications such as *Creation Liturgy, Earth Prayers, Celebrating Earth Holy Days, Environmental Education and Ministry, World's Religions and Ecology,* and *Religion's Role in Preserving the Environment.*

NACRE's programs include an annual fall program, "Caring for Creation," which emphasizes global stewardship, and a habitat program for local congregations and communities. NACRE also has a Leadership Education Program for Global Stewardship to empower the clergy and secular leaders, and an Eco-Ethics and Public Policy Program to identify emerging global social change (NACRE's *EcoLetter*, Fall 1992).

National Religious Partnership for the Environment. During the late 1980s, several national religious denominations embarked on environmental study and action. To encourage other faith groups and denominations to examine the environmental agenda, thirty-four prominent scientists, including Carl Sagan, the well-known astronomer from Cornell University, released "An Open Letter to the Religious Community" (January 1990) on the peril to planetary ecology. "Problems of such magnitude and solutions demanding so broad a perspective must be recognized from the outset as having a religious as well as a scientific dimension" (NRPE 1994). Religious and political leaders responded, began many shared discussions, and made a joint appeal to encourage national religious bodies to initiate environmental programs, to measure interest in grassroots religious environmental activity and to facilitate formal consultations between religious leaders and scientists. Thus leaders from the religious, political, and environmental areas in the Joint Appeal consulted and concluded (June 2–3, 1991) that "We believe a consensus now exists, at the highest level of leadership across a significant spectrum of religious traditions, that the cause of environmental integrity and justice must occupy a position of utmost priority for people of faith" (NRPE 1994).

Further explorations during the following year led to the formation in May 11, 1992 of the National Religious Partnership for the Environment (NRPE), which has drawn together a collaboration of the United States Catholic Conference, the National Council of Churches of Christ, the Coalition on the Environment and Jewish Life (a coalition of major national organizations of American Judaism), and the Evangelical Environmental Network (an association of evangelical Christian bodies). They outlined objectives for a three-year program of action; prepared and received approval from their respective governing bodies on specific projects; developed a timetable; and, by mid-1993, had received foundation funding of $3 million. Their board of trustees includes fourteen religious leaders and two scientists (Carl Sagan and Henry Kendall). The Partnerships Program "seeks to broaden exponentially the base of mainstream commitment, integrate the issues of social justice and environmental concern, and urge behavioral changes in the lives of congregants" (NRPE 1995). Paul Gorman was selected as executive director of NRPE. Collaborative projects undertaken through the member groups during their Phase 1 (1993–96) include: clergy and lay leadership training programs; legislative updates; and testimony and action alerts, particularly those written on "environmental justice." Later, in Phase 2 (1996–99), they will explore joint initiatives with eminent scientists and their national scientific organizations, summit meetings for leaders of black and Orthodox Christian churches, environmental curricula, teleconferences, videos, etc.

Union of Concerned Scientists. NRPE is also unique in having a direct organizational connection with scientists, namely the Union of Concerned Scientists (UCS). This organization, which began in 1969, has a staff of about sixty, a membership of about 80,000, a 1996 budget of about $4.8 million, and a newsletter, *Nucleus*. UCS has worked to curtail nuclear weapons, to minimize their production, to curtail the aftereffects of the Three Mile Island nuclear power plant accident, to demilitarize international conflict, and to promote renewable safe and cost effective energy technologies.

In 1994, UCS issued a statement, "World Scientists' Warning to Humanity," with signatures from 1,600 distinguished scientists around the world (UCS 1994; see appendix G), which led to a new UCS focus and related program to encourage responsible stewardship of the global environment, its life-sustaining resources, and the promotion of sustainable agriculture (UCS 1994). In working to present accurate information about global environmental issues to policymakers and the media, UCS has recently focused on biodiversity, climate change, ozone depletion, and population growth. The Science Office of NRPE, which is located at the UCS office, serves "as an essential resource for all program areas of the Partnership's mobilization" and as a "vehicle to sustain the dialogue between religious leaders and scientists (NRPE 1994). More specifically, the science director participates in NRPE's strategy meetings, provides current scientific information and public policy recommendations in formats accessible to people of faith communities, maintains a speakers bureau, and encourages opportunities for dialogue and fellowship of the faith communities.

Green Cross. The newest interdenominational entity, the Christian Society of the Green Cross, began in 1993 at a planning conference at the Carter Presidential Centre in Atlanta to be "a biblically-based ecology action organization created to promote Earth healing." Green Cross (its short name) was incubated by NACCE and twenty other Christian organizations, many of which are cited in appendix I. Their short motto is, "serving and keeping creation." Their mission statement declares,

> As followers of Jesus Christ, we join in the restoration of God's creation and the formation of new ecologically responsible life-styles through: (1) assessing our values in light of Scripture; (2) learning to think, talk and act responsibly; and (3) creating new Earth-keeping opportunities for our lives, churches and communities. . . .

One of their key themes "will involve each chapter taking spiritual and ecological responsibility for a self-defined area." Their executive committee includes Job Ebenezer (ELCA), Cal DeWitt, Mel West (UMRF), and Paul Thompson (World Vision , Monrovia, Calif.) (see appendix I for these acronyms). The director of Green Cross is Frederick Krueger (see appendix I). Green Cross has a quarterly magazine, *Green Cross*, a special thirty-page issue on endangered species, a *Chapter Handbook*, and a publication program (see *Fruits of Creation, The Lord's House: A Guide to Creation Careful Management of Church Facilities, Thorns in the Garden Planet*, and eight other books). Green Cross has work projects and has initiated chapters on college campuses.

To summarize, the synergy of religious communities, whether Catholic, Jewish, or Protestant groups, and the environmental movements has commenced in a major way and can be facilitated by writing directly to one or more of these vital organizations (see appendix I, parts 1 and 2).

Several years hence the subject should be reviewed to assess the outreach of these programs. Another subject open for exploration is the connections of religious communities and environmental movements with their respective denominational colleges and universities.

Concern and Commitment within Denominational Groups

Simultaneously with the rise of the above interdenominational groups has been the development over the past decade of the denominational environmental committees, teams, networks or programs. To prepare this chapter, I have corresponded or telephoned with many respective church leaders within the Brethren, Catholics, Friends, Episcopalians, Lutherans, Methodists, Presbyterians, and the United Church of Christ. A beautiful panoply of ideas, devotions, programs, and resources is available through the groups described in appendix I, part 2. Unfortunately, space prevents a longer description of each group. The mission of one group, **Presbyterians for Restoring Creation,** follows:

- To seek support and implementation of Restoring Creation through all the agencies and ministries within the church
- To foster networks of Presbyterians of all walks of life in order to share gifts and skills for restoring and preserving creation for future generations
- To cooperate with others who are actively engaged in living lightly on the earth through ecumenical, national and community environmental/justice organizations
- In all, to be faithful to the call of our Redeemer, Jesus Christ.

As another example of outreach, the **Environmental Justice Program of the United States Catholic Conference** distributed a quite comprehensive parish resource kit, "Renewing the Face of the Earth," in 1994 and another kit, "Peace with God the Creator—Peace with All Creation," in 1995 to about 180 dioceses for about 18,000 parishes. In response to Pope John Paul II's messages on overdevelopment and materialism, EJP has a new project on Consumption Study, along with small grants, scholar's consultations, videos, public policy/legislation, and network activity.

For further information on each religious group, write to the appropriate address in appendix I, parts 1 and 2. The reader should note that a parallel section, "Concern and Commitment among College Students," is presented in chapter 11.

To conclude, this chapter and its interconnecting triangles (figure 1) have aimed to "close the loop" from values (penetrating insights, spiritual depth, moral vigor and expressed justice) to ecological integrity, environmental concerns, and sustainability. These considerations plus related scientific observations are pertinent to the academic disciplines and programs presented in other earlier chapters. Each factor helps connect and rebuild the needed "web of life."

Overall Summary for This Book

Academic and religious leaders, along with their respective organizations, curators, trustees, and governing boards, are invited to join with others in this challenging, multidisciplinary teaching endeavor. Many professors and some departments or colleges have already begun these tasks. We, professors and administrators, are called to be faithful participants in the proposed changes in values, attitudes, and teaching content, and to understand the resources placed in our Garden, or planet, our home on this Earth.

Literature Cited

Albrecht, Paul, et al., eds. 1978, 1979. *Faith, Science and the Future.* Philadelphia: World Council of Churches and Fortress Press.

Bailey, Liberty Hyde. 1943, 1988. *The Holy Earth.* Reprint. Columbus, Ohio: National United Methodist Rural Fellowship.

Bernard, Ted. 1995. Reconnecting with Radical Quaker Witness for the Earth. *BeFriending Creation,* Vol. 5, 3-4.

Berry, Thomas. 1988. *The Dream of the Earth.* San Francisco: Sierra Club Books.

Berry, Thomas and Thomas Clarke. 1991. *BeFriending the Earth–A Theology of Reconciliation Between Humans and the Earth.* Mystic, Conn.: Twenty-Third Publications.

Boulding, Elise. 1989. *One Small Plot of Heaven.* Wallingford, Pa.: Pendle Hill Publications.

Davison, Steven. 1994. 9½ Principles of Earth Stewardship–Scripture References. In *Becoming a Friend to the Creation–Earthcare Leaven for Friends and Friends Meetings,* edited by Lisa L. Gould. Burlington, Vt.: Friends Committee on Unity with Nature.

DeWitt, Calvin B. 1994. *Earth-Wise–A Biblical Response to Environmental Issues.* Grand Rapids, Mich.: CRC Publications.

Fox, Matthew. 1988. *The Coming of the Cosmic Christ.* San Francisco: Harper and Row.

Friends Committee on Unity with Nature. 1987. FCUN Goals, etc. Burlington, Vt.: Friends Committee on Unity with Nature.

Friends Committee on National Legislation. 1987, 1994. Statement of Legislative Policy. Washington, D.C.: Friends Committee on National Legislation.

Gould, Lisa L., ed. 1994. *Becoming a Friend to the Creation: Earthcare Leaven for Friends and Friends Meetings.* Burlington, Vt.: Friends Committee on Unity with Nature.

Granberg-Michaelson, Wesley. 1984. *A Worldly Spirituality.* San Francisco: Harper and Row.

Hall, Douglas John. 1990. *The Steward: A Biblical Symbol Come of Age.* Grand Rapids, Mich.: Eerdmans Publishing Co.

Hamilton, Stanley. 1968. *Rural Life Association Papers.* Richmond, Ind.: Friends Collection, Box 1, Lilly Library, Earlham College.

Hessel, Dieter A. 1995. Religion and Ethics to Meet the Environmental Challenge, p. 30. In *Proceedings of a Conference, 'Just and Sustainable Community–A Conference on Environmental Values,' June 1–2, 1995,* edited by Betty Little and Franklin Vilas. Chatham, N. J.: Partners for Environmental Quality.

Illinois Yearly Meeting. 1987. Minutes for Annual Session, July 29–August 2, 1987. McNabb, Ill.: Illinois Yearly Meeting.

Kinsley, David. 1995. *Ecology and Religion–Ecological Spirituality in Cross-Cultural Perspective.* Englewood Cliffs, N. J.: Prentice Hall.

Lerner, Michael. 1994. *Jewish Renewal.* New York: Putnam's Sons.

Mangelsdorf, Paul. 1979. Faith, Science and the Future. *Friends Journal,* Vol. 25, No. 19, 14-17.

McFague, Sallie. 1987. *Models of God: Theology for an Ecological, Nuclear Age.* Philadelphia: Fortress Press.

North American Coalition on Religion and Ecology. *EcoLetter* (newsletter).. Series of environment-related articles, 1992, 1995. Washington, D.C.: North American Coalition on Religion and Ecology.

Nash, James A. 1995. An Urgent Need: The Ecological Reformation of Our Religious Tradition. In *Proceedings of a Conference, 'Just and Sustainable Community–A Conference on Environmental Values,' June 1–2, 1995,* edited by Betty Little and Franklin Vilas. Chatham, N. J.: Partners for Environmental Quality. See also his 1991 *Loving Nature: Ecological Integrity and Christian Responsibility.* Nashville: Abingdon Press.

National Religious Partnership for the Environment. 1994. Statement of goals; history and organizational background; and goals of the Science Office. NRPE, UCS; plus oral information from Dr. Charles Puccia, science director for NRPE. Cambridge, Mass.: National Religious Partnership for the Environment.

North American Conference on Christianity and Ecology. 1995. *Earth Keeping News* (newsletter). Saint Paul, Minn.: North American Conference on Christianity and Ecology.

Oelschlaeger, Max. 1994. *Caring for Creation– An Ecumenical Approach to the Environmental Crisis.* New Haven: Yale University Press.

Phillips, Jack. 1994. Preface to 'The Earth and the Bible'. In *Becoming a Friend to the Creation: Earthcare Leaven for Friends and Friends' Meetings,* edited by Lisa L. Gould, 55. Burlington, Vt.: Friends Committee on Unity with Nature.

Teilhard de Chardin, Pierre. 1965. *Hymn of the Universe.* English trans. by Simon Bartholomew. New York: Harper and Row.

———. 1960. *The Divine Milieu—An Essay on the Interior Life.* New York: Harper.

Union of Concerned Scientists. 1994. *World Scientists' Warning to Humanity; World Scientists Warning Briefing Book;* and subsequent newsletters. Cambridge: Union of Concerned Scientists.

Woolman, John. 1720-72. *The Journal of John Woolman*, edited by Amelia Mott Gurnmere. New York: McMillan, 1922, 157,462.

Appendix A

Purposes and Goals of
Friends Association for Higher Education and
Friends Committee on Unity with Nature

The purpose of **Friends Association for Higher Education** shall be to strengthen the Quaker mission in higher education by:

- Providing a supportive relationship and opportunities for fellowship among all who share Quaker ideals of higher education, whether on Quaker or non-Quaker campuses
- Enhancing members' appreciation of Friends' religious heritage and nurturing the individual and corporate search for Truth
- Lending support to the Quaker ideal of integrating spiritual commitment, academic excellence and social responsibility
- Lending support and encouragement to scholarly research directed toward perceiving and achieving a more perfect human society
- Helping to clarify and articulate the distinctively Quaker vision of higher education, in terms of both curriculum and teaching
- Assisting Friends colleges in their efforts to affirm their Quaker heritage
- Fostering greater communication and cooperation among Friends educational institutions and the various Friends constituencies to which they may be connected.

The goals of **Friends Committee on Unity with Nature:**

- To search for the life which affirms the unity of all Creation
- To apply Friends' practice to live in deep communion with all life spirit
- To be guided by the Light within us to participate in the healing of the Earth
- To be a reflective and energetic forum within the Religious Society of Friends to strengthen and deepen our spiritual unity with nature.

[Note. The addresses for FAHE and FCUN are in the front of this book. Please see **Foreword** for further comment.]

Appendix B

Twenty-Seven Principles of the *Earth Charter* (UNCED)*

Preamble

The United Nations Conference on Environment and Development, having met at Rio de Janeiro from 3 to 14 June 1992, reaffirming the Declaration of the UN Conference on the Human Environment, adopted at Stockholm on 16 June 1972, and seeking to build upon it, with the goal of establishing a new and equitable global partnership through the creation of new levels of cooperation among States, key sectors of societies and people, working towards international agreements which respect the interests of all and protect the integrity of the global environmental and developmental system, recognizing the integral and interdependent nature of the Earth, our home,

Proclaims that:

Principle 1: Human beings are at the centre of concerns for sustainable development. They are entitled to a healthy and productive life in harmony with nature.

Principle 2: States have, in accordance with the Charter of the United Nations and the principles of international law, the sovereign right to exploit their own resources pursuant to their own environmental and developmental policies, and the responsibility to ensure that activities within their jurisdiction or control do not cause damage to the environment of other States or of areas beyond the limits of national jurisdiction.

Principle 3: The right to development must be fulfilled so as to equitably meet developmental and environmental needs of present and future generations.

Principle 4: In order to achieve sustainable development, environmental protection shall constitute an integral part of the development process and cannot be considered in isolation from it.

Principle 5: All states and all people shall cooperate in the essential task of eradicating poverty as an indispensable requirement for sustainable development, in order to decrease the disparities in standards of living and better meet the needs of the majority of the people of the world.

Principle 6: The special situation and needs of developing countries, particularly the least developed and those most environmentally vulnerable, shall be given special priority. International actions in the field of environment and development should also address the interests and needs of all countries.

Principle 7: States shall cooperate in a spirit of global partnership to conserve, protect and restore the health and integrity of the Earth's ecosystem. In view of the different contributions to global environmental degradation, States have common but differentiated responsibilities. The developed countries acknowledge the responsibility that they bear in the international pursuit of sustainable development in view of the pressures their societies place on the global environment and of the technologies and financial resources they command.

Principle 8: To achieve sustainable development and a higher quality of life for all people, States should reduce and eliminate unsustainable patterns of production and consumption and promote appropriate demographic policies.

Principle 9: States should cooperate to strengthen endogenous capacity-building for sustainable development by improving scientific understanding through exchanges of scientific and technological knowledge, and by enhancing the development, adaptation, diffusion and transfer of technologies, including new and innovative technologies.

Principle 10: Environmental issues are best handled with the participation of all concerned citizens, at the relevant level. At the national level, each individual shall have appropriate access to information concerning the environment that is held by public authorities, including information on hazardous materials and activities in their communities, and the opportunity to participate in decision-making processes. States shall facilitate and encourage public awareness and participation by making information widely available. Effective access to judicial and administrative proceedings, including redress and remedy, shall be provided.

Principle 11: States shall enact effective environmental legislation. Environmental standards, management objectives and priorities should reflect the environmental and developmental context to which they apply. Standards applied by some countries may be inappropriate and of unwarranted economic and social cost to other countries, in particular developing countries.

Principle 12: States should cooperate to promote a supportive and open international economic system that would lead to economic growth and sustainable development in all countries, to better address the problems of environmental degradation. Trade policy measures for environmental purposes should not constitute a means of arbitrary or unjustifiable discrimination or a disguised restriction on international trade. Unilateral actions to deal with environmental challenges outside the jurisdiction of the importing country should be avoided. Environmental measures addressing transboundary or global environmental problems should, as far as possible, be based on international consensus.

Principle 13: States shall develop national law regarding liability and compensation for the victims of pollution and other environmental damage. States shall also cooperate in an expeditious and more determined manner to develop further international law regarding liability and compensation for adverse effects of environmental damage caused by activities within their jurisdiction or control to areas beyond their jurisdiction.

Principle 14: States should effectively cooperate to discourage or prevent the reloca-
tion and transfer to other States of any activities and substances that
cause severe environmental degradation or are found to be harmful to
human health.

Principle 15 : In order to protect the environment, the precautionary approach shall
be widely applied by States according to their capabilities. Where there
are threats of serious or irreversible damage, lack of full scientific certainty
shall not be used as a reason for postponing cost-effective measures to prevent environmental degradation.

Principle 16: National authorities should endeavor to promote the internalization of
environmental costs and the use of economic instruments, taking into
account the approach that the polluter should, in principle, bear the
cost of pollution, with due regard to the public interest and without distort-
ing international trade and
investments.

Principle 17: Environmental impact assessment, as a national instrument, shall be
undertaken for proposed activities that are likely to have a significant
adverse impact on the environment and are subject to a decision of a
competent national authority.

Principle 18: States shall immediately notify other States of any natural disasters or
other emergencies that are likely to produce sudden harmful effects on
the environment of those States. Every effort shall be made by the international community to help States so afflicted.

Principle 19: States shall provide prior and timely notification and relevant information to potentially affected States on activities that may have a significant adverse transboundary environmental effect and shall consult with
those States at an early stage and in good faith.

Principle 20: Women have a vital role in environmental management and development. Their full participation is therefore essential to achieve sustainable development.

Principle 21: The creativity, ideals and courage of the youth of the world should be
mobilized to forge a global partnership in order to achieve sustainable
development and ensure a better future for all.

Principle 22: Indigenous people and their communities, and other local communities, have a vital role in environmental management and development
because of their knowledge and traditional practices. States should recognize and duly support their identify, culture and interests and enable
their effective participation in the achievement of sustainable
development.

Principle 23: The environment and natural resources of people under oppression,
domination and occupation shall be protected.

Principle 24: Warfare is inherently destructive of sustainable development. States
shall therefore respect international law providing protection for the

environment in times of armed conflict and cooperate in its further development, as necessary.

Principle 25: Peace, development, and environmental protection are interdependent and indivisible.

Principle 26: States shall resolve all their environmental disputes peacefully and by appropriate means in accordance with the Charter of the United Nations.

Principle 27: States and people shall cooperate in good faith and in a spirit of partnership in the fulfillment of the principles embodied in this Declaration and in the further development of international law in the field of sustainable development.

*Derived from United Nations (1993) *Agenda 21.*

[See **chapters 1, 2, and 11** for comment.]

[Note. The correct name for these twenty-seven principles is the Rio Declaration on Environment and Development, which has also been loosely labeled the "Earth Charter." Many citizens feel that the substance of the Rio Declaration does not satisfy the concept of an Earth charter.]

222

Appendix C

Agenda 21 Contents (UNCED)*

*Derived from United Nations (1993) *Agenda 21.*

[See **chapters 1, 2, and 11** for comment.]

Appendix D

Principles on Population and Development*

The implementation of the recommendations contained in the Programme of Action is the sovereign right of each country, consistent with national laws and development priorities, with full respect for the various religious and ethical values and cultural backgrounds of its people, and in conformity with universally recognized international human rights.

International cooperation and universal solidarity, guide by the principles of the Charter of the United Nations, and in a spirit of partnership, are crucial in order to improve the quality of life of the peoples of the world.

In addressing the mandate of the International Conference on Population and Development and its overall theme, the interrelationships between population, sustained economic growth and sustainable development, and in their deliberations, the participants were and will continue to be guided by the following set of principles:

Principle 1: All human beings are born free and equal in dignity and rights. Everyone is entitled to all the rights and freedoms set forth in the Universal Declaration of Human Rights, without distinction of any kind, such as race, colour, sex, language, religion, political or other opinion, national or social origin, property, birth or other status. Everyone has the right to life, liberty and security of person.

Principle 2: Human beings are at the centre of concerns for sustainable development. They are entitled to a healthy and productive life in harmony with nature. People are the most important and valuable resource of any nation. Countries should ensure that all individuals are given the opportunity to make the most of their potential. They have the right to an adequate standard of living for themselves and their families, including adequate food, clothing, housing, water and sanitation.

Principle 3: The right to development is a universal and inalienable right and an integral part of fundamental human rights, and the human person is the central subject of development. While development facilitates the enjoyment of all human rights, the lack of development may not be invoked to justify the abridgment of internationally recognized human rights. The right to development must be fulfilled so as to equitably meet the population, development and environment needs of present and future generations.

Principle 4: Advancing gender equality and equity and the empowerment of women, and the elimination of all kinds of violence against women, and ensuring women's ability to control their own fertility, are cornerstones of population and development-related programmes. The human rights of women and the girl child are an inalienable, integral and indivisible part of universal human rights. The full and equal participation of women in civil, cultural, economic, political and social life, at the national, regional and international levels, and the eradication of all forms of discrimination on grounds of sex, are priority objectives of the international community.

Principle 5: Population-related goals and policies are integral parts of cultural, economic and social development, the principal aim of which is to improve the quality of life of all people.

Principle 6: Sustainable development as a means to ensure human well-being, equitably shared by all people today and in the future, required that the interrelationships between population, resources, the environment and development should be fully recognized, properly managed and brought into harmonious, dynamic balance. To achieve sustainable development and a higher quality of life for all people, States should reduce and eliminate unsustainable patterns of production and consumption and promote appropriate policies, including population-related policies, in order to meet the needs of current generations without compromising the ability of future generations to meet their own needs.

Principle 7: All States and all people shall cooperate in the essential task of eradicating poverty as an indispensable requirement for sustainable development, in order to decrease the disparities in standards of living and better meet the needs of the majority of the people of the world. The special situation and needs of developing countries, particularly the least developed, shall be given special priority. Countries with economies in transition, as well as all other countries, need to be fully integrated into the world economy.

Principle 8: Everyone has the right to the enjoyment of the highest attainable standard of physical and mental health. States should take all appropriate measures to ensure, on a basis of equality of men and women, universal access to health-care service, including those related to reproductive health care, which includes family planning and sexual health. Reproductive health-care programmes should provide the widest range of services without any form of coercion. All couples and individuals have the basic right to decide freely and responsibly the number and spacing of their children and to have the information, education and means to do so.

Principle 9: The family is the basic unit of society and as such should be strengthened. It is entitled to receive comprehensive protection and support. In different cultural, political and social systems, various forms of the family exist. Marriage must be entered into with the free consent of the intending spouses, and husband and wife should be equal partners.

Principle 10: Everyone has the right to education, which shall be directed to the full development of human resources, and human dignity and potential, with particular attention to women and the girl child. Education should be designed to strengthen respect for human rights and fundamental freedoms, including those relating to population and development. The best interests of the child shall be the guiding principle of those responsible for his or her education and guidance; that responsibility lies in the first place with the parents.

Principle 11: All States and families should give the highest possible priority to children. The child has the right to standards of living adequate for its well-being and the right to the highest attainable standards of health, and the right to education. The child has the right to be cared for, guided and supported by parents, families and society and to be protected by appropriate legislative, administrative, social and educational measures from all forms of physical or mental violence, injury or abuse, neglect or negligent treatment, maltreatment or exploitation, including sale, trafficking, sexual abuse, and trafficking in its organs.

Principle 12: Counties receiving documented migrants should provide proper treatment and adequate social welfare services for them and their families, and should ensure their physical safety and security, bearing in mind the special circumstances and needs of countries, in particular developing countries, attempting to meet these objectives or requirements with regard to undocumented migrants, in conformity with the provisions of relevant conventions and international instruments and documents. Countries should guarantee to all migrants all basic human rights as included in the Universal Declaration of Human Rights.

Principle 13: Everyone has the right to seek and to enjoy in other countries asylum from persecution. States have responsibilities with respect to refugees as set forth in the Geneva Convention on the Status of Refugees and its 1967 Protocol.

Principle 14: In considering the population and development needs of indigenous people, States should recognize and support their identity, culture and interests, and enable them to participate fully in the economic, political and social life of the country, particularly where their health, education and well-being are affected.

Principle 15: Sustained economic growth, in the context of sustainable development, and social progress require that growth be broadly based, offering equal opportunities to all people. All countries should recognize their common but differentiated responsibilities. The developed countries acknowledge the responsibility that they bear in the international pursuit of sustainable development, and should continue to improve their efforts to promote sustained economic growth and to narrow imbalances in a manner that can benefit all countries, particularly the developing countries.

*Derived from United Nations, 1995. *Population and Development.* Report of the International Conference on Population and Development—Programme of Action, Cairo, Egypt, September 5-13, 1994.

[See **chapters 2** and **5** for comment.]

Appendix E

Principles of the President's Council on Sustainable Development (PCSD)*

We Believe Statement

There are certain beliefs that we as Council members share that underlie all of our agreements. We believe:

1 To achieve our vision of sustainable development, some things must grow—jobs, productivity, wages, capital and savings, profits, information, knowledge, and education—and others—pollution, waste, and poverty—must not.

2 Change is inevitable and necessary for the sake of future generations and for ourselves. We can choose a course for change that will lead to the mutually reinforcing goals of economic growth, environmental protection, and social equity.

3 Steady progress in reducing disparities in education, opportunity, and environmental risk within society is essential to economic growth, environmental health, and social justice.

4 The United States made great progress in protecting the environment in the last 25 years, and must continue to make progress in the next 25 years. We can achieve that goal because market incentives and the power of consumers can lead to significant improvements in environmental performance at less cost.

5 Economic growth based on technological innovation, improved efficiency, and expanding global markets is essential for progress toward greater prosperity, equity, and environmental quality.

6 Environmental regulations have improved and must continue to improve the lives of all Americans. Basic standards of performance that are clear, fair, and consistently enforced remain necessary to protect that progress. The current regulatory system should be improved to deliver required results at lower costs. In addition, the system should provide enhanced flexibility in return for superior environmental performance.

7 Environmental progress will depend on individual, institutional, and corporate responsibility, commitment, and stewardship.

8 We need a new collaborative decision process that leads to better decisions; more rapid change; and more sensible use of human, natural, and financial resources in achieving our goals.

9 The nation must strengthen its communities and enhance their role in decisions about environment, equity, natural resources, and economic progress so that the individuals and institutions most immediately affected can join with others in the decision process.

10 Economic growth, environmental protection, and social equity are linked. We need to develop integrated policies to achieve these national goals.

11 The United States should have policies and programs that contribute to stabilizing global human population; this objective is crucial if we hope to have the resources needed to ensure a high quality of life for future generations.

12 Even in the face of scientific uncertainty, society should take reasonable actions to avert risks where the potential harm to human health or the environment is thought to be serious or irreparable.

13 Steady advances in science and technology are essential to help improve economic efficiency, protect and restore natural systems, and modify consumption patterns.

14 A growing economy and healthy environment are essential to national and global security.

15 A knowledgeable public, the free flow of information, and opportunities for review and redress are critically important to open, equitable, and effective decisionmaking.

16 Citizens must have access to high-quality and lifelong formal and nonformal education that enables them to understand the interdependence of economic prosperity, environmental quality, and social equity—and prepares them to take actions that support all three.

*Derived from *PCSD Final Report* (1996).

[See **chapter 2** for comment.]

Appendix F

Message to the Academic Community*

Whereas the students have the responsibility to make themselves aware of environmental issues and problems threatening their future, and

Whereas the upcoming generations will inherit the ecological problems of past generations, and must work to rectify these problems and prevent future problems from escalating, so that our children will have a planet to live on; and

Whereas the students of today will be the leaders of tomorrow, and must make decisions regarding the well-being of our Earth and its inhabitants,

We, the members and supporters of the **Student Earth Day Coalition,** do hereby make the following recommendations to the **students of the University of Missouri,** in response to the support of Earth Day 1990 and the environment as a whole:

1. Take an active role in environmental activities as organizations.
2. Reuse all non-renewable resources and products.
3. Reduce your energy consumption (water, electricity, fossil fuels, etc.).
4. Recycle all possible resources and materials.
5. Support environmentally sound businesses, products, legislation, organizations, etc., and become aware of what these are.

Whereas the faculty has the power to influence student knowledge, thought, attitudes and actions concerning environmental issues,

We, the members and supporters of the **Student Earth Day Coalition,** do hereby make the following recommendations to the **faculty of the University of Missouri,** in response to the support of Earth Day 1990 and the environment as a whole:

1. Spend necessary class time to discuss the ecological ramifications of the courses' subject matter.
2. Encourage thought and constructive action discussion of pertinent environmental issues, of which every person should be knowledgeable.
3. Reduce the amount of disposable materials used in the course.
4. Use recycled paper for course materials.
5. Use both sides of paper in preparing course handouts, lab manuals, tests, etc.
6. Recycle as much as possible.

We, the members and supporters of the **Student Earth Day Coalition,** do hereby make the following recommendations to the **curators and administrators of the University of Missouri,** in response to the support of Earth Day 1990 and the environment as a whole:

1. Take a leadership role in the environmental community by making decisions and implementing changes that are environmentally sound.
2. Create a University of Missouri System panel, to review and extend decisions made on all four UM campuses, based on the environmental impact of those actions.

For students, faculty, administration, and curators:

1. **Make every day Earth Day; think globally, act locally.**
2. **Encourage others to do the same.**

*By the Earth Week Student Coalition at the University of Missouri-Columbia; distributed at the main event, April 26, 1990.

[See **chapter 11** for comment.]

Appendix G

The Talloires Declaration*

from the **Association of the University Leaders For a Sustainable Future**
(formerly University Presidents for a Sustainable Future)

We, the presidents, rectors and vice chancellors of universities from all regions of the world are deeply concerned about the unprecedented scale and speed of environmental pollution and degradation and the depletion of natural resources. . . .

University heads must provide the leadership and support to mobilize internal and external resources so that their institutions respond to their current challenge. We, therefore, agree to take the following actions:

1. Use every opportunity to raise public government, industry, foundation and university awareness by publicly addressing the urgent need to move toward an environmentally sustainable future.
2. Encourage all universities to engage in education, research, policy formation, and information exchange on population, environment, and development to move toward a sustainable future.
3. Establish programs to produce expertise in environmental management, sustainable economic development, population, and related fields to ensure that all university graduates are environmentally literate and responsible citizens.
4. Create programs to develop the capability of university faculty to teach environmental literacy to all undergraduate, graduate and professional school students.
5. Set an example of environmental responsibility by establishing programs of resource conservation, recycling, and waste reduction at the universities.
6. Encourage the involvement of government (at all levels), foundations, and industry in supporting university research, education, policy formation, and information exchange in environmentally sustainable development. Expand work with non-governmental organizations to assist in finding solutions to environmental problems.
7. Convene school deans and environmental practitioners to develop research, policy, information exchange programs, and curricula for an environmentally sustainable future.
8. Establish partnerships with primary and secondary schools to help develop the capability of their faculty to teach about population, environment, and sustainable development issues.

9. Work with United Nations Environment Programme and other national and international organizations to promote a worldwide university effort toward a sustainable future.

*c/o University Leaders for a Sustainable Future
Thomas H. Kelly, director, Tufts University, 177 College Avenue, Medford, MA 02155, USA, (617) 627-3464; Fax (617) 627-3099; Internet: ULSF@Infonet.tuft.edu

[See **chapter 11** for comment.]

Appendix H

World Scientists' Warning to Humanity (UCS)*

The Union of Concerned Scientists, established in 1969, and now an organization of leading scientists, initiated a Global Resources Project in 1993. Their objectives were "to encourage responsible stewardship of the global environment and life-sustaining resources; promote energy technologies that are renewable, safe and cost effective; reform transportation policy; and curtail weapons proliferation." *The World Scientists' Warning to Humanity,* signed by 104 Nobel laureates and over 2,000 other scientists, describes critical environmental stresses (atmosphere, water resources, oceans, soil, forests, and living species) and unrestrained population growth (UCS 1994). The next section, "What We Must Do," is particularly relevant to educators and indeed all citizens:

"What We Must Do"—five inextricably linked areas must be addressed simultaneously:

1. **We must bring environmentally damaging activities under control** to restore and protect the integrity of the Earth's systems we depend on. We must, for example, move away from fossil fuels to more benign, inexhaustible energy sources, to cut greenhouse gas emissions and the pollution of our air and water. Priority must be given to the development of energy sources matched to Third World needs—small scale and relatively easy to implement.
2. **We must manage resources crucial to human welfare more effectively.** We must give high priority to efficient use of energy, water, and other materials, including expansion of conservation and recycling.
3. **We must stabilize population.** This will be possible only if all nations recognize that it requires improved social and economic conditions, and the adoption of effective, voluntary family planning.
4. **We must reduce and eventually eliminate poverty.**
5. **We must ensure sexual equality, and guarantee women control over their own reproductive decisions.**

The developed nations are the largest polluters in the world today. They must greatly reduce their overconsumption, if we are to reduce pressures on resources and the global environment. The developed nations have the obligation to provide aid and support to developing nations, because only the developed nations have the financial resources and the technical skills for these tasks.

Acting on this recognition is not altruism, but enlightened self-interest: whether industrialized or not, we all have but one lifeboat. No nation can escape from injury when global biological systems are damaged. No nation can escape from conflicts over increasingly scarce resources. In addition, environmental and economic instabilities will cause mass migrations with incalculable consequences for developed and undeveloped nations alike.

Developing nations must realize that environmental damage is one of the gravest threats they face, and that attempts to blunt it will be overwhelmed if their populations go unchecked. The greatest peril is to become trapped in spirals of environmental decline, poverty, and unrest, leading to social, economic, and environmental collapse.

Success in this global endeavor will require a great reduction in violence and war. Resources now devoted to the preparation and conduct of war—amounting to over $1 trillion annually—will be badly needed in the new tasks and should be diverted to the new challenges.

A new ethic is required—a new attitude towards discharging our responsibility for caring for ourselves and for the Earth. We must recognize the Earth's limited capacity to provide for us. We must recognize its fragility. We must no longer allow it to be ravaged. This ethic must motivate a great movement, convincing reluctant leaders and reluctant governments and reluctant peoples themselves to effect the needed changes.

The scientists issuing this warning hope that our message will reach and affect people everywhere. We need the help of many:

- **We require the help of the world community of scientists— natural, social, economic, political.**
- **We require the help of the world's business and industrial leaders.**
- **We require the help of the world's religious leaders.**
- **We require the help of the world's peoples.**
- **We call on all to join us in this task.** (UCS 1994)

*UCS has additional valuable books, pamphlets, briefing papers, and leaflets that may be useful in the university/college classroom; their books are recommended for college libraries. Please write for a full copy of the above warning or other educational materials to:

Union of Concerned Scientists, 26 Church Street, Cambridge, MA 02238-9105; (617) 547-5552; (617) 864-9405 (fax).

[See **chapter 14** for comment.]

Appendix I*

Religious Organizations with an Environmental Emphasis

1. National Interdenominational Environmental Organizations

Name / Address	Short Name/ Date Started	Newsletter	Phone Number
Christian Society of the Green Cross Inc. Fred W. Krueger, dir. 10 E. Lancaster Ave. Wynnewood, PA 19096	Green Cross,1993	*Green Cross*	(610) 645-9393 (610) 649-8090 (fax)
Evangelical Environmental Network Stan Le Quire, dir. 10 W. Lancaster Ave. Wynnewood, PA 19096	EEN,1993		(610) 645-9392
National Council of Churches Lynne West 475 Riverside Dr. #572 New York, NY 10115	NCC,1991 Economic and Environmental Justice/ Hunger Concerns	No newsletter	(212) 870-2386 (212) 870-2265 (fax)
National Religious Partnerships for the Environment Paul Gorman, exec. dir. 1047 Amsterdam Ave. New York, NY 10025	NRPE,1993	No newsletter	(212) 316-7441
NRPE's Science Office at UCC, Charles Puccia, science dir. P.O. Box 9105 Cambridge, MA 02238	NRPE,1993	No newsletter	(617) 547-5552
North American Coalition on Religion and Ecology c/o Donald B. Conroy 5 Thomas Circle NW Washington, DC 20005 (also Caring for Creation Project)	NACRE 1989	*EcoLetter*	(202) 462-2591

North American Conference on Christianity and Ecology c/o Elizabeth U. Dyson P.O. Box 40011 St. Paul, MN 55104	NACCE 1986	*Earthkeeping News*	(612) 698-0349

2. Denominational Environmental Organizations:

Environmental Justice Program c/o U.S. Catholic Conference Walter E. Grazer, director Jill Ortman-Fouse, program specialist 3211 Fourth St. NE Washington, DC 20017	EJP, 1993	No newsletter	(202) 541-3180 (202) 541-3334 (fax)
Environmental Steward- ship/ Hunger Education Div. for Church in Society, Evangelical Lutheran Church in America Job S. Ebenezer, director 8765 W. Higgins Rd. Chicago, IL 60631	ELCA 1988		(312) 380-2708 (o)
Friends Committee on Unity with Nature c/o Ruah Swennerfelt, general secretary 179 North Prospect St. Burlington, VT 05401-1607 E-mail: fcun@together.org or **FCUN Sustainability Committee** Robert L. Wixom, clerk (chair) Dept. of Biochemistry M121 Med. Sci. Bldg. University of Missouri- Columbia, MO 65212	FCUN 1987	*BeFriending Creation*	(802) 658-0308 (573) 882-5670 (o) (573) 442-0426 (h)
Episcopal Environmental Coalition c/o Jack S. Winder, co-chair 4900 Bradley Blvd. Chevy Chase, MD 20815 or Sally G. Bingham, co-chair	EEC 1991		(202) 564-4292 (o) (301) 657-4532 (h) (415) 929-1589 (h)

Episcopal Environmental Network Episcopal Church Center 815 Second Ave. New York, NY 10017	EEN		(212) 922-5204 (o)
Ministry of God's Creation Jaydee Hanson, asst. general secretary Board of Church and Society Maria Paz Artaza Regan United Methodist Church 100 Maryland Ave. NE Washington, DC 20002 (see also United Methodist Rural Fellowship)	1980	*Environmental Justice News*	(202) 488-5600 (o)
Network for Environ- **mental and Economic** **Responsibility** c/o United Church of Christ Albert G. Cohen 696 S. Madison Pasadena, CA 91106	NEER 1986	*NEER News-* *letter*	(818) 796-2051 (o)
Office of Environmental **Justice** National Ministries Div. Presbyterian Church USA William Somplatsky- Jarman, associate 100 Witherspoon #3069 Louisville, KY 40202-1396	OEJ, 1987	*Networker/* *Interfaith*	(502) 569-5809 (o) (502) 569-8116 (fax)
Presbyterians for **Restoring Creation** c/o Bill Knox P.O. Box 2146 Boone, NC 28607	PRC, 1995		(704) 262-3881
United Methodist **Rural Fellowship** Melvin E. West, field representative. 108 Balow Wynd Columbia, MO 65203	UMRF 1990	*Creative* *Awareness* *Newsletter*	(573) 445-9397 (573) 445-3788

3. Major National Environmental Organizations*

Name	Date Started	Name of Periodical
The Cousteau Society	1973	*Calypso Log* and *Dolphin Log*
Earthwatch	1971	*Earthwatch Magazine*
Environmental Defense Fund	1967	*EDF Letter*
Greenpeace	1971	*GP Newsletter*
National Arbor Day Foundation	1971	*Arbor Day*
National Audubon Society	1905	*Audubon*
National Geographic Society	1888	*National Geographic*
National Park and Conservation Association	1919	*National Parks*
National Wildlife Federation	1936	*National Wildlife*
National Resources Defense Council	1970	*Amicus Journal*
The Nature Conservancy	1951	*Nature Conservancy*
Sierra Club	1892	*Sierra*
Student Environmental Action Coalition	1988	*Threshold*
Student Pugwash	1979	*Pugwatch*
Union of Concerned Scientists	1969	*Nucleus*
United Nations Associations		*The Interdependent of USA*
The Wilderness Society	1955	*Wilderness*
Wildlife Conservation Society	1895	*Wildlife Conservation*
Zero Population Growth	1968	*ZPG Reporter*

[*Note: Further information on the organizations in part 3 and several in part 1 may be found in the *Encyclopedia of Associations* (1995) or the *Conservation Directory* (1995).]

Index